Fieldwork in Educational Settings

This book is designed to encourage readers to seek the truth, tell it
eloquently, and find an audience to buy it. Most books emphasize the
search for truth and neglect the reporting and marketing of the findings.
This one demands that you should be poet, pilgrim and merchant.

From Sara Delamont's introduction to the first edition

Extensively revised and updated, this new edition of *Fieldwork in Educational
Settings* will be welcomed by researchers and academics in education and the
social sciences. Embracing both sociological and anthropological approaches
to qualitative research, the book covers education inside and beyond schools.
The emphasis is upon writing up ethnographic research and getting the
project finished, and the text is packed with examples from research in
progress and the current literature.

As practical, accessible and amusing as its predecessor, this new edition
brings the original text right up to date for new researchers. There is an additional chapter on computer software for data handling and attention is given
to the implications of postmodernism for writing up research. The examples
given have been taken from the latest research, replacing those from the first
edition.

An optimistic, encouraging and down-to-earth take on qualitative research,
Fieldwork in Educational Settings is an indispensable handbook by an author
whose work on this subject is widely recognized as being an essential resource
for the researcher in education.

Sara Delamont is a Reader in Sociology at Cardiff University. She is the
author of many books on qualitative research and feminism including
Knowledgeable Women.

Fieldwork in Educational Settings

Methods, pitfalls and perspectives

Second edition

Sara Delamont

London and New York

First published 2002
by Routledge
11 New Fetter Lane, London EC4P 4EE

Simultaneously published in the USA and Canada
by Routledge
29 West 35th Street, New York, NY 10001

Routledge is an imprint of the Taylor & Francis Group

© 2002 Sara Delamont

Typeset in Bembo by Taylor & Francis Books Ltd
Printed and bound in Great Britain by MPG Books Ltd, Bodmin

British Library Cataloguing in Publication Data
A catalogue record for this book is available from the British
Library

Library of Congress Cataloging in Publication Data
A catalogue record for this book has been requested

ISBN 0–415–24836–1 (hbk)
ISBN 0–415–24837–X (pbk)

Contents

Tables

Preface
The golden journey

This book has a poetic theme woven through it, taken from James Elroy Flecker's *The Golden Journey to Samarkand* (1922). My theme is that doing research is a similar exercise to going on a voyage of discovery, and that we undertake scholarly studies to make the familiar strange. In Flecker's poem, merchants, poets and pilgrims set out for Samarkand, each with their own mission. The pilgrims search for knowledge, the merchants for trade, the poets tell stories. Qualitative research involves the same three goals. Researchers seek enlightenment and understanding, tell stories about them, and finally exchange that knowledge for goods (the PhD, a job, publications, royalties). If the poetic theme annoys you, skip those bits. For me, each research project is a mental golden journey.

Preface to the second edition

The people asked about the changes I needed to make were kind enough to say that its general structure and content were fine. It needed updating and the inclusion of some new material, and that has been done.

Caveat

Do you really want to do qualitative research?

You have probably picked up this book because you are thinking of doing qualitative research. If you think that qualitative research is the soft option, is easy, is common sense, is simple, then (a) you are wrong and (b) you will not enjoy this book. Qualitative research is harder, more stressful and more time-consuming than other types. If you want to get your MEd dissertation or whatever finished quickly and easily, do a straightforward questionnaire study.

Qualitative research is only suitable for people who care about it, take it seriously, and are prepared for commitment. It must be done properly or not at all – so unless you are fired with zeal, don't do it!

Acknowledgements

This book draws on all the research I have been lucky enough to conduct since 1968. The ESRC funded my PhD study at 'St Luke's', the ORACLE project, and the research on PhD students and their supervisors. SCRE funded my observations of computing and statistics teaching in Scotland. The DES funded the PhD/PGCE chemistry project, and the Welsh Office sponsored (with the DHSS) the domestic violence research, (with IFAPLAN, Cologne) the evaluation of industrial training units for slow learners, and the locational integration project. In the 1990s I have also been privileged to work on a variety of Welsh Office funded projects on social pharmacy. Irene Williams acted as research assistant for the redraft and prepared the text. Twenty-five people who had used the first edition of the book gave me their ideas on what needed updating. Cate Whittlesea won a bottle of champagne in the draw; the others get no reward but intellectual satisfaction.

I dedicated the first edition to Paul Atkinson: he deserves this version even more.

Chapter 1

For lust of knowing

Introduction to the scope and purpose of the book

> We travel not for trafficking alone;
> By hotter winds our fiery hearts are fanned:
> For lust of knowing what should not be known,
> We take the Golden Road to Samarkand.
>   (Flecker, 1922: 182)

Flecker's poem comes at the end of his play *Hassan*, when the 'great summer caravan' leaves Baghdad 'for the cities of the Far North East, divine Bokhara and Happy Samarkand' (p. 169). One group of travellers are pilgrims who are hoping that they will find 'a prophet' who 'can understand why men were born' (p. 181). There are also poets, merchants, Jews, as well as the professional guides and camel drivers, and each group has its own reasons for travelling. In this way they resemble the disparate origins of those who set out to do research.

In their search for knowledge, pilgrims are prepared to face deserts and heat, thirst and hunger, fear and loneliness. The theme of this book is that researchers should be motivated like those pilgrims by lust of knowing. However, just discovering things is not enough: the findings must be written up and eventually 'sold' to an audience. Flecker's caravan also contained poets 'who sing to find your hearts', and merchants, carrying trade goods as well as being driven by that 'lust of knowing'. This book is designed to encourage researchers to seek the truth, tell it eloquently, and find an audience to buy it. Most books emphasize the search for truth and neglect the reporting and marketing of the findings. This one demands that you should be poet, pilgrim and merchant.

This chapter introduces the book, outlines the author's qualifications for writing it, and explains what the book does and does not do. Key terms are explained, and the different types of ethnographic research are outlined.

The scope and purpose of the book

There are already plenty of books available on qualitative methods in general and ethnography in particular (Hammersley and Atkinson, 1995; Burgess, 1984a; Lofland and Lofland, 1995; Spradley, 1979; Denzin and Lincoln, 2000; and Atkinson *et al.*, 2001, for example). There are also several texts about qualitative methods in educational research (Dobbert, 1982; Le Compte and Preissle, 1994; Woods, 1996; Walker, 1985; Hitchcock and Hughes, 1989). Many of the books on feminist methods (e.g. Eichler, 1988; Stanley and Wise, 1993) contain advice on qualitative techniques. Coffey and Atkinson (1996) deal with analysis in more detail than I have done here. Coffey (1999) reflects on the relationships between the researcher's self and the impact of that self on the field.

Since the first edition of this book, alongside feminist methods we have the methodological implications of the new men's studies, the rise of queer theory. The implications of feminism, men's studies, queer theory, critical race theory and postmodernism for qualitative research in educational settings are rehearsed in the journal *Qualitative Studies in Education*. There have been special issues on queer theory (vol. 12, no. 5, 1999) and critical race theory (vol. 11, no. 1, 1998). There is also a growing collection of autobiographic accounts by researchers which outline the pitfalls of various methods (see, for example, Hammond, 1964; Burgess, 1984b, 1985a, 1985b, 1985c; Walford, 1987, 1994, 1998; Messerschmidt, 1982; Spindler, 1982; Spindler and Spindler, 1987; McKeganey and Cunningham-Burley, 1987; Carter and Delamont, 1996; de Marrais, 1998).

Throughout the past twenty-five years there has been a steady acceleration in the acceptability of qualitative methods in the social sciences generally. The existence of a second edition of this book, is of course, part of the growth. The early 1990s saw a culmination of this trend when two big handbooks were published. In 1994 Denzin and Lincoln produced their *Handbook of Qualitative Research*, which contained 650 pages of commentary and reflection on qualitative research. Two years earlier, Le Compte, Millroy and Preissle had edited their handbook of *Qualitative Research in Education* (1992), which had 870 pages. Denzin and Lincoln had thirty-six chapters written by forty-seven authors, Le Compte *et al.* includes eighteen chapters by thirty authors. There are no overlaps at all: seventy-seven different people produced these 54 chapters. Planned in the 1980s, these books appeared in the 1990s. Both have been commercially successful and mark an achievement for qualitative research. Denzin and Lincoln (2000) went into a second edition in only six years, reinforcing the popularity of qualitative research.

With these two handbooks, the rapid growth in qualitative research in the social sciences in general, and education in particular, which had been taking place over the previous twenty-five years was embodied, made manifest, revealed in all its enormity. With the establishment of qualitative methods alongside the traditional quantitative ones, it is appropriate to take stock of their growth and subject them to critical scrutiny. In particular, it is vital that the use and development of qualitative methods in educational research is scrutinized in comparison with their use and development in the other disciplines (especially sociology, social psychology and anthropology) which are close to educational research, and the use and development of qualitative methods in other empirical areas such as research on health and illness, gender or urban life.

This books aims to be different from the texts already available, in seven main ways.

1　It is multidisciplinary, because it draws on the sociological and anthropological traditions of qualitative research in education.
2　It is about all kinds of education, not just schools.
3　It gives priority to reading and writing as central parts of the ethnographic process.
4　It is cheerful and optimistic, while it does not gloss over the tedious, boring and unpleasant bits.
5　It is non-sexist.
6　It is reflexive.
7　It makes the familiar strange.

These principles are explained below. Most of the existing books are grounded in only one discipline (either sociology or anthropology); focus on schools and ignore every other aspect of education; make research seem dull and boring; are sexist; or take too much for granted. Some of the existing books (e.g. Spradley, 1979) concentrate on instructing the researchers in techniques, while others (e.g. Silverman, 1995) are more concerned with the philosophy and ideology of ethnographic research. This book mixes the two, and is intended both for the novice and as a provocative read for the expert.

Precisely because there are so many books on qualitative methods available today, this one was designed to fill some of the gaps they leave. Themes developed in this volume – such as leaving the field, how to read productively, collecting urban legends and using school histories as a data source – are those absent from the other books. Other issues, such as interviewing, which are dealt with fully in the existing guidebooks, are dealt with briefly or not at all here.

Interviewing is probably the most commonly used qualitative method, and there are several good books on how it should be done. Spradley (1979) is a detailed guide to ethnographic interviewing, Plummer (1983, 2000, 2001) a central text on life history collection, Hammersley and Atkinson (1995) deal with the use of questioning in ethnographic work, and Measor (1985) is a reflexive account of interviewing teachers and pupils in British schools. As there are plenty of good books on how to do interviews, and useful accounts of how they have *been* done, such as Measor's, little space is given to that aspect of qualitative methods in this book. Although interviewing is relatively neglected in this book compared to observation, documents and more observation, it does get some coverage. During the 1990s the unstructured interview, the collection of narratives (Atkinson, 1997b) or life histories and the focus group became very popular, and even, for many people, became qualitative research. I have argued elsewhere, alone (Delamont, 1997, 2000b) and with colleagues (Atkinson *et al.*, 1999; Delamont, Coffey and Atkinson, 2000), that this is pernicious. Interviewing of individuals or groups can produce data quickly, but they are different from, and inferior to, proper observational fieldwork.

There has been one new arena for qualitative research since 1992: the Net. Many scholars are now using varieties of qualitative techniques to gather data from informants all over the world on the Net. Lori Kendall (2000), an American, did a form of participant observation in an on-line forum (known as a 'mud'). Shelly Correll (1995) is an ethnography of an on-line lesbian bar. In the UK, Matthew Williams (2000), who is conducting a study of crime and deviance in virtual reality communities, also describes his work as participant observation. In some ways, for example the need for keeping careful reflexive records, the Net is only a new setting that does not change the method. In other ways, however, such as the removal of the limits of time and space from the 'field', the research techniques are different. Some of the insights of qualitative researchers working on-line are drawn on in this second edition.

However, the major topic in qualitative research which is totally neglected in this volume is language use in educational settings. This is a deliberate omission of a very important research topic and set of methods which must be explained. Language in educational settings is the sole concern of Edwards and Westgate's (1994) outstanding book. They deal with all the main qualitative perspectives on the study of language: conversation analysis, sociolinguistics, ethnomethodology and discourse analysis. These are explained with clarity, and nothing I could say would add anything but confusion to their lucid presentation. Any readers who think that their focus will be on language use would be well served by starting with Edwards and Westgate, and then looking at some of the publications by authors such as Shirley Heath (1983) and Grace Guthrie (1985). Atkinson, Delamont and Hammersley (1988) contains a summary review of British literature on language use in educational settings. Some empirical topics, such as gender, are particularly illuminated by a focus on language use (e.g. French and French, 1984). In summary, research on language in educational settings is a valid and productive enterprise which is *not* covered in this volume. Here, language is not studied as a topic in its own right, but merely treated as one of the ways in which meanings are conveyed between actors and between informants and researchers. See Hymes (1996) for the best introduction to this area.

The third topic which is shamefully neglected in this book is the use of microcomputers to help analyse qualitative data. Most of the 'classic' texts on qualitative methods predate the rapid growth of excellent software produced specifically for social scientific work, and the spread of micros in social science departments. In the 1960s nobody expected ethnographers to use computers for analysis; today a qualitative researcher who does analysis by hand has to defend their decision *not* to use the hardware and software. The main reason for neglecting the topic in this book is that the potential is changing so fast that it quickly becomes hopelessly outdated. The capacity of the hardware keeps expanding and its price falling, while the available software is in constant flux. The basic parameters are well described in Coffey and Atkinson (1996). Any reader who knows nothing about using microcomputers needs to find out about their potential before embarking on a qualitative research programme.

The style and tone of the book

The tone of the book is uneven. In each chapter there is a mixture of three types of writing. There are statements of a general nature ('qualitative researchers need to concentrate on ...'), autobiographical accounts ('in this project I found that ...') and direct injunctions to prospective researchers ('you must not ...'). Experienced researchers will no doubt find the direct instruction tedious, while those desperate for practical advice may want to skip the general discussions. The mixture of the three is never easy for readers or writer, but has been done deliberately.

The aim of the book is to make reflexive, non-sexist, high-standard qualitative research a pleasure. If research is not enjoyable, then it should not be done. It may also be frightening and difficult, but it should be satisfying. My intention is to convey the sheer exhilaration of doing research: the joy of reading, the luxury of writing, the excitement of a new field setting, the pleasure of good field relations, and the thrill of analytical work. To communicate these delights the book is personal and autobiographical. The pleasures of reading are illustrated by my favourite books, of writing by examples that give me happiness, and so on. Some of the material used in the book is from my own projects. Fieldnotes taken in classrooms and schools as part of investigations into how far ESN(M) pupils were being functionally or locationally integrated in Welsh comprehensive schools (Upton et al., 1988) are used to illustrate ethnographic research. Documentary research is illustrated with 217 scary stories concerning transfer to secondary school, written for me by 'Ledshire' sixth formers in 1988 and 1989, and 40 published girls' school histories (Delamont, 1991, 1993a, 1993b). Interviewing is represented by a study of social science and science PhD students and their supervisors which began in 1990 (Delamont, Atkinson and Parry, 2000). Writing and publishing is enriched by an analysis of the pseudonyms for schools used by contemporary British ethnographers. The idea of using on-going research projects is to show that investigations, analysis, reading and writing are a continual process: a never-ending golden journey.

The organization of this book

This book is structured in a deliberately novel way. Before anything else it starts with reading. Chapter 2 explains why reading widely, and critically, and with a purpose, is the most important task for the ethnographer. The subsidiary aim of Chapter 2 is to show how experienced readers recognize good-quality ethnographic work when they read it. Then Chapter 3 explores what problems have arisen in past qualitative research, and how they can be avoided in future projects. Writing is central to ethnography, and it is discussed in Chapter 4, before any of the other practical issues. The heart of the book, Chapters 5–12, covers the progress of a research project: how to choose a topic, gain access, start the research, manage to stay in the field, gather data, analyse them, leave the field, and produce the written report at the end. Each chapter ends with a reference to one *key* piece of literature – a text which carries the central issues of that chapter onward. There is a suggestion for a follow-up reading at the end of each chapter, plus a full bibliography.

There is now a large amount of published material on qualitative methods in educational settings. In the first edition I used thirteen monographs regularly through the text, so the reader could get some familiarity with them. For this edition I have retained some of these, and added some newer texts. The monographs retained are worth reading for what they teach about the joys and disasters of ethnography, and it does not really matter if a text is five years old or forty-five if it 'works' as a learning tool. The most regularly cited books in this edition are: Abu-Lughod (1986), Atkinson (1997a), Beynon (1985), Cusick (1973), Eickelman (1985), Finders (1997), Fine (1983, 1987, 1996, 1998), Lubeck (1985), Mac an Ghaill (1994), Reed-Danahay (1996), Valli (1986), Walker (1988). These cover settings from an American kindergarten to a Bedouin tent, from mushroom hunting to rugby football, from a French primary school to a Scottish medical school. Teaching and learning are going on in all these settings: Islamic learning, leisure learning, vocational learning, academic learning. The monographs and articles chosen for special attention are not those thought to be particularly good, or those felt to be exceptionally bad. They were chosen to represent work by women and by men, by anthropologists, sociologists and educationalists, by Americans, Australians, British (not just English) and others. Some are about conventional schooling, others (such as Fine and Abu-Lughod) are not. The articles are either crucial to the understanding of the current state of ethnography, or allow a detailed examination of one text which can be consulted by the reader. Authors criticized in this book are not necessarily any less competent than the author or other scholars; those not cited at all are not considered worse than those included.

Key terms explained

Three terms have been used – ethnography, qualitative methods, and reflexivity – which need to be explained.

In the book *qualitative research* is the wide-ranging term, used to cover interviewing with open-ended questions, life history interviews, oral histories, studying personal constructs and mental maps, and observational studies, whether the observer is a participant or non-participant. *Ethnography*, my preferred term, can be used to mean most of the above, but here is used to cover observational research (which will include talking to the people in the setting, of course). 'Participant observation' is used interchangeably with 'ethnography' in this book. Both these terms imply that the researcher values the views, perspectives, opinions, prejudices and beliefs of the informants, actors or respondents she is studying, and is going to take them seriously. This does not mean being naive or credulous – informants may lie to you, or be deluded or misinformed themselves. But it does mean paying attention to the outlook of the people in the setting or culture you are studying. Your job is to find out how the people you are researching understand *their* world.

Participant observation has a long history in social science research, especially in urban sociology and anthropology, but had not been widely used in educational policy and administration until the 1970s. In the last thirty years ethnographic methods have grown in popularity and accessibility to the extent that one of the founding fathers (Spindler, 1982) could write:

> It is a rare research project today that does not have somewhere in the table of operations at least one ethnographer and somewhere in the research design some ethnographic procedures ... The sudden wave of popularity is exhilarating.
>
> (p. 1)

With the growth and proliferation of studies has come what Louis Smith (1982) calls 'zesty disarray' among different groups of ethnographers, which can be seen in the review essay by Jacob (1987) and the critique of it by Atkinson, Delamont and Hammersley (1988). The range of ethnographic methods used in education is reviewed in Delamont and Atkinson (1995) I do not attempt to map or evaluate all the schools of thought here; instead I have summarized the 'common core' of ethnography.

Most of the earliest ethnographers were either anthropologists – who lived in alien cultures – or social scientists focusing on 'strange' ethnic groups in their own society. They suffered 'culture shock' and were forced to rethink their *own* preconceptions about everyday life by living among people who saw 'the same' phenomena differently or, indeed, did not even 'see' the same things at all. The focus of good ethnographic work is on what the educator takes for granted.

> We took the challenge provided by our mentors to provide a mirror for educators. Our intent was to help educators look at themselves ... to turn their attention to what actually goes on in schools rather than to be so singularly preoccupied with what ought to go on in them.
>
> (Wolcott, 1981: 7)

The central method of ethnography is observation, with the observer immersing himself/herself in the 'new culture'. Ethnographies involve the presence of an observer (or observers) for prolonged periods in a single or a small number of settings. During that time the researcher not only observes, but also talks with participants; significantly, the ethnographer calls them informants, rather than subjects. Also, the anthropologist does not make a strong category distinction between observer and observed. Gussow and Vidich put the anthropological case most clearly.

> When the observers are physically present and physically approachable the concept of the observer as non-participant, though sociologically correct, is psychologically misleading.
>
> (Gussow, 1964: 240)

> Whether the fieldworker is totally, particularly or not at all disguised, the respondent forms an image of him and uses that image as a basis of response. Without such an image, the relationship between the field-worker and the respondent, by definition, does not exist.
>
> (Vidich, 1955: 35)

This relationship between observer and respondent leads on to the other key concept, reflexivity, which is the central topic in Hammersley and Atkinson's (1995) excellent textbook on ethnography.

The importance of reflexivity

Reflexivity is a social scientific variety of self-consciousness. It means that the researcher recognizes and glories in the endless cycle of interactions and perceptions which characterize relationships with other human beings. Research is a series of interactions, and good research is highly tuned to the interrelationship of the investigator with the respondents.

Hammersley and Atkinson (1995) provide a full account of the need for reflexivity in social research and, indeed, of the inescapable fact that 'there is no way in which we can escape the social world in order to study it' (p. 15). There is no location where the researcher can base herself to do research which is outside or beyond the social world. The scholar must use what knowledge she has, while, as Hammersley and Atkinson argue, 'recognizing that it may be erroneous and subjecting it to systematic enquiry' (p. 15). The researcher, therefore, should not waste time trying to eliminate 'investigator effects': instead, she should concentrate on *understanding* those effects. Data should be collected at different levels of reactivity, and theories made explicit. Finally, everything we develop to explore the world should also be used to expose the way in which we do that exploration.

Throughout their text Hammersley and Atkinson use the concept of reflexivity, which should be deployed at all stages of the research from design to writing up. It is essential to be as self-conscious about the construction of texts as one is about the processes of interviewing or doing participant observation. The permeation of all aspects of the research process with reflexivity is essential. Each researcher is her own best data-collection instrument, as long as she is constantly self-conscious about her role, her interactions and her theoretical and empirical material as it accumulates. As long as qualitative researchers are reflexive, making all their processes explicit, then issues of reliability and validity are served. These issues are developed in Coffey (1999).

Conclusions

This chapter has made it clear that the book is polemical, personal and partial. Qualitative research is hard work – exhaustingly hard work – but enormous fun. In the next ten chapters the reader will be led on a golden journey, in search of wisdom and worldly goods.

Key reading

The key reading suggested for this chapter is Alison Lurie's novel *Imaginary Friends* (1978), which follows the course of an ethnographic research project. It is a fictionalized account of a real research project by Festinger *et al.* (1964 [1956]).

Chapter 2

Tales, marvellous tales

Recognizing good fieldwork and reading wisely

Yorgo was a fair-haired, friendly but rather silent man.
  'You shouldn't go to sleep under a fig tree,' he said ...
  'Why not?'
  'The shadow is heavy.'

(Patrick Leigh Fermor, 1958. 15)

Do you immediately want to know what Yorgo meant? What is a heavy shadow? Why is it dangerous? Why a fig tree? If your response to that extract was a flurry of questions, then you are on your way to being an ethnographer. Patrick Leigh Fermor was travelling into Mani – the remote, desolate peninsula in the south of mainland Greece – and while he is known as a travel writer rather than a social scientist, his work is beautifully written and full of intriguing glimpses into Greek folklore and everyday life. This chapter starts with him because *Mani* captures the three passions you must have if you are to be an ethnographer: reading, writing and curiosity.

Reading To be an ethnographer you need to be an omnivorous reader: of ethnographies, of travel books, of detective stories, of biography, of sociological theory, of history, of everything.

Writing You have to like writing. Ethnographies involve doing lots of writing and you must enjoy it (or choose another research method). The persuasiveness of ethnographies lies in the ways they are written, so you need to recognize good styles, appreciate them, and be prepared to strive for them.

Curiosity You need to have the insatiable curiosity of Miss Marple or the Elephant's Child. Whatever you heard, saw or smelt, it should raise dozens of questions in your mind, and you should be eager to ask them.

If you do not like reading, hate writing and lack curiosity, you should not choose ethnographic research. Do a survey, where the results, presented in tables, are much easier to write about.

To do a decent ethnography yourself, you need to develop criteria for judging ethnographies, and that means reading them. This chapter is all about reading different kinds of texts, being reflexive about them, and learning what questions to ask of them. In Flecker's poem the poets aim to 'beguile' the pilgrimage with 'tales, marvellous tales of ships and stars and isles where good men rest' (p. 90). Ethnographies have authors who are trying to beguile you, and it is important both to enjoy their tales and to discover how they recount them and make them plausible. This chapter first discusses types of reading, sets out some guidelines for finding and recording the literature, and then focuses on some pieces of writing to expose their flaws, so the readers can learn how to read critically in order to do better themselves.

Lack of wide and critical reading can lead to statements that make their author appear idiotic. Julia Stanley (1989: 173), for example, states that 'Paul Willis was the first English writer to use ethnography to document the school days of ordinary "lads", in his book *Learning to Labour*'. A simple literature search should have produced at least seven authors in the UK who had studied ordinary 'lads' before Willis.

Similarly, Paul Connolly (1998: 2) states that 'Within the sociology of education, for instance, we find a distinct lack of attention paid to young children's own experiences and concerns.' While it is possible to argue that more of the literature sees children through the eyes of the teacher rather than seeing school through the eyes of the pupil, or the eyes of the whole child, Connolly is actually revealing that he has not read much. From the UK there is work by Hamilton (1977), Nash (1973), Prout (1986), Lloyd and Duveen (1992), Waterhouse (1991) and Willes (1983). There is also the research on transfer from home to pre-school called *The First Transition* (Blatchford *et al.*, 1982) and from pre-school to school *And So to School* (Cleave *et al.*, 1982). In the USA, there has been the work of Adler and Adler (all pulled together in their 1998 book, but in journals before) and all the papers in the *Annual Review of Research on Childhood* they edited for a decade. There is also William Corsaro, who has been doing ethnographic work on young children in the USA and in Italy for twenty years (see Corsaro, 1981, 1997; Eder and Corsaro, 1999). Gilmore and Glatthorn (1982) is a collection of papers by leading scholars. Fine (1987) is famous for his work on small boys, Paley (1981, 1984, 1986) for her reflections on life in the early years as children see it. Hart (1979) is an ethnography of how children see their own neighbourhoods. These works are all cited in easily available secondary sources in the UK, and can be obtained from Boston Spa on inter-library loan. The anthropology of education has also dealt with life as seen by small children, for example Shultz and Florio (1979), Hatch (1987) and de Marrais *et al.* (1992). Wide reading, and careful attention to what is read, will prevent newcomers to ethnographic research making such elementary blunders in their own writing.

The three types of reading

There are three types of reading to look forward to. First there is the reading about, and around, the topic you have chosen for your own research. Second is the reading designed to contrast with the area you plan to work in to keep yourself alert, sceptical and curious. Third there is the social science reading intended to help you generate your analytical and theoretical categories. All three types of reading should go on throughout your research, starting long before you settle upon a topic and continuing to the day your thesis goes to the binders or your manuscript to the printers. (And by then you should be reading for your next project or publication.) Throughout your fieldwork there will be reading, throughout your analysis there will be reading, and as you write the final version you will be reading. Each type is explained next.

Reading on your topic

There is always lots of reading to be done in and around a topic, even if there is no orthodox social science scholarship on it. As soon as you have a vague idea for a research area or research problem you can usefully begin searching for reading about it. The first rule is that any kind of text may be relevant: journalism, serious fiction, popular fiction, academic writing from other disciplines, poetry, drama, comics, anything. Atkinson (1992) demonstrates this using the topic of TB sanatoria with examples from Thomas Mann to Betty MacDonald. Below are some examples of the imaginative thinking around a topic that will produce a good 'starter' reading list.

To give some concrete examples, imagine that you and four of your colleagues have to carry out the following five research projects:

1   A case study of a Roman Catholic sixth form college in Lancashire where a pupil has just died of CJD.
2   A comparison of two primary schools in Cardiff and Edinburgh to see how far, if at all, devolution has made an impact on pupils, teachers or teaching.
3   A study of medical students being taught the new curriculum required by the General Medical Council, set out in *Tomorrow's Doctors* (1993).
4   An ethnography of a private catering school in a cathedral city, where the students run a restaurant.
5   Life history interviews with women science lecturers in universities.

For each of these projects we can plan reading on the topic, reading for contrast, and reading for theorizing and analysis. Where a topic has generated a large literature – such as primary schooling – the studies of the UK are treated as 'central to the topic' and those from other countries as 'contrasting'.

Where a topic is not often researched I have put all the Anglophone reading together as 'central to the topic' and drawn my contrast ideas from a more 'off the wall' range. There are three other examples of reading in Delamont *et al.* (1997: 57–8), one sociological, one historical and one literary.

The Roman Catholic sixth form college and CJD

There are four sets of reading directly on the topic

- on Roman Catholic schooling in the UK and elsewhere;
- on sixth form colleges;
- on adolescents and death;
- on CJD.

On Roman Catholic schooling in the UK, an obvious place to start the reading would be Robert Burgess's (1983) monograph on Bishop MacGregor, a Roman Catholic comprehensive in the English Midlands. As Burgess has done research in Bishop MacGregor twice, all the later papers (e.g. Burgess, 1989a) would also need to be traced and read with attention. The next step would be to look for other studies of UK comprehensives, and other studies of Catholic schooling. The former can be traced from a review article (e.g. Atkinson, Delamont and Hammersley, 1988), the latter involve some creative searching. Without undue exertion, it is easy to trace Angus's (1988) Australian monograph, and two Canadian ones: McLaren (1986) on a Catholic school in Toronto which served a clientele of Azorean (Portuguese) and Italian adolescents, and Kleinfeld (1979) on a rural school serving a Catholic Inuit (Eskimo) community. In the USA, Schneider (1997) is a study of a Roman Catholic school for Polish–American girls in a northern city parallel to Lesko's (1988) done in an urban area serving several ethnic groups. All those books are easily identifiable, and provide insights into Catholic schooling in the industrialized, capitalist world.

On sixth form colleges, the starting point is Aggleton (1987), followed by Quicke (1993) and more recently Hodkinson and Bloomer (2000). On adolescents and death, a good starting point is Bluebond-Langer (1978) on dying children. There is unlikely to be much social science literature on CJD because it is both new and rare. However, as there are more deaths and more research, the literature will build up. It would be more productive to look in recent issues of the journals which publish medical sociology (*Sociology of Health and Illness*) and watch for new publications by the scholars who study death and dying, such as J. Hockey (1990), Lindsay Prior (1989) and David Field (1989) in the UK. There is also an American journal on death and dying (*Journal of Thanatology*) and it would be shrewd to check its contents and book review pages regularly.

Primary schools and devolution

There are three sets of reading on this topic:

- on primary schooling in the UK, especially in Wales and Scotland;
- on citizenship and political literacy among primary children and primary teachers;
- on devolution in the UK.

On primary schooling in Wales there is Nash (1977) and in Scotland Nash (1973) and Hamilton (1977). There has been a rural emphasis in the Welsh and Scottish research, with several studies focused on small, country schools. Nash (1973) and Hamilton (1977) are about Edinburgh, but Cardiff primary schools are largely unstudied. In England, there is a large literature covered in the critiques of Woods (1996) and Connolly (1998) (pp. 11 and 74 of this book).

Researchers interested in citizenship and political literacy have more frequently focused on older children, adolescents and young adults. Education for citizenship is supposed to be a cross-curricular theme in English secondary schools, but as Whitty et al. (1993) showed, it was very unpopular with teachers. The relevant government document in England does not face up to whether 'citizenship' might mean something different in Wales and Scotland. A starting point would be Gordon et al. (2000), which contrasts secondary schooling and citizenship in London and Helsinki. On devolution there is a small, recent literature, such as Taylor and Thomson's (1999) Scotland and Wales: Nations Again, Morgan and Mungham (2000), Jones and Balsom (2000).

Medical students and the new curriculum

There are two sets of reading to be done on this topic:

- the GMC (1993) Tomorrow's Doctors which is setting the agenda for the whole project;
- the main studies of the UK medical students and medical education.

There are two monographs based on participant observation of medical education, Atkinson (1981, 1997a) on Edinburgh and Sinclair (1997) on UCL. There is a relatively small but important literature on the occupational socialization of medical students done from a sociological perspective. There is a very extensive professional literature deriving from medical educators themselves, in journals such as Academic Medicine, Medical Teacher, Medical Education and the Journal of Medical Education which is relevant as a source of insight into policy and practice but does not provide a model for sociological or anthropological research itself.

The catering school in the cathedral city

There are three sets of reading directly on the topic:

- the studies of catering students;
- research on restaurants;
- studies of private vocational training.

The starting point on catering students will be Riseborough (1993a) on BTEC catering students at a state-funded tertiary college in a city in the north of England and Fine's (1985, 1996) study of catering trainees in Minneapolis. There is Gleeson and Mardle (1980) on a further education college, while Geer (1972) is a collection of papers on vocational training. However, beyond the academic literature, it would be highly relevant to read Tom Sharpe's (1978) comic novel *Wilt*, in which the hero is struggling to teach liberal studies to trainee butchers and plumbers.

On restaurants the starting place would be Fine (1996). Much of the research on the sociology of food and eating has focused on restaurants, but the emphasis has been on the customers and their use of restaurants, not on the chefs and waiting staff (see, for example, Warde *et al.*, 1999). However, following up the studies in Murcott (1998) would be a useful starting point. The rise of celebrity chefs on TV means there are autobiographies which can be skimmed, or autobiographical 'bits' threaded between the recipes. It would also be sensible to get hold of the textbooks produced for such courses, and the syllabuses of the exams they are scheduled to take, if any.

If there are any studies of private vocational training, and I was not able to find any British ones myself, they would be published in the *Journal of Education and Work*. Private vocational courses exist in secretarial skills, in fashion modelling, in fine art and in drama, but most of the research on vocational training has been done in state-run institutions.

Life history interviews with women scientists

As a final example, suppose you were planning to do life history interviews with women lecturers in science and engineering in UK universities. There are four sets of reading here:

- on women scientists;
- on women in universities today;
- fiction about university life;
- historical studies of women in higher education.

On women scientists: British higher education was criticized for gender inequalities in pay (Bett, 1999) and for the low percentage of women in tenured, especially promoted, posts. The lack of women in science and engineering disciplines is seen as a particularly serious part of the overall problem. The CVCP has set up the Athena initiative as the latest attempt to address this. There is, however, relatively little research in Britain (as opposed to the USA) on the gendered nature of science in higher education. The USA has produced a rich literature on gender and science in higher education (Keller, 1995) with publication grounded in philosophy (Harding, 1986), history (Rossiter 1982, 1995; Noble, 1992; Wertheim, 1997; Schiebinger, 1989, 1993, 1999) and empirical investigations of the contemporary scene (Gornick, 1990; Zuckerman et al., 1991; Sonnert and Holton, 1995). The American sociological research has been produced by scholars grounded in the Columbia School, founded by Merton. This group works mostly with quantitative methods and a positivist philosophy in their approach to science and technology studies (STS). The small amount of research in Britain has been primarily descriptive/demographic (Burrage, 1983; Evetts, 1996) and lacks a clear grounding in the sociology of higher education, or the sociology of professions or the sociology of scientific knowledge (SSK). Britain has been pre-eminent in SSK work, but the SSK scholars have not been interested in gender at all (Delamont, 1987a; Ashmore et al., 1995). (One exception is the special issue of *Science, Technology and Human Values*, vol. 20, no. 3, 1995).

There is a small literature on women in universities in the UK, which can be traced from Brooks (1997), Morley (1999) and the two collections edited by Morley and Walsh (1995, 1996). There is a very large corpus of novels about university life (Carter, 1990). Carter traced 204 fictional portrayals of British universities, mostly about Oxford and Cambridge. Women academics are rare in these, and women scientists even rarer. Worse, the novelists treat women in a caricatured and hostile way. However, there are more rounded portraits of women academics in the novels of Alison Lurie and Carol Shields, and a rich vein of detective stories produced by women who have been academics themselves from Sayers's (1935) *Gaudy Night*, through Amanda Cross (1970, 1971, 1976, 1981, 1984, 1988, 1990, 1992, 1995) to Janet Neel (1993) and Michelle Spring (1994). However, in the general fiction and in the detective stories, women scientists are very rare: the heroines and the victims are overwhelmingly lecturers in English, history, modern languages or social sciences. They are not chemists or engineers, or professors of anatomy or genetics. The historical background is to be found in Dyhouse (1995), and that text is the best place to learn about the role of women in higher education in Britain since 1848.

Reading for contrast

The aim of reading for contrast is exactly the opposite of that for reading around the topic. Instead of searching for texts that give you fresh angles on the topic you have already chosen and help you generate hypotheses and foreshadow problems or neat parallels to put into your text, the task now is to search for contrasts. The role model here is Goffman, whose freshness and appeal comes from his juxtapositioning of previously unrelated items (see Atkinson, 1989). The explanatory power of his writing came from comparing and contrasting the barracks and the monastery, the asylum and the boarding school. It is not feasible for everyone to be as good an author as Goffman, but all social science writing is improved by apposite comparisons and contrasts. Even if we cannot all have Goffman's flair and creativity, it is possible to train yourself to make careful contrasts and comparisons which help your reader to locate and visualize the topics in your writing if they are strange, or to see them in a new light if they are familiar. Not everyone likes Goffman's style, of course. Mary Jo Deegan (1987: 15) complains that he 'plays with words', and states 'The temptation to be humorous and clever *weakens* the writings of Goffman' (my emphasis). If you agree with Deegan this is not the right book for you!

Taking each of the five projects, starting back from the hypothetical ethnography of Fatima RC Comprehensive, the 'on topic' reading was on non-Catholic secondary schools in the UK and on Catholic ones anywhere in the world. The contrastive reading needs to be done in a principled way, so, for example, one could read more widely about Catholicism in Britain (i.e. keep the RC but vary the 'education' element), and read about schools for other denominations and religions (i.e. hold 'religious schooling' constant and vary the 'Catholicism'). The former strategy would suggest Hornsby-Smith's (1987) survey of Catholics in Britain, the Ranson et al. (1977) survey on the Catholic clergy, anything on seminaries, *In Habit* (Campbell-Jones, 1979), a study of nuns, and the novel by David Lodge (1980) *How Far Can You Go?* To vary the denomination, the obvious literature is Peshkin's (1986) *God's Choice* and Susan Rose's (1988) *Keeping Them out of the Hands of Satan*, both about American evangelical fundamentalist schools, Bullivant (1978) on Orthodox Jewish schooling and Eickelman (1978, 1985) on Islamic education. Additionally there is Schoem (1982) on an American Jewish elementary school attached to a synagogue, Dewalt and Troxell (1989) on Old Order Mennonites, and Seaford (1991) on evangelical students forced to confront Darwinian theory. The point of this last idea is to contrast students facing Darwin with Catholic students facing an 'unjust' death: both are potentially destructive of a basic faith.

Contrastive reading for the study of two primary schools since devolution would be of two kinds: primary schooling in other minority cultures, especially where there has been devolution or where it is being fought for; and on ideas about citizenship and devolution among adults like teachers in Wales and Scotland. Reed-Danahay (1987, 1996) is a useful starting point for reading on primary schooling and marginal regional identities. Her study of parents, teachers and pupils in a small village in the mountains of the Auvergne found simultaneously a rejection of 'Parisian' intrusions and a strong sense of a French identity. Maryon McDonald (1989) studied primary schooling in rural Brittany, where there is a minority language (Breton) parallel to Welsh and Gaelic and a campaign for devolution. Heiberg (1989) contains material on Spanish Basque schooling and its role in the Basque struggle for independence. Beyond Europe the studies of American anthropologists on minority schooling, especially of First Americans such as Navajo, Inuit and Hawaiians, would provide good contrasts. Kathryn Hu-pei Au's (1980) work on Hawaii, Lipka and McCarty (1994) on Navajo and Yup'ik are typical papers.

The views of the teachers on devolution, citizenship and identity would be usefully contrasted with the material in McCrone (1992), Osmond (1994), Morgan and Mungham (2000). McCrone *et al.* (1995) link the rise of modern Scottish nationalism and identity with the rise of a Scottish heritage industry. Suiting their research to this belief, the team have studied the heritage industry, life members of the National Trust for Scotland, and members of the arts elite and the landed elite (McCrone *et al.*, 1998). Heritage is an 'intensely personal matter' (1995: 165) combined with 'a broad sense of nationalism' (166). This sense of Scottishness is strong and growing stronger. By 1997, 61 per cent of Scots said they felt more Scottish than British, 48 per cent said they had more in common with a Scot of another social class than an English person of the same class. An outsider might argue that privileging national identity over class identity is romantic nonsense, because class and its associated matters of life chance, wealth and taste mean that a Scots lawyer and a Welsh doctor have more in common than a Scots lawyer has with an unemployed member of the Glasgow underclass as personified by Rab C. Nesbitt, but the *myth* is itself interesting. If Scots are claiming the priority of nationality above class, it is an interesting *claim*.

For the research on medical students there is reading on medical education outwith the UK, on socialization into other health-related occupations and other professions, and on the introduction of new curricula in other settings. There is an extensive literature that has documented professional and institutional barriers to innovation in North American medical schools (Kaufman, 1985). Colombotos (1988), Bloom (1988) and Light (1988) all argue that curricular reforms do not reach the everyday practice of faculty in medical schools, and so the student experience is not radically different from those of previous periods – such as that studied by Becker *et al.* (1961) – see Ludmerer (1999). The pioneering American studies *The Student Physician* (Merton *et al.*, 1957) and *Boys in White* (Becker *et al.*, 1961) are the work of giants, and all subsequent work is in their debt. Canada's landmark studies are Shapiro (1978) on McGill and Haas and Shaffir (1987) on McMaster. Israel's major contribution is by Shuval (1980). The American tradition subsequent to the first classic studies includes Bucher (1970), Miller (1970), Mumford (1970), Bloom (1973, 1979, 1988), Fredericks and Munday (1976), Bucher and Stelling (1977), Coombs (1978), Light (1980), Eichna (1980), Leserman (1981), Mizrahi (1980), Broadhead (1983), Johnson (1983), Klass (1987), Konner

(1987), Hafferty (1988, 1991), Muller (1992). From a more explicitly anthropological tradition there are also studies by Del Vecchio Good (1989), Good (1994) and Good and Del Vecchio Good (1993). These research publications include studies of initial MD training and also the socialization of interns and residents. There is also a tradition of autobiography, often thinly disguised as fiction (see reviews by Stoeckle, 1987, and Conrad, 1988). There is a further literature on everyday life and work in hospitals that – while not explicitly about medical education *per se* – provides insight into the socialization of hospital medical staff. The American literature up to 1988 was systematically reviewed by Colombotos (1988), which is a useful starting point.

For the research on the private catering school in the cathedral city, there are two possibilities: research on vocational training for other occupations and research on catering and other service occupations and settings. The reading for contrast could be all aspects of catering outside education (holding 'cooking' constant and varying the context) and material on people learning to do professionally what they have experienced in their everyday lives (i.e. holding 'learning to work' constant and varying the cookery). This latter might lead one to learner drivers, student nurses, trainee teachers, people studying to be employed as gardeners, or nursery nurses, or prostitutes, or, to take a classic from the Chicago School era, taxi-dancers (paid dance partners in a public dance hall). Masingila (1994) is a study of people learning how to lay carpets. All these are cases of people learning to perform as their paid work activities they have learnt already as amateurs.

The wider research on food and eating is growing rapidly (Murcott, 1998). To stretch one's mind, James Davidson's (1997) *Courtesans and Fishcakes* contains a chapter on food, which starts from Socrates' question 'for what kind of behaviour a man is called an *opsophagos*?' (p. 3). Simply it is someone who loves eating fish – today someone who saved up to eat at Rick Stein's restaurant – but in practice, as Davidson shows, the word is more subtle than that. His detailed analysis of ancient texts and pictures is an excellent way to think about food, cooking, eating and restaurants. As a complete contrast, Fine (1998: 129) found that people who happily spent hours searching for edible fungi often did not choose to spend any time cooking them carefully in elaborate recipes. Instead they just fried them or added them to ordinary dishes like quiche and soup. Strahan (1998) is the autobiography of a man who wanted to be an American historian, but spent twenty years managing Lucky Dogs, the carts selling hotdogs on the streets of New Orleans. It gives an inside view of the bottom end of the catering trade. Lisa Adkins (1995) studied workers in tourist industries, which offers a perspective on other service and tourist occupations.

Moving to the life history interviews with women scientists and engineers in higher education, the 'on topic' reading would have covered women staff in higher education and women scientists and engineers. The contrastive reading needs to focus on higher education subjects/departments where men are the minority among the lecturers, and on women teachers/researchers in non-educational settings who are unusual/unfeminine/deviant. The former would suggest male lecturers in nursing and other 'female' areas, the latter women teaching in seminaries, police academies, driving schools, women football coaches, and even Barbara Heyl's (1979) life history of a brothel madam who taught her girls to be high-earning prostitutes rather than low-paid ones.

Generating analytical and theoretical concepts

It is not easy to explain how reading helps with the generation of theoretical or analytical concepts. However, the deployment of theoretical or analytical concepts is what separates social science from journalism, and it is therefore essential to find some from somewhere. Few of us are able to 'theorize' unaided, and most of us therefore turn to previous thinkers for inspiration. Reading to help generate analytical and theoretical concepts may be the least or the most rewarding, depending on your tastes. If you enjoy wrestling with theoretical ideas then it will be the best part of doing a piece of research, while if you find theorizing frightening or pointless you may resist doing it. However, the analytical and/or theoretical side of an ethnography is what separates it from journalism, so there is no escaping it.

When reading there are three levels of theory or analysis that can be found. There is the grand theory which is used to explain and generalize about 'life', the universe and everything. Ideas such as Weber's charismatic, patriarchal and bureaucratic authority come into this category, like his theory about the 'Protestant Ethic' and its relations with the origins of capitalism. Then there are much more 'homely' concepts which are useful for generalizing or pulling together material. Goffman's analysis of 'total institutions' would come into this category, as would Willis's ideas about 'resistance'. Then there are analytical concepts which have been generated from the respondents, who may not realize they have something in common, but when the researcher analyses all the responses, it is there. For example, Sikes *et al.* (1985) found that their sample of teachers had a shared concept of 'the proper teacher', Murcott (1983a, 1983b) discovered that all her South Wales sample had a shared idea of 'a proper dinner'. Neither group would necessarily have realized that these were analytical concepts, but once the researchers had spotted them, they could be used to do analytical work. A similar point can be made about Fermor's (1966) discussion of Greeks' usage of *Hellene* or *Romios* (96–115) which has parallels in educational discussions about 'dons', 'lecturers' or 'teachers' in higher education, or the union membership of school teachers.

It is sensible, when reading, to look for all three types of theorizing or analytical work. It is unlikely that much grand theory or even middle-order theory will be found in fiction or travel books or any of the other non-academic types of reading that have been suggested in similar or contrasting sources in the two previous sections. However, David Lodge's (1989) *Nice*

Work probably explains de-constructionist ideas in literary scholarship better than any text on it, so there may be science fiction stories which use Weber or travel writing which deploys grounded theory. In general, theory has to come from academic writing.

Keeping one's eyes open for theoretical ideas that can be borrowed, plundered or adapted in whole or in part is the best way forward. When reading, or at seminars, or when teaching other people, think about whether any theories or analytical approaches can be useful to your work. Two different kinds of 'usefulness' apply here. There is the direct kind: Walford (1983 and 1994) has used Bernstein's (1971) classification and framing to analyse his data on PhD students in chemistry, so you can use Bernstein's ideas to analyse your research on occupational therapists, or students of pharmacy, or ballet classes. There is also the indirect usage. Seeing how Walford used Bernstein may help you use Mary Douglas or Dorothy Smith or Marilyn Strathern in your work. There is also the negative example: seeing how Delamont (1989a) used Bernstein's (1971) ideas about the new middle class might make it clear to you that you do not want to theorize that way. Such negative decisions can be just as useful as positive ones. For example, when I read Sharp and Green's (1975) Marxist ethnography of infant schooling it crystallized for me a conviction that one should not collect data in one framework (e.g. symbolic interactionism) and then retrospectively analyse them in another (e.g. Marxist). If there is a book in which the theory seems unconvincing, stop and explore why the theorizing 'fails'. Negative examples can be very useful.

Some guidelines for finding and recording literature

It is important to remember, when you are looking for literature, that the search in itself is part of the research, and notes should be kept. What does not exist in the literature may be just as important as what other researchers have already written about. If there are no studies of blind trapeze artists, or albino policewomen, or transvestite doctors, this absence is, in itself, a finding. You may have defined 'relevant' too narrowly, or be looking in the wrong places – but if there really is a gap in the literature then you are doing an original piece or research.

When doing an article on the sociology of science education, the negative findings of the literature search became, themselves, part of the argument eventually framed (Delamont, 1989c). It transpired that introductory texts in the sociology of education did not mention science at all. Then a search of the first ten volumes of the *British Journal of Sociology of Education* revealed that fourteen of the 152 articles had focused on science, technology or maths, compared to twenty-five on gender. The fourteen articles provided some literature to review, but the relative scarcity of material was also a finding about the priority given to scientific issues by sociologists of education in the UK. A careful scrutiny on the science education journals (like *School Science Review*) revealed very few papers which deployed any sociological theories or concepts. Finally, a review of the sociology of science literature showed that educational or learning contexts were hardly ever studied by the exponents of that sociological speciality. Having checked three different sets of journals and books it was possible to argue that there was nothing that could reasonably be called 'the sociology of science education'. The eventual paper established this with detailed references (so a sceptical reader could check the negative conclusion), and then explored what the research agenda for 'the sociology of science education' should be. A similar scrutiny of four journals on the history, philosophy and sociology of science, searching for articles and book reviews on gender, forms the basis of Delamont (1987a).

Booth *et al.* (1995), Cuba and Cocking (1994) and Hart (1998) are good on how to search the literature. The general rules are the same in all areas:

1   Ask your supervisor/other lecturers/other students what studies they know which are particularly relevant to your work. (Specially ask if they know of any bibliographies on your topic.) People may know of things you have not heard of that you need to read, or they may merely reiterate the same items you are finding for yourself. If the former, that is priceless. If the latter, you can feel reassured *and*, equally relevant, you are learning what the taken-for-granted literature is.

2   Make friends with the relevant library staff. Always be polite, patient and remember to thank them. (And acknowledge their help in everything you write.)

3   See if there are any bibliographies in the library on your areas, particularly annotated ones, but remember that these become out of date. A bibliography compiled in 1998 will only give sources up to about 1996. Chaff (1977) contains little published after 1974, while Rosenberg and Bergstrom (1975) and Een and Rosenberg-Dishman (1978) are much stronger on the pre-1970 literature than that of the 1970s.

4   Pay careful attention to the citations in each item that you read, and follow up the ones that sound most relevant/interesting/important.

5   Make yourself familiar with the main journals in the field, not only skimming the articles but also noticing the books which are reviewed and advertised. When you are new to a field, reading some book reviews is a quick way to get a sense of what the active scholars (who are reviewing the books) think is important.

6   Before you spend hours and hours doing computer searches, think hard about how to focus your searches so they generate useful references and not an undifferentiated mass. Take advice from library staff on how to search effectively.

Taking notes on the literature

Reading is not enough on its own. A permanent record of what has been read is necessary. In the long run, taking good notes always pays off, and is certainly quicker than having to re-read whole books to check one's memory or scramble around the library searching for a reference that is dimly recalled. Students are not always aware of all the things that should be in their notes about a book or paper, so some basic features that should be recorded are listed below. The notes should always include:

1   Full bibliographic details:

  • the author(s) with full names and all initials;
  • the full title of the book/article;
  • the date the study was published originally (so you know if it is an old or a new study) and of the edition you are using;
  • the publisher and the place of publication (if it is a book);
  • the name of the journal with full details of the volume and issue numbers;
  • if an edited collection, the editors' names, the title of the book and page numbers of any particular article.

2   The Library Catalogue Number (e.g. LC5146 1127) so you can find it again! (And the ISBN is useful if you ever want to buy the book yourself or order it for another library.)

In addition there should be a record of the key features of the book or paper, such as:

3   Is it an original study, or a report of other people's work? (Primary or secondary source?)
4   Is it empirical (has data in it) or theoretical or polemical (argumentative)?
5   What methods were used (e.g. questionnaires, interviews, experiments, observation, etc.)?
6   What theory is cited (Marxist, Weberian …)?
7   What are the author's conclusions (i.e. what did she find out/prove)?
8   What date was the research done? (Maybe many years before it was published.)
9   The number of respondents/subjects (and the response rate).
10   Sex and race of respondents/subjects.

If your notes on the reading you have done always contain at least this amount of detail, the writing of the literature review and the incorporation of the literature into your arguments will be much more straightforward.

Reading critically and learning

In the 1992 edition I devoted six pages to a critique of one paper to illustrate the need for wide, deep and thoughtful reading. Many colleagues feel that it was unfair to savage one paper by one person, so for this edition I have kept the categories of critique, but drawn on ten other articles and a book to illustrate them. The critique of Riseborough (1988) is paralleled and amplified by examples from ten other publications. The categories are:

- the title
- the pseudonyms
- the literature
- basic information
- the ethics
- language use.

The articles chosen have all been published in peer-reviewed journals that reject over 90 per cent of the papers submitted to them.

The title

Riseborough (1988), the paper I criticized in 1992, was called

> Pupils, recipe knowledge, curriculum and the cultural production of class, ethnicity and patriarchy: a critique of one teacher's practices

Equally clumsy and unattractive titles are still found in leading journals. For example:

> Why aren't teachers being prepared to teach for diversity, equity and global interconnectedness? A study of lived experiences in the making of multicultural and global educators
>
> (Merryfield, 2000)

> The effects of aggregation method and variations in the performance of individual students on degree classifications in modular degree courses
>
> (Simonite, 2000)

> The importance of gender as an aspect of identity at key transition points in compulsory education
>
> (Jackson and Warin, 2000)

> Some signposts for medical and nursing educational policy formulation for aboriginal healthcare
>
> (Jordan et al., 2000)

All these are too long, and none is memorable. In the same issues of the same journals there were titles that work better:

> Small-town college to big-city school: preparing urban teachers from liberal arts colleges
>
> (Sconzert *et al.*, 2000)

> Factors influencing successful submission of PhD theses
>
> (Wright and Cochrane, 2000)

> When the 'rot' set in: education and research, 1960–75
>
> (Nisbet, 2000)

> Learning to write in the street
>
> (Kalman, 2000)

These all work much better. They are shorter, they are simpler, they convey the contents of the paper just as well and they are not boring. The Merryfield title, like the Riseborough, suffers from packing far too many concepts into the title. The Riseborough is only about one teacher, the Merryfield is only about a few university lecturers in the USA and Canada who are less ethnocentric than their colleagues. To coin a cliché it is not rocket science.

My personal preference is for the two-part title with a colon, so people citing it only have to put a short title in their bibliography, which saves them time. I usually aim for a catchy, jokey or literary short title to try and make the paper distinctive and memorable, so the Nisbet and the Sconzert *et al.* titles are more attractive to me than the others. Gamradt (1998) has a section in a paper on surgeons called 'Romancing the gallstone' which is exactly the sort of title one *remembers*. In 2000 I published papers called 'The anomalous beasts' and 'The twilight years', just as in 1981 there was 'All too familiar?' and in 1991 'The HIT LIST' and other horror stories'. When you read, think about the titles, so that when you write you can think of good ones.

The pseudonyms

Riseborough (1988) used 'Cosmopolis' to disguise a city in the north of England (which sounded like the home of Batman), and 'Annie Body' to disguise his heroine, a gentile teacher in a Jewish school, which diminished her (anybody) rather than preserving her gentile identity or her starring role in the paper. If Riseborough had good reasons for his choices he did not share them with his readers. Tony Sewell (1997) calls his London comprehensive 'Township' deliberately, because the pupils commuted to it: 'There is a parallel with the townships in South Africa. Poor Black people travel to rich areas each day to work and then return home to their neighbourhoods at night' (p. 26).

This is a political choice of pseudonym. Fordham's (1996) Capital High for a high school in Washington DC and Datnow's (1998) Central High School for a city institution in a western American state are more successfully neutral. There is an extensive analysis and discussion of pseudonyms in Chapter 12, so all that needs saying here is: note and consider the applicability of the pseudonyms as you read, to help you choose good ones yourself.

The literature

Sconzert *et al.* (2000) is an example of a paper weakened by the authors' failures to read and cite the literature. Their paper 'Small-town college to big-city school: preparing urban teachers from liberal arts colleges' is about bringing student teachers from small towns into Chicago to practise in the city's schools. The students live together in a former convent, attend seminars, explore Chicago, and do a placement in one of the city's 500 plus schools. The paper describes the programme and some students' responses to it carefully. However, it totally misses a great opportunity to locate the students in the long tradition of research on Chicago teachers. There is American educational anthropology done in Chicago (e.g. Burnett 1973), and classic sociology of education (Becker, 1952a, 1952b; Geer, 1966). Chicago has been intensively studied for over a century (Abbott, 1999), often with school-aged people as the focus (e.g. Abbott and Breckinridge, 1916; Thrasher, 1927) but none of this rich heritage is mentioned by Sconzert and her colleagues. The problems of teachers in urban Chicago have a long history, and the readers of the paper deserve to know that.

Jackson and Warin (2000) studied gender issues during school transfers, from home to school at ages 4 and 5, and from primary to secondary school. They fail to use Best (1983) or Lloyd and Duveen (1992), any of Measor's (1984, 1989) work on gender at the primary–secondary transfer, or anything from the ORACLE project (e.g. Delamont and Galton, 1986), nor had they found Merton (1994), an ethnography of transfer to junior high school in a suburb outside Chicago. Their analysis would be richer and deeper if they used that literature.

Basic information

Authors owe their readers a duty to provide basic data about their research: the country it was done in, the date the data were collected, the age, sex, race and location of the respondents, the basics of the data collection methods, and some mention of how the data were analysed. Many papers fail these simple tasks. Solorzano (1998), in an article called 'Critical race theory, race and gender microaggressions, and the experience of Chicana and Chicano scholars' which appeared in *QSE*, does not say his paper is about America for five pages, and then only by mentioning 'California' as the location of the research. The study is about PhD students and 'post docs' who are Chicana and Chicano: Solorzano never explains what those terms mean. He also refers to Latino/Latina Americans and Puerto Ricans, so the reader who is not clear about the differences between Chicana, Latina, Hispanic and Puerto Rican women is never enlightened. Notice as you read which authors fail to give you basic information, and make sure you do not fail in the same ways when you write yourself.

The ethics

While reading, keep alert for the ethical dimension of what you are reading. The Merryfield (2000) paper is grounded in a concern that student teachers in the USA are not learning about globalization or multiculturalism. She wrote to 730 institutions who were members of the American Association of Colleges for Teacher Education, asking for the names of outstanding teacher educators who are preparing their students for a global age. She also used personal networks to trace such people, and ended up with eighty respondents who sent her autobiographical reflections and teaching materials. (At least one is from Canada, although this is not marked out by the author for the reader.) The paper is an analysis of the eighty teacher trainers' accounts of their 'lived experiences' (p. 431). Extensive quotes from the writings of these eighty are presented in the rest of the paper. Ethical issues arise. First, Merryfield does not discuss the ethics of her paper at all. She is using the real names and locations of her respondents. She does not say she has had their permission to do this, or that each respondent has agreed the quotes she has used. There is no acknowledgement to the respondents, and they are not credited with co-authorship. You can decide whether this offends you: the important point is to notice the ethical issues.

Language use

When you are reading it is important to think about the ways the author uses language, both their own and that of their respondents. Riseborough (1988) has a distinctive style, which is idiosyncratic and recognizable. Among the features are puns and new coinings, which are examined below. Puns are present at several levels of the paper. The phrase 'recipe knowledge' in the title is itself a pun when the subject is known to be a cookery teacher. The social science use of the phrases 'recipe knowledge' and 'cookbook knowledge' come from the phenomenologist Schutz (1971), and so there is a pun on a pun: one pun for the reader who does not know about Schutz, two for the insider who does. Each reader has to decide whether this annoys or amuses her, each author whether s/he wishes to write that way. Annie Body is also a pun for Anybody, as Riseborough (1988) hammers home on p. 50.

Coinings of new words or phrases can be a creative way to present unfamiliar worlds to the reader – just as using the terms and language of the respondents can give a sense of immediacy. Thus, in *The Jack-roller* (Shaw, 1930/1966, and Snodgrass, 1982), a classic life history of a 'mugger', his vocabulary is used. Similarly in *The Fantastic Lodge* by Helen MacGill Hughes (1961), the life history of a woman jazz groupie and heroin addict, the reader is given a glossary including terms like 'pad' and 'chick' used in that subculture. Spradley (1979) concentrates on strategies for the systematic collection of such language, which if properly deployed give authenticity to accounts. Dan Mannix (1951) realized this, as one can tell from the following passage. Captain Billy, a tattooed man who lay on a bed of nails, is telling Mannix, the novice, about carnival life:

> Most grind men would like to be talkers, but they don't have the talent for it. Sometimes you'll hear people say of a poor talker 'That gee's a grind man who thinks he's a talker.'
>
> (Mannix, 1951: 63)

and

> In some places, the crabbers raise too much of a beef with the town clowns and the word is passed to lay off the grift ... Then the joint men don't pay off in cash but in slum.
>
> (p. 64)

Mannix was being introduced to life in a travelling carnival in the USA in the 1930s. All the specialist terms needed to be learnt by a new recruit (or an ethnographer). 'Slum' is prizes (cuddly toys, clocks, pure wool blankets), 'joints' were gambling places, a 'talker' is the person who persuades, using improvised speech, the public to come into a sideshow, as opposed to a 'grind man' who merely repeats a set formula, 'crabbers' are local people who object to carnivals, and 'town clowns' are the police. In his study of fungi collectors, Fine (1998: 87) lists:

> The range of folk names given to the morel also speaks to its popularity: merkels, honeycomb mushrooms, hickory chicken, sponge mushrooms, and roons.

In Riseborough's paper, Hebrew and Yiddish words are used – some relatively familiar (*Shabbat*), others (*Siccot, minion, schlect, frummy*) unfamiliar. These work well to convey both the teacher's familiarity with Jewish culture and its centrality in the school. Riseborough is not content to use the words of respondents alone. He adds coinings of his own: 'chalkfacial' and 'chalkfront', 'trialectical' and 'lowerarchy'. Then there are the words and phrases that will send readers to a dictionary: 'procrustean', 'osmosis', 'aeonic', 'proclivities'. Again, the use of such words or phrases is a matter of personal choice. It is crucial to be aware what effect they may have on a reader. Then there is the social science language, some used with its source (like 'ideological counter-hegemony' being attributed to Gramsci), some not ('resistance' in pupils and 'symbolic violence' in schools are not linked to Willis and Bourdieu).

Finally, the sentences of data and analysis make an illuminating contrast. Annie says things like

So the Chief Rabbi has actually breakfasted in my room with the boys

and

So when I tried to find out about this chopped and fried fish, I had terrible trouble. I asked the Rabbi's wife, I asked the Senior Mistress.

Annie Body specifically says that she will not discuss sex roles in the Jewish home or in the Synagogue with the pupils.

that is their culture and that school is specially set up to foster that culture and I would not undermine it in any way. I wouldn't feel it was ethical.

(p. 49)

In contrast, Riseborough talks of

Chalkfacial mediated commonsense which makes Annie support a 'home orientated role for women' ... rather than simple top-down arbitrary imposition by the powerful.

(p. 48)

Her pupils were not 'mindless' tabula rasa. Given their culture-carrying humanity the fixity of the categories of teacher and taught fluxed.

(p. 42)

She has dialectically slurred 'curriculum-as-process' into 'curriculum-as-fact' ... She has been relationally turned into the kind of person the situation demanded.

(p. 45)

The contrast is considerable. Riseborough's sentences are very hard to follow and difficult to understand. They are stereotypically sociological: the *Daily Telegraph* would enjoy mocking them. In these extracts it is not the socio-logical analysis that produces the awkwardness of the Riseborough sentences, but Riseborough's style. The life story of Annie Body is a marvellous tale, fit to beguile any pilgrimage. You, as a reader, can decide how far Riseborough's coinages, his vocabulary (both general and sociological) and his sentence constructions help or hinder the reader's access to it. The more you reflect as you read, the better your own writing will be. Writing about the literature you've read is discussed in Chapter 4.

Conclusions

Qualitative research is dependent on voracious reading. This chapter has explored how to find the 'marvellous tales' of others, and record them. Whether they are of ships, stars or 'isles where good men rest', the researcher should always be searching out such tales.

Key reading

The key reading suggested for this chapter is B.M. Bullivant (1978) *The Way of Tradition*.

Chapter 3

Beyond that last blue mountain

Impediments to good fieldwork and how to overcome them

I arrived in Libya in August 1975 on the day after an attempt to over-
throw Qaddafi's Government. I went to Benghazi, and in various
government offices and at the university proclaimed my desire to study
traditional trade. It took me three months to get the necessary permissions ... In late November I went to Kufra ... that visit lasted until
September 1976. I returned for six weeks in December 1977, and again
in the following July. My hosts were at war and it was a difficult time to
be a foreigner who asked questions ... I was able to return for the last
time in August 1978 and stayed for a year ... Altogether I spent 26
months in Libya.

(J. Davis, 1987: 7)

Few readers of this book are likely to find their informants muzzled by a
war, although Nordstrom and Robben (1995) collected papers from thirteen anthropologists who did fieldwork during violent conflicts. But when
a person is trying to do a piece of good fieldwork any impediments seem
equally insurmountable. This chapter deals with five common impediments
to good fieldwork:

1   not finishing the process;
2   sexism and racism;
3   going native;
4   being bored;
5   reporting the familiar.

Each of these barriers may appear to the researcher like the 'last blue
mountain barred with snow' facing Flecker's pilgrims. The first impediment – not finishing – is rather different in kind from the other four,
which are all concerned with data collection. The chapter therefore starts
with a section on finishing, and then has a longer section on the fieldwork
problems.

Failing to finish

One of the worst things that can happen to fieldwork is not finishing it. Until the research is written up, the thesis submitted and the book and/or article published, the fieldwork is not finished. Coming out of the field is not the end: the polished research report is. Mandy Llewellyn (1980), for example, did a year's ethnography in a girls' grammar school and a girls' secondary modern school. The glimpse of her material we get from one published paper is tantalizing: her PhD was never written and submitted, so her data are lost. Peter Levi (1980: 73) offers this sad vision of the scholar who does not finish her work. He is describing the wide range of people he found working at the British School in Athens:

> Then there was the boy everyone loved who plunged into the Greek countryside like a dolphin into the sea, who had the most Greek friends and spoke the best Greek, who had not a talent but a genius for his subject, but who could never finish any piece of work

Another example is explored by Mitchell (1993): Joe Gould's 'Oral History of Our Time'. Joe Gould was a scrounger who lived on the streets of New York and in various hostels and cheap hotels in the 1920s, 1930s and 1940s. He talked endlessly about a great literary project, 'The Oral History of Our Time', which occupied all his waking hours and was part history, part autobiography, part urban ethnography. He declared that it ran to 8,800,000 words, and that after his death it was to go to Harvard and the Smithsonian (two thirds and one third). Mitchell tried to help him get extracts published; after all, Gould said it was superior to Gibbon's *Decline and Fall of the Roman Empire*. After several abortive meetings with publishers, Mitchell realized that the Oral History did not exist. There were four or five short essays, rewritten endlessly, but no Oral History. Gradually Mitchell realized that Joe Gould

> hadn't been talking about the Oral History all those years ... only in order to dupe people like me but also in order to dupe himself. He must have found out long ago that he didn't have the genius or the talent, or maybe the self-confidence or the industry or the determination, to bring off a work as huge and grand as he had envisioned ... he very likely went around believing in some hazy, self-deceiving, self-protecting way that the Oral History did exist ... he had it all in his head and any day now he was going to start getting it down.
>
> (1993: 690)

Joe Gould died a pauper in an asylum in 1957. He lives on in Mitchell's fine writing: but most of us will only live after our deaths if we finish our projects.

Much of this book is designed to help people finish their work, but here are a few general pointers. One reason people do not finish projects is that they want them to be perfect, or at least their very best attempt at perfection. This is understandable but can be self-defeating. Higher degrees are not meant to be perfect work, they are meant to show that their author has learnt something of the craft. At the other extreme, some people cannot finish because they believe their work is so bad no one else will want to see it. When Penelope Peterson was a graduate student of Nate Gage's, she was slow to produce a paper for him, to be told robustly 'The world is waiting, Penny.' If the work is not finished, the world will never know whether it was worth waiting for or not, and the world has the right to decide.

Sometimes a project is unfinished because it is too large, unwieldy or ambitious. An MPhil of 40,000 words, finished and in the library, is better than an uncompleted PhD; a journal article published is better than a book manuscript half completed; a brief research report to the sponsors is better than an ambitious set of reports lying unfinished in the investigator's office. Sometimes losses are better cut, and half-loaves are better than no bread.

To motivate yourself to complete a piece of research, think how relieved you will be to get rid of not only the work but also the guilt of not finishing; think how much time and effort will be wasted if you stop now; and think about never having to face your supervisor, or editor, or publisher, or funding body, again. If the people waiting for the work to be finished are nice, you can be friends again when the work is done. If they are unpleasant you can cut them out of your life for ever, with no hard feelings, once you have delivered the goods.

Leaving the topic of failure to complete the research process, the rest of this chapter deals with five problems which are concerned with the data collection: sexism, racism, going native, being bored, and familiarity.

Sexism

In Flecker's poem, the caravan for Samarkand is a 'men only' affair. The men march joyfully out of Baghdad, leaving the women complaining that 'They have their dreams, and do not think of us', while the gatekeeper comments:

> What would ye, ladies? It was ever thus,
> Men are unwise and curiously planned.

Apparently the golden journey could only be undertaken by males, and in that mythical but Islamic society, men and women led segregated and separate lives. Very few places in the modern world are like that, although sometimes educational ethnographies imply that schools, universities and other educational settings are. In James Watson's (1968) famous book, *The Double Helix*, about the 'discovery' of the structure of DNA, he paints a portrait of Rosalind Franklin as an unsociable, unfriendly, prudish, difficult woman, with whom it was impossible to relax and be collegial. At the time she was employed at King's College, London, all the eating, drinking and leisure facilities for staff at King's were for men only. In the 1950s King's was dominated by white male Anglicans, and, as Sayre (1975: 96) points out, 'was not distinguished for the welcome that it offered to women'. The facilities of the college were designed to reinforce male solidarity, for women were banned from the senior common room eating facilities:

> Male staff at King's lunched in a large, comfortable, rather clubby dining room though the female staff – of any age or distinction whatever – lunched either in the students' hall, or off the premises.
>
> (Sayre, 1975: 97)

This meant, of course, that informal socialization was ruled out at mealtimes. Watson's failure to mention this means he was not a very astute ethnographer.

There are several ways in which qualitative research can fall into sexism. Avoiding sexism in writing about the research is discussed in Chapter 12, and reading in non-sexist ways has been covered in Chapter 2. An extract from a large study of primary education in Malta (Darmanin, 1990) will illustrate the importance of paying attention to issues of sex and gender, and avoiding sexism. Darmanin observed Miss Ximenes, who had taught in a girls' primary school but now worked in a mixed one. Both staffroom and pupils' play-ground relationships became problematic for Miss Ximenes.

Miss Ximenes and amalgamation

The amalgamation of the single sex girls' primary school with the boys' primary can be seen as a critical incident for Miss Ximenes. The second day of term, a chance playground remark about the teachers getting on well together was followed by a more detailed account when I showed interest in the initial remark. Miss Ximenes said that when the schools were single sex, she and the other women teachers used to 'have a great time'. Staffroom humour (Woods, 1979) was more unguarded and even the ex-headmistress would join in. On occasion, the neighbouring male teachers from the boys school were asked to join the female staff. A ficti-tious engagement followed by a wedding was held between Mr Adami (now of Minsilja, Year 6G) and the ex-head teacher (now head of Primary A). Miss Ximenes gets on with the male teachers, but 'it was more fun when it was women only'. Miss Ximenes found pupil–pupil relationships in the newly mixed schools raised difficulties for her too. Her critique of the amalgamation extends to the effects it has on the children. Her explicit objection to mixed schooling is precipitated by Godwin's whispered remark to Maryanne on the 13th October, and following a heavy storm in which a roof collapsed on a married couple and killed them as they were in bed. Godwin tells Maryanne, who then tells the teacher 'I wish that the roof would fall on us as we are in bed, and you would be in your knickers'. Miss Ximenes is worried about the moral tone of her pupils and spends the lesson on a sermon in which she describes the moral code she expects them to follow. In keeping with her custodial orientation to the children and her specific religious beliefs, she concludes the session with Prayers and the aside to me:

In break, I'm not going to let them play together. God knows what they'll do. At home they can do what they like, but not here, during the break. Me, that's why I'm against it, mixed schooling at this age. We're not English, we're Latins and it's different.

For the researcher who meets a teacher with these views, it is crucial neither to ignore them as 'old fashioned' nor to accept them uncritically. The change in schooling, from single-sex to mixed, is a critical incident which allows a researcher to explore with the teacher how gender articulates with her career, her ideas of fun and colleagueship, her teaching, her religion and her perceptions of pupils and parents.

Working hard to make sex and gender problematic in the research setting is a useful strategy. Avoiding sexism does not mean focusing on women and ignoring men. It is just as much sexism to treat men as stereotypes as it was to stereotype women; and focusing on one gender rather than the other is equally blameworthy. Much of the force of feminist critiques of existing educational research has come from pointing out that only half the story is being told.

In the early years of contemporary feminism, women scholars pointed out how the existing disciplines ignored women or stereotyped them. Landmark studies were then conducted to fill the gaps, so that data were collected on women in education, and theories about gender produced. During the 1990s two new approaches came to prominence, men's studies and work on sexuality or, rather, sexualities. Mac an Ghaill (1994) is an exemplary ethnography of a co-educational comprehensive which treats masculinity among pupils and teachers as problematic while paying careful attention to the lives of female pupils and teachers, and explores sexualities in the school. Epstein has pioneered the thoughtful exploration of sexualities in schools, with their interplay with gender issues carefully mapped (see Epstein and Johnson, 1998; Steinberg et al., 1997). In the UK the policy context has become 'gendered', because there has been a moral panic about 'failing' boys (see Epstein et al., 1998; Delamont, 1999, 2000a). It is unlikely that it will disappear as a research topic in the shelf life of this book. However, it is still true that gathering data on females is an important step in rectifying bias in the literature. Becoming reflexive about feminist methods is also important, and would probably begin to generate research to close the gaps in our knowledge about masculinity/ maleness.

Research on boys and men in education has now become a paradoxical topic. When we need to know something about men's different experiences compared to women's, we typically have no available data. In a society where most people live in a mixed world, and where most educational institutions are mixed, this is distinctly odd. There are still many areas of research where data on males as males would be of considerable educational value. The impact of feminist methods has potential to challenge familiarity and assuage our lust of knowing. As Morgan (1981) has pointed out, 'taking gender seriously' is not a simple operation.

Everyone else needs to bear in mind the following points when carrying out qualitative educational studies:

1   Be conscious of gender differences, or possible gender differences, in all fieldwork settings.
2   Include males and females in all enquiries, or be self-conscious about the reasons for choosing a single-sex sample.
3   Never extrapolate findings from males to females.
4   Avoid taken-for-granted gender roles when framing interview schedules, planning observation, etc.
5   Avoid gender-specific language unless essential to the sense of your writing.
6   Avoid sexist wording whenever possible and listen for it from informants.

A good piece of fieldwork will be reflexive about the sex of the investigator and its impact on the data, will explore the importance of gender in the setting, and will be written in a non-sexist style. The informants may be women with sexist ideas, radical feminists or chauvinist males: the fieldwork should make gender problematic in all three settings.

Racism

It is much easier for me, a woman who has done research on girls and women, to make gender problematic than it is for me, as a 'white' person, to make racism problematic. Michelle Fine, Lois Weis, Linda Powell and L. Mun Wong (1997) make a similar point when they argue that 'we have witnessed a flurry of scholarship on multiculturalism, but across these texts there rings out a consistent silence, a silence on questions of whiteness' (p. vii).

Convinced that 'white standpoints, privileged standpoints, are still taken as the benign norm' (p. viii), they edited a book, *Off White*. In it they put 'whiteness' in the centre of the analytic spotlight to analyse it, to stop it being 'both invisible and dominant' (p. ix). Fine and Weis (1998) had been collecting, during the 1990s, data from 154 working-class and poor women and men aged 23 to 35 in Jersey City and Buffalo, two cities suffering from de-industrialization. Buffalo, for instance, lost 21 per cent of its manual jobs between 1960 and 1990. White working-class men suffered most from this – because they held the 'best' manual jobs. The men in Fine and Weis's research did not blame the American economy, globalization or the owners and shareholders of big business for their plight: they blamed Afro-American men. Such findings led them to focus on whiteness and 'all its glistening privilege' (p. xi).

The four editors of *Off White* are brave enough to claim that future students are able to draw on 'smart theory, vivid research and powerful pedagogies' to 'struggle with whiteness' (p. xii), Certainly that is the best way to avoid racism in research. In the UK there is a twist to racism, or rather to the best attempt at anti-racism. Too many researchers equate 'Britain' and 'England': they do not 'see' the other three nations. As long as people in England cannot 'see' Northern Ireland, Scotland and Wales, they are perpetuating forms of ethnocentrism and colonialism that impede any programme of anti-racist analysis or non-racist research.

To conduct non-racist ethnography, we all need to bear in mind the following points:

1   Be conscious of racial differences, or possible racial differences, in all fieldwork settings.
2   Include all races in all enquiries, or be self-conscious about the reasons for taking a less diverse racial sample.
3   Never extrapolate findings from one race to another.
4   Avoid taken-for-granted racial stereotypes when framing interview schedules, planning observation, etc.
5   Avoid racially stereotypical language unless you are quoting informants directly.
6   Do not leave informants' racist language unremarked on in your text.

A good piece of fieldwork is reflexive about the race of the investigator and its impact on the data, will explore the importance of race in the setting, and will be written in a non-sexist style. Mac an Ghaill's (1994) use of his own Irishness is exemplary; Rapport's (1993) Jewish/Welsh identity problems during a study of Cumbrian farmers is salutary. The views of Rapport, and of his key informants, are equally inducing of culture shock.

Going native

'Going native' is an objectionable term, deservedly, for an objectionable phenomenon. It means over-identifying with the respondents, and losing the researcher's twin perspectives of her own culture and, more importantly, of her 'research' outlook. Many classic anthropological jokes or folk tales turn on 'going native': stories of reaching the sacred burial ground of a tribe to find a ceremony in progress, only to discover that the leading ritual expert is another anthropologist, whipping lazy locals into the correct form of the dances. Students are warned of the last great Kwakiutl potlatch, attended by ten bored Kwakiutl and twenty eager anthropologists.

Anthropologists have particular problems trying to handle this. Loring Danforth (1989) highlights the problems of 'contemporary anthropology in a post-modern world' (p. 189). He describes how he began his Greek research (on death rituals and firewalking):

> I was an American, a graduate student in anthropology, and I had been brought up as a member of a liberal Protestant church in a white, upper-middle class suburb of Boston. I was going to live in a Greek village, a warm emotional place where people ate exotic food outdoors late at night and men embraced each other in public ... Greek churches were filled with candles, incense, bearded priests dressed in splendid robes.
>
> (p. 189)

Of course, once he had done his research this simplistic contrast dissolved. In some ways Danforth had 'become' partly Greek (he spoke the language, and he had a new sense of identity as a 'native' of Ayia Eleni, 'his' village). Danforth shows how the simple ideas of Americans versus Greeks, anthropologists versus firewalkers, scientists versus primitive believers, all dissolved in the face of the complex realities of contemporary Greek life. As a contrast to the 'traditional' Greek firewalking, Danforth also studied modern 'alternative' firewalking in Maine, confusing the distinctions even further, and not 'going native' anywhere.

In the 1980s many anthropologists began to explore how their discipline created 'the other' in their writing and became much more reflexive about their own processes. The rapid development of anthropological work on reflexive autobiography can be appreciated by reading the papers in Okely and Callaway (1992) with those in Reed-Danahay (1997). From such autobiographies we can see that the world of the ethnographer 'at home' is more problematic. It is harder to generate the initial sense of strangeness that characterizes anthropology, but equally easy to 'over-identify' and 'go native'.

Philip Cusick (1973) offers a typical example of a researcher 'going native' in an American high school. He was studying student culture, and had gone in at the top of the hierarchy of cliques, among the sportsmen and their cheerleading female companions who ran the school clubs and societies. Cusick could 'see' the social structure of tightly bounded, exclusive dyads, triads and cliques in ways the teachers could not. Yet, as Cusick spent time with the high-status groups – and especially with the young sportsmen – he 'went native', as he cheerfully admits.

> There was an important question about those who apparently did not have any friends. One person in particular was a boy named Nick who would frequently stand around the student lounge by himself. In the first few minutes I knew him, he volunteered, 'You probably noticed that I'm not too popular. I don't have many friends.'

Of Nick and others like him, Bill said, 'Them, they're just standing around leaning against the wall. They're out of it.' Which, as far as I could see, was a good description of what Nick did. I occasionally asked others about students who had no friends and would mention Nick as an example. Although he had been in the class for years they would say, 'Who? Who do you mean?' They did not even see him, and I found that as I became closer to the members of one particular group, *I, too, stopped seeing Nick.*

(Cusick 1973: 67–8, emphasis mine)

In the years after Cusick, other researchers fell into the same trap: they became over-identified with one sub-group of the participants in their setting. It is a fine line between doing excellent research, which enables the researcher and then her readers to see the world as the actors see it, and becoming so over-identified with that viewpoint that the others in the setting become stereotyped, or are ignored. It may not be possible, or desirable, to try and see the setting from all the possible angles, but if a study is partial that needs to be explained to its eventual audience. For example, in Merryfield (2000) one of her respondents, Joyce King, describes a formative experience:

I visited Stanford's campus as a high school student and sought out a young woman from my home town. She went to my church and our parents grew up together in the South. Although she had been at Stanford for two years, no one seemed to know her; she was invisible even to the other women in her dorm.

(p. 435)

Joyce King and her family friend are both African-American. If an ethnographer had been studying that dorm or that class at Stanford along the lines of Moffat (1989) or Holland and Eisenhart (1990) it would have been all too easy not to 'see' Joyce King's friend: to ignore her as Cusick ignored Nick.

Marqusee (1994) is an American, a Jew, a Marxist, who loves cricket. He came to England in 1971 and fell in with some friends who listened to *Test Match Special*. In 1976, when the West Indies destroyed England, he 'fell in love with the game' (p. 6). Knowledgeable about baseball, he began to study cricket as an American outsider. By 1994 he knew he had 'gone native':

Over the years I have come to take for granted many of the peculiarities of English cricket. Nowadays when I take Americans to a cricket match … I find myself taken aback by their enquiries … many products of cricket's history have become invisible to me, a distressing sign that I may be becoming 'English'.

(p. 26)

In the sphere of educational research, 'going native' means over-identifying, or over-empathizing, with either all teachers or all pupils, or some subset of the staff or the children. No one has ever accused an educational ethnographer of over-empathy with a secretary, nurse, lab technician or caretaker. Generally, critics of education ethnographies accuse the researchers of going native among the pupils, and therefore being biased against teachers and good order in schools. Where class, race and sex are involved, these accusations about going native are particularly likely to arise. To illustrate this point, a specific example of such an accusation from 1980 is explored, and then the topic is brought up to today and set in the context of Becker's (1967) classic paper on bias.

In 1980 David McNamara published a polemical attack on the educational ethnographies enjoying popularity in Britain at the time. He accused the authors of being arrogantly anti-teacher, and blamed the authors for being 'outsiders' to schools, who misrepresented what they saw or misreported it. In fact, as the example below will show, McNamara has identified a real problem, but got its nature wrong. All the papers he objected to were attempts by researchers to show what the school and the classroom look like through the eyes of the pupil. If they had a fault, it was over-identifying with the pupil and becoming too involved with their worldview rather than remaining outsiders. McNamara complained:

> In his study of school discipline Woods (1975) clearly indicates where his unexamined sympathy lies and while indicating that the teacher has a problem he fails to appreciate how it may appear to the teacher and how, within the context of an actual lesson, he might resolve it. Woods is concerned with an aspect of unofficial punishment in schools: the public showing up of pupils who deviate from the norm. He recognized the importance of this punishment technique during a two-term period of field study in a secondary modern school and his discussion is based upon transcripts of lessons and recorded interviews with pupils. An example of what are called 'officially sponsored embarrassments' (124) is illustrated in the following passage.
>
> (p. 119)

McNamara then quotes a passage of transcribed group interviews from Woods (1975).

Christine: I don't like that subject because I can't stand the teacher. I've never really liked him since I got caught skiving, and he made that right fool of me, and I sat next to Kevin ... don't you remember! ... I've never been so bright red in all my life.
Interviewer: What did he say?
Christine: Oh nothing, I'm not telling you.

Interviewer: Come on, tell us what he said.

Christine: I was sitting next to Kevin and he'd got his cartridge in his pen
and he was going like that *(she indicates an obscene gesture)*, and I
just pushed him away, and the teacher was writing on the board
and he must have eyes in the back of his head ... and he says ...
he turns round with a fuming face and he says 'will you two stop
fiddling with each other!' I never went so bright red in all my
life, and he pushed me over one side and him on the other ...
and everybody turned round, didn't they ... in front of all my
friends! You know ... he made such a ... mockery ... can't stand
him! Everybody was scared stiff in that class, everyone just sits
there, all quiet.

(*ibid.*)

Before reading either Woods's original commentary on this or McNamara's
attack on Woods, it is important to notice that these particular pupils were
girls, and that Kevin was apparently making an obscene gesture to Christine.
In 1990 an ethnographer might well use this incident as an illustration of
sexual harassment. In 1975 Woods commented:

This vividly portrays the consumer's experience and a common teacher
problem. So acutely had she felt the embarrassment that she found it very
difficult to relate, but having started almost by accident, she responded to
her three friends present, and addressed most of her remarks to them.
There was no doubting the intensity of the hostility felt towards the
teacher in question, chiefly based on that one incident. According to
Christine's account, she was the victim of both Kevin and the teacher.
With Kevin, however, it was privatized. The teacher made the matter
public, implied illicit sexual activity, very plausibly to others perhaps
because the pair were sitting at the back unseen, and everyone discontinued activity to turn around and gaze. This sudden transformation of
position vis-à-vis others, from being at the back one moment to being at
the front the next, is a necessary feature of the 'Shock' show-up. That her
closest friends were present made things worse, and that it was a
'mockery' of what had actually been happening compounded her sense
of injustice.

(pp. 134–5)

Woods was emphasizing how teenagers resented and were repelled by this
disciplinary strategy: being 'shown up'. This paper formed part of a literature
which demonstrated how adolescents responded better to teachers who were
not sarcastic and did not use humiliations to keep order.

McNamara is apparently unable to accept that studying how pupils see
classroom life is a useful or valid research activity. Worse, he appears to believe

that there is one reality and that the teacher is the only participant who should be studied. He attacked Woods as follows:

> The interesting point about this interpretation of the evidence is that the researcher's sympathy is clearly for the pupil. Why? By her own admission Christine has been skiving and there has been something rather interesting taking place on the back row. Yet she is a 'consumer' who has been embarrassed. She is a victim, she has been shocked and shown up in public among her closest friends. But what about the circumstances of the teacher who has been trying to write on the blackboard and, it would seem, has been disturbed by the sexual games in the back row? How would the observer have him respond? Was he to ignore the event? Was he to interrupt his blackboard work and talk to the pupil quietly? Was he to request the pupils come and see him later in the day in private? Of course not. Teachers must remove their attention from the class from time to time and if older children do not behave responsibly ... then they must be publicly rebuked. In this case a short sharp admonition was probably more effective, in that it stopped the bad behaviour and reminded the rest of the class to behave, than an investigation of the rights and wrongs of the event and the formal punishment of the guilty parties. Woods is concerned that the attack on corporal punishment has over-shadowed other punishments which 'may impinge on the pupil to a great extent'. But he never reports any conversations with teachers and thus examines how activities of pupils may impinge upon their efforts to teach. For the beginning teacher, the problem is to find out about craft techniques which can be used when faced with disruptive pupils. The teacher's response to Christine's behaviour is probably a good example of the way in which the experienced teacher rapidly copes with a potentially disruptive situation.
>
> (p. 120)

McNamara attacked Woods because his 'sympathy' is 'clearly for the pupils', when Christine had been misbehaving in class and therefore deserved to be punished. Taking the 'side' of a teacher, McNamara claims that 'a short, sharp admonition' was 'probably' effective. This analysis is clearly wrong. First, the pupils concerned were so angry about the master's disciplinary style they were no longer prepared to learn anything from him. While they may have been 'in the wrong', the teacher had alienated them to the detriment of their subsequent education. Second, if either experienced or trainee teachers are to consider disciplinary strategies, information about how they are interpreted and received by pupils is vital. A professional cannot make an informed decision about how to respond to scuffling in the back row without some recognition of how reprimands will be 'heard'. Any student teacher who understood the literature on the pupil's eye view of humiliation as a form of classroom control would look for alternatives. Woods's analysis shows that, in McNamara's own terms, 'showing up' pupils is counterproductive.

In 2001 it is striking that neither Woods nor McNamara saw this as an example of sexual harassment between pupils. Kevin is harassing Christine, and the teacher, instead of seeing her as a victim, effectively labelled her as a 'slut' – the kind of girl who lets Kevin fiddle with her in class. Sue Lees (1986) and similar authors (e.g. Herbert, 1989) have shown us how vulnerable young women are to accusations of this kind.

Woods could have asked teachers who routinely used humiliation as a control strategy about their reasons for doing so, and discovered if they even realized they were doing it. That would be an interesting piece of research which has yet to be done as systematically as the work on how pupils feel about being disciplined. Such an investigation would, however, be a different task from the one Woods set himself in his 1975 paper.

As most school and classroom ethnographies end up over-identifying with either the pupils – or some sub-set of the student body – or with the teachers, or some faction of the staffroom, McNamara had a point, even if he himself had missed it.

The argument and counter-argument was more bitter about race than gender, and can be found in Woods and Hammersley (1993) and Foster et al. (1996). On race, the main ethnographers attacked were David Gillborn, Cecile Wright and the late Barry Troyna. The collection edited by Connolly and Troyna (1998) is the counterweight to the Hammersley position. The level of discussion has not risen beyond that in the dispute between McNamara and Woods: the late Peter Foster's arguments were essentially the same as McNamara's.

Rather than rehearse details of these debates, it is more sensible to go back and remind ourselves of Becker's (1967) famous essay 'Whose side are we on?' Becker started from the position that it is impossible to do research 'that is uncontaminated by personal and political sympathies' (p. 123), and that it is inevitable that all researchers will take sides. Therefore, 'whose side are we on?' is the crucial question. He illustrated his argument with examples from the study of deviance, but all the points raised could have come out of his earlier work on education, in the Chicago public schools and the University of Kansas. Becker chose deviance because sociologists of deviance are frequently told they are 'too sympathetic' to the deviants, and that this sympathy has distorted and biased the research. As he summarizes the charge:

1 we fall into deep sympathy with the people we are studying;
2 we believe they are more sinned against than sinning;
3 we do not give a balanced picture;
4 we neglect to ask those questions that would show that the deviant has done something pretty rotten;
5 we product a whitewash of the deviant;
6 we produce a condemnation of respectable citizens.

(pp. 124–5)

Becker then examines the precise circumstances in which such charges are levelled at sociologists and concludes that the accusation of bias is levelled at investigations which give 'credence' to 'the perspective of the subordinate group in some hierarchical relationship' (p. 125). In deviance research, the subordinate group are criminals, prisoners, deviants; the respectable are police, prison officers, judges, lawyers and the 'law-abiding' citizen, especially in the middle classes.

Becker then compares deviance research with educational studies, pointing out that 'Professors and administrators, principals and teachers, are the super-ordinates, while students and pupils are the subordinates' (p. 125). In all hierarchies, Becker points out, 'credibility and the right to be heard are differentially distributed through the ranks of the system' (p. 127). Researchers who refuse to abide by that 'hierarchy of credibility' are actually expressing 'disrespect for the entire established order' (p. 127). Accusations of bias arise when the researcher has not accepted the established hierarchy of credibility.

Given that 'we must always look at the matter from someone's point of view' (p. 131) and 'we can never avoid taking sides' (p. 132), Becker argues that the real question is whether our work is so distorted that it is useless. The central point of his paper is that good researchers have to strive to do projects which are not rendered useless by our biases. We must ensure that 'our unavoidable sympathies do not render our work invalid' (p. 132). The Becker strategies for valid research are:

1   Do not misuse the techniques of our discipline.
2   Use our theories impartially.
3   Avoid sentimentality.
4   Inspect our methods and theories to ensure they could disprove our beliefs.
5   Make clear the limits of what we have studied (i.e. the vantage point adopted).

(pp. 132–4)

Throughout his paper, Becker had distinguished between research settings which were explicitly political and those which were held to be not political, such as schools, hospitals and prisons. Accusations of bias were less frequently made, Becker claimed, when explicitly political settings are studied, because the disputed claims of the participants are overt and have spokespeople in the setting. Becker's careful discussion of bias is also an excellent discussion of the dangers of 'going native', and an explanation of where Foster et al. really disagreed with Gillborn, Wright and Troyna.

It is extremely hard to collect the perspectives of all the participants, it is harder to empathize with all viewpoints, and it is hardest of all to produce an account of a setting which gives equal status to the lives of males and females, 'lads' and 'ear 'oles', the 'good old boy' male staff (Datnow, 1998) and the feminist ones, the caretaker and the senior mistress, the head and the newest probationer, and make it all seem coherent. Mac an Ghaill (1994) manages to present the views and experiences of many different groups: that is why it is exemplary.

Being bored

Being bored can be a serious problem. If a researcher is bored with the whole idea of research, as well as with the specific project, then a change of career seems indicated. As research, done full time, is not well paid, lacks security and is highly stressful, it is not a career for anyone except the insatiably curious. If a person is trying to do it part time, the boredom might be resolved by spending more time and getting the project finished. However, few people read a book about something with which they are bored, so I am assuming none of my readers finds research tedious: the types of boredom that concern us here are finding the data collection, or the analysis, or the writing up, boring.

One solution to any one of those three problems is to mix the three stages up. If analysis seems boring, mix it with more data collection (perhaps in the library rather than the field) and with writing. Some tasks are boring, and it is better to plan short bursts interspersed with other activities. Coding, transcribing, entering data on to computer files and into a software package, and sorting out the referencing can all be dull jobs – so they are best done in stages with different tasks interwoven.

If the fieldwork/data collection is boring, there is something wrong. It may be time to stop. It may be time to take a break and do some serious thinking, collating and analysing. However, it is also possible that the boredom is a signal for the researchers to change their focus, or play a new role, or ask different questions. Boredom can grow because the setting becomes too familiar, so the devices in the next section may help.

Deliberately seeing things from another view can help. For example, in a school, try sitting in different places in class and staffrooms, 'hanging out' with groups or even isolates who have been previously neglected. If you have been in a school among teachers or pupils, try a day with the dinner ladies, or inside the kitchen with the cooks, or with the school bus driver, or with the secretary or nurse. Try breaking up the routine: if you have been following 3C, make a change by spending a whole day based in the art room, or in the swimming pool, or in the library, or behind the bike sheds. In an infant classroom try basing yourself in a different corner. Lisa Serbin (1984) found that nursery school teachers very rarely went to certain bits of their rooms and rarely played with some of the toys (especially cars/trucks/bricks). It is entirely possible that a researcher can slip into a cosy pattern of sitting in the same place day after day, and a fresh seat can give a fresh insight. If the fieldwork is boring, a day 'out' re-reading all the notes and memos while self-consciously listing hypotheses to be tested, or ways of changing the angle, is a day well spent.

It is possible that the fieldwork site, or the content of the interviews, is boring for the researcher because it is boring for the participants. Some experiences are boring. For example, exam invigilation is not an exciting, challenging or brain-stretching task, and an observational study of invigilators would probably find they were bored, so it would be hard to keep the researcher's interest up too. David Lodge's (1962/1984) novel drawing on his experiences in the army doing national service, *Ginger, You're Barmy*, is a skilful evocation of how boring the peacetime army in Britain was: 'Nothing but a bleak prospect of windswept barracks, cold water in the early mornings, the harsh cries of stupid authority, the dreary monotony of slow-moving days' (1984: 126). A Belgian social scientist who read the book was convinced that Lodge was a conscript in the Belgian army, as the boredom is the same and is so well captured in Lodge's novel. Much of soldiering in wartime is also boring, as Colin Thubron (1968: 32) captures it in his account of walking through the Lebanon:

> After two hours I reached another post where iron obstructions stood and some men were being searched for weapons, and a sentry let me through unwillingly. I walked between tank blocks and followed the road into the empty valleys ... The miles to Israel dwindled ... Somewhere in front the soldiers faced one another, lost in the boredom which is the better half of war.

A vivid ethnography of boredom is a real challenge to the researcher and the author. See, for example, the study of guard duty on US air bases by Charlton and Hertz (1989). Tom Hall (2000) captures the sheer boredom of the lives of Britain's young homeless, 'killing' time. If the setting is not in itself boring, then the researcher's boredom may be the result of over-familiarity with the setting, the most frequent impediment to good fieldwork.

Fighting familiarity

The problem of over-familiarity is a central one in qualitative research. This point was made by Blanche Geer (1964) long ago:

> Untrained observers ... can spend a day in a hospital and come back with one page of notes and no hypotheses. It was a hospital, they say; everyone knows what hospitals are like.
>
> (p. 384)

Such a response (which is not entirely confined to untrained observers) reflects the 'natural attitude' of thinking as usual, and a corresponding failure to suspend such commonsense assumptions. It is a particular problem in educational research and the familiarity trap was graphically described by Howard Becker (1971: 10):

> We may have understated a little the difficulty of observing contemporary classrooms. It is not just the survey method of educational testing or any of those things that keeps people from seeing what is going on. I think instead, that it is first and foremost a matter of it all being so familiar that it becomes impossible to single out events that occur in the classroom as things that have occurred, even when they happen right in front of you. I have not had the experience of observing in elementary and high school classrooms myself, but I have in college classrooms and it takes a tremendous effort of will and imagination to stop seeing the things that are conventionally 'there' to be seen. I have talked to a couple of teams of research people who have sat around in classrooms trying to observe and it is like pulling teeth to get them to see or write anything beyond what 'everyone' knows.

Expressed by Becker, the problem of familiarity may not sound too serious. Consider, however, the following extract, which is all an untrained observer managed to record about an English lesson lasting forty minutes at Guy Mannering (9–13) School, taught by Mr Evans:

> Children supposed to work in silence on an essay 'a foolish thing I did'. Terence, of course, had done three foolish things in his life, according to his mum, and whispered them to Mr Evans who advised him on the most foolish. Dominico Grillo seems to get a fair share of friendly attention and Norris a lot of chivvying

Even if one accepts that a lesson in which an essay is written by docile 9-year-olds cannot be expected to produce observational fireworks or massive insights into Gramscian hegemony, this extract reveals the familiarity problem. Nothing has been recorded about the time of day, the weather, the room, the teacher's dress or demeanour, what Mr Evans did for forty minutes, the number of pupils present, their seating arrangements, what they wrote with or on, whether the board was used, if dictionaries were available, and so on. There were twenty-nine children in the class, fourteen girls and fifteen boys (Delamont and Galton, 1986: 248). Noticeably, while twelve boys are not written about, three are, yet no girl is mentioned at all. A reader who knew nothing else about Guy Mannering could have decided it was a single-sex school.

These notes are a perfect illustration of the point Becker and Geer were making: a researcher too familiar with schooling to 'see' anything going on.

Yet novices are not the only people to fall into the trap of being 'too close' to schooling, especially schooling in our own culture. The great strength of Hammersley and Atkinson (1995) is that they widen the horizons of educational researchers by showing that methods used in, and findings from, other social settings (prisons, Spanish villages, public lavatories, Brazilian umbanda ceremonies, hospitals or nude beaches) are not only parallel to those from educational contexts, but also, by providing a contrast, can stimulate fresh insights into education. The arguments for fighting familiarity and detailed examples of strategies for doing so are the subject of Delamont and Atkinson (1995).

Novice and experienced teachers would benefit from adopting the aims of researchers: fighting familiarity. Many social settings, and especially educational institutions, are too familiar. Central features of education are so taken for granted that they are invisible. Wolcott (1981: 253) made this point about his own practice when he wrote that it took a colleague from outside educational research 'to jolt me into realizing that the kinds of data teachers gather "on" and "for" each other so admiringly reflects the dominant society and its educator subculture'.

This colleague was 'particularly intrigued' by the research about 'time on task' and commented:

> How incredible ... that teachers would measure classroom effectiveness by whether pupils appear to be busy. How like teachers to confuse 'busyness' and learning.
>
> (p. 253)

Wolcott then pointed out that he and his educational research colleagues

> have not systematically encouraged our students ... to go and look at something else for a while. We keep sending them back to the classroom. The only doctoral student I have sent off to do fieldwork in a hospital was a nurse-educator who returned to her faculty position in a school of nursing!
>
> (p. 260)

Wolcott and Becker's comments appeared in American 'anthropology of education' collections, just as M.F.D. Young was issuing his clarion call to British sociologists. While there are significant differences between British and American researchers in their use of qualitative methods (Atkinson and Delamont, 1980; Delamont and Atkinson, 1995), it is clear that, in 1971, on both sides of the Atlantic there were similar feelings about researchers taking too many features of schooling for granted.

The central argument in Young's (1971) piece was, of course, that sociologists had focused so much on structures that they had neglected to study the content of education and who had power over it. Young did offer a solution for sociologists, that instead of taking as obvious the problems of teachers, they should make the curriculum problematic. Becker (1971) did not offer any solution to the familiarity problem for educational researchers, although he found one in his own area of occupational socialization. Consequent upon his desire to treat all types of occupation as potentially similar in sociologically interesting respects, Becker and Geer followed their studies of medical students with liberal arts undergraduates, and then turned their attention to occupational learning in different contexts. Rather than mounting yet another study of a single institution, they directed a number of small related projects (mostly undertaken single-handed by junior colleagues). These were deliberately focused on topics other than 'professions': a barber school, apprentice high steelworker; learning door-to-door selling; a county jail school; workers learning new jobs in an electronic plant (Geer, 1972). Becker did not offer his readers any strategies for challenging the familiarity of normal school and college classrooms. It is my contention, however, that the Becker/Young diagnosis was correct, and that little has changed since.

Our task, as researchers now, is to devise strategies to deal with the familiarity problem and to empower teachers to challenge the familiarity of schooling. This could be done by insisting that all teachers had periods in other occupations, rather than through the academic study of schools. All the deadening aspects of the occupational culture of teaching (Hargreaves, 1980) would be dispelled by systematic exposure to other occupational cultures. Rather than focusing the sociology of education ever more closely on teachers and teaching, the sociology of education should look outwards to other social settings, and campaign for teacher-researchers to have the challenging experience too.

Humans learn and teach in many types of setting, but the rich potential of incorporating the study of such settings into British educational research has not been exploited. If the sociology of education in the UK has ignored Becker and Young, the other major tradition of qualitative research in education, American applied anthropology, is no better.

The decade following the publication of the Spindler (1982) and the Popkewitz and Tabachnick (1981) volumes saw a continuing stream of qualitative research on American education being produced. Spindler and Spindler (1987) contains nineteen chapters, two by a British researcher, Paul Yates (1987a and 1987b). The Eisner and Peshkin (1990) collection on qualitative research reverts to being all-American, as does de Marrais (1998). Studying back issues of *Anthropology and Education Quarterly* and *Qualitative Studies in Education* is salutary for non-Americans: we and our countries do not exist. The lack of challenge to the American authors' and readers' sense of familiarity did not alter, nor did their ethnocentric citation patterns. Overall, a perusal of these volumes forces the conclusion that the anthropology of education is still as all-American as Yellowstone Park, and that the booming field of education ethnography is equally isolationist.

Neglect of research outside the USA forgoes the opportunity to make use of national differences in educational experience and organization to point out features of the US scene that might otherwise be taken for granted. Many features of American education are immediately thrown into relief, made visible and illuminated, by systematic comparison with other educational practices. Finders (1997) is an ethnography of girls' literacies in Northern Hills Junior High, a good school in the rural Midwest of the USA.

Finders starts her monograph with an event from the end of the school year: the 'sale and distribution of the school yearbook' (p. 31). This event, while important to many staff and pupils at Northern Hills, signifying the move to adolescence (for elementary pupils do not have a yearbook), needs far more context and explanation for readers outside the USA than Finders provides. For American readers, Finders raises good questions about the yearbook; but to someone reading the monograph in Wales, the chapter is puzzling. What *is* a yearbook? Why do American schools have them? Why are Americans happy that producing the yearbook 'counts' as 'work' and is done as a course, in work time? It is inconceivable that French, German or Japanese teenagers would 'waste' time producing a largely photographic record of themselves rather than studying Latin, ancient Greek, French or calculus.

At Northern Hills, sixty-five pupils prepared the 48-page yearbook. Pupils took the photographs for it, overwhelmingly of after-school clubs and team activities. Teachers saw the yearbook as the symbol of the school as a community, and regarded participation in sport, clubs and drama as a central part of the school's life. Yet, as Finders points out, the 'community' was an exclusive one. Teachers said repeatedly that 'everybody' buys a yearbook and 'everyone' loves it. In fact, in the year Finders was doing her study the school had 531 pupils but only 397 of them bought a yearbook. A quarter of the pupils were 'invisible' to teachers, excluded from the community. Finders contrasts two girls who were 'social queens' (Tiffany and Angie) and two who were tough cookies (Cleo and Dottie). The latter, from a trailer park, were not involved in any extra-curricular activities, took no part in the 'social' life of the school and did not buy a yearbook. This was partly financial, but also because 'I don't know why I would want one. None of my friends are in there anyway' (p. 35).

The published research on American junior high schools and high schools from Hollingshead (1947) through to the ethnographies of the past forty years such as Cusick (1973), Martin (1976), Larkin (1979), Metz (1978, 1986), Grant and Sleeter (1986), Gibson (1988), Lesko (1988), Wexler (1992), Peshkin (1986), Abi-Nader (1990), Fordham (1993), Merton (1994), Mehan *et al.* (1994), Hemmings (1996), Merton (1996), Schultz (1996), Goto (1997), Datnow (1997) and Lustig (1998), consists of studies which make the massacre at Colombine High in Colorado seem entirely understandable. Study after study has shown that the 'leading crowd' who do well in school work *but are resolutely anti-intellectual* come from the wealthiest homes served by that school, play team games (mostly the boys) and are cheerleaders (the girls), who write the yearbook and elect each other Prom Queen and Homecoming Queen, are lauded and cherished by the staff. Pupils who prefer to be intellectual, those who avoid the school's social life, and those who are outcasts because of poverty, race, religion, language, drink, drugs or just 'not belonging', have an appalling experience. To a non-American, the number of 'lessons' which are actually not lessons at all is also striking. Pupils who are cheerleaders learn their routines as lessons; producing the yearbook is a lesson.

Other American disciplines are equally ethnocentric. American authors and editors practise routine, casual, unthinking ethnocentrism which makes all of *us* second-class citizens of *their* global colonialism. For example, Ellis and Bochner (1996) has fourteen chapters, all but one by Americans. Jessor *et al.* (1996) has twenty-one chapters, all by Americans. The second edition of Denzin and Lincoln (2000) has forty-one chapters written by fifty-six authors. Four are Australian, three British and one Norwegian.

Our task, as researchers now, is to devise strategies to deal with the familiarity problem. The four strategies outlined below do not exhaust the ways in which familiarity can be contested, but are good weapons to consider. Accordingly, it is useful to run through four of the possible strategies suggested to combat familiarity and the other impediments outlined earlier.

Making the familiar strange

There are four strategies available to the sociologist for making the familiar bizarre, unusual and novel. If we take classrooms and schools as our empirical area, there are the following possibilities for action:

1   Study unusual, bizarre or different classrooms, such as those for adults rather than children, the deaf, blind and physically handicapped rather than the able-bodied, or unusual subjects such as PE or pottery rather than English or maths. The 'familiarity' is thus thrown into relief by contrast with the unfamiliar.
2   Study schools and classrooms in other cultures, such as Orthodox Judaism, Islamic instruction, Maoist regimes or native Amerindian societies. This has been mainly the province of the anthropology of education, but there is no reason why it should not provide a contrasting locale to aid the sociologist.
3   Study non-educational settings chosen for their parallel features by theoretical sampling (Glaser and Strauss, 1967). Research on aspects of hospitals, prisons, factories, shops, street corners and TV studios (to take a few examples) should help to give a novel perspective to school research.
4   Adopt gender, race or sexuality as the main focus of the study. The attempt to focus on a neglected, taken-for-granted feature of school life can highlight other aspects of it.

These four strategies are not mutually exclusive, but what is chiefly notable about educational research in Britain (and in the USA and Canada) is that none of them has been adopted except by one or two 'eccentrics'. When we examine each strategy in turn, the most notable finding is that researchers have not tried it.

Studying 'different' classrooms and schools

The majority of school and classroom studies have been carried out on able-bodied, normal ability range pupils in state schools, taking academic subjects. We lack studies of interaction in elite schools (in the UK of preparatory schools, public schools for boys, convents and public schools for girls). We have few data on sixth form colleges (Aggleton, 1987 is an exception), little on the nursery age group, and little on adults learning. Britain is short of observational work on learning-disabled pupils, on the physically handicapped, the blind or the deaf. We have no ethnographic work on the Welsh–medium schools in Wales, and little on Gaelic schools in Scotland. The Catholic schools throughout Britain have not been researched except for Burgess's (1983) study of Bishop McGregor Comprehensive, and there are no published accounts of Islamic, Jewish, Seventh-Day Adventist or other fundamentalist Christian schooling. The many Saturday schools for Italian, Polish, Greek, Sikh and Islamic children to learn their own languages have been neglected.

Teaching and learning go on in medical schools (Atkinson, 1997a, 1984a, 1984b) and there are parallels between bedside teaching and school science (Delamont and Atkinson, 1995). The teaching of student architects, accountants, plumbers, taxi drivers and hairdressers should all be part of educational research.

When scholars have collected data on any of these 'unusual' schools or classrooms (e.g. Evans and Wragg, 1969) the payoff is considerable. When Evans and Wragg (1969) were observing learning-disabled classes, using FIAC (Flanders, 1970), they found that the children's utterances could not usefully be confined within the two categories of 'response' and 'initiation'. Instead, pupils made contributions which were 'praise', 'encouragements' and so on. In other words, the children talked like teachers – that is, inappropriately. This is interesting at two levels. It tells us something useful about learning-disabled pupils. But it also tells us something about 'normal' pupils, 'normal' classrooms, and about Flanders's member's knowledge about them. Mainstream pupils do not make comments of this kind, and when Flanders was constructing his system he made no allowance for any pupils to do so. Mary Darmanin's (1990) ethnography of Maltese primary schooling included a deliberate contrast. She wrote:

> In order to 'make strange' classroom practices in state schools, I also
> spent some weeks in private fee-paying schools. I found that it was

precisely in the question of constraints and strategies that the differences lie which serve to separate the two sectors. Shortly after my fieldwork observation the very questions of differences between the two sectors became a political issue in the Maltese scenario and has remained so ever since. The history of this issue as well as an analysis of organizational policies of the two sectors will be presented in this thesis, as a way of 'making strange' practices in state schools. Some attention will be given to the political implications of a differentiated system. in fact the Maltese data indicate that the private sector is in itself a constraint on the state sector.

Study 'other cultures'

Paul Atkinson and I (Delamont and Atkinson, 1995) have reviewed the field of educational anthropology, which is almost non-existent in Britain, and shown how little cross-referencing there is between the sociology and anthropology of schooling. Apart from one or two 'classic' papers popularized by the Open University (e.g. Dumont and Wax, 1971) the large body of work produced by applied anthropologists has been shamefully neglected by British sociology of education. Curriculum researchers do not refer to Wolcott (1977), researchers in inner cities ignore Rosenfeld (1971) and the journal of the American anthropologists of education (AEQ) is not widely available in Britain. The potential intellectual mileage gained by comparisons with other cultures, whether of minority groups in our own mass society or different countries long ago and far away, is great. When educational researchers have made such comparisons, they have inevitably focused upon a 'disadvantaged', under-achieving group to show how they 'fail' in school because they have a culture of their own which is contradictory to that of the school. The material on First American groups by Dumont and Wax (1971) is regularly cited, and so is that on African-Americans collected by Labov (1972). Yet it is probably more fruitful to look at the opposite case: highly successful pupils in other cultures. Singleton's (1967) material on Nichu, a Japanese school, raises many important questions about British education. The work of Maryon McDonald (1989) and Deborah Reed-Danahay (1987 and 1996) on Breton and French schooling is unlikely to be read by British educational researchers because it appears as anthropology. McDonald's work, published during the 1980s, has not had the impact on the study of Welsh schooling it deserves. Gibson's (1987a, 1987b, 1988) study of Punjabi pupils in a Californian high school focuses on adolescents who are regarded as peculiar by the staff because they work too hard and do not 'party' like WASP teenagers. Two concrete examples, one American, one Australian, will illustrate the point. Hostetler and Huntington's (1971) *Children in Amish Society* describes school life for the Old Order Amish in the USA. They are strict Anabaptists, who reject all modern technology and most modern beliefs, and have to fight to be allowed to run their own schools in which their children learn only Amish ideas and practices. Their children are very successful in school, and so unlike the native Indian groups, but the schooling is diametrically opposed to standard American schooling. Similarly, the Orthodox Lubavitcher (Chassidic) Jews in Australia studied by Bullivant (1978) are highly successful in their school. Yet they reject much of the 'Australian' knowledge in the syllabuses and adhere to Chassidic beliefs and practices. These books show two contrasting minority schools, each judged 'successful' by its community, in which knowledge, teacher–pupil interaction and pupil behaviour are all quite startlingly different from the majority culture with which they are surrounded. These two books, read alongside each other, contrast Protestant and Jew, rural and urban, agricultural and industrial, American and Australian, mixed and single-sex schooling. Neither book is about deviant or rebellious pupils, only those who are dancing to a different drummer from any that most ethnographers know. Therefore all our taken-for-granted assumptions about what school is for are challenged.

Study 'non-educational' settings

Sociologists of education in Britain are very bad at using published material from other empirical areas of sociology. Research on teachers and teaching is detached from the sociology of work (Delamont and Atkinson 1995). Despite Goffman's insights and pioneering work, research has not used material on hospitals, factories or shops to draw parallels and contrasts with educational settings. Howard Becker and Blanche Geer's educational work is cited, but that on other contexts for work learning (Geer, 1972) is not. People learn and teach in many settings which are not conventional schools and colleges, and studying such settings is always fruitful for educational researchers. Leacock and Leacock (1972: 173–88) have provided a vivid account of teaching and learning in the *terreiros* of Belem in northern Brazil. Terreiros are centres of spirit possession, where mediums receive *encantados* (spirits), go into trances and may act as counsellors and curers. Leacock and Leacock show how mediums have to learn their role: the role of a person possessed by an encantado who behaves properly while in trance:

> The expression they use is 'development'. When a person is possessed for the first time, it is expected that he will fall on the floor, stagger about, and be unable to sing. As he 'develops', however, the medium gains 'control' and is able to dance, sing and speak as the encantado.

Some terreiros run classes in which novices can practise going into a trance, and therefore practise the appropriate behaviours. The apprentice medium is told what spirit is possessing him or her, and is taught how to behave in the expected manner. A medium possessed by a dolphin spirit must learn a dance routine based on hopping, Curupiras are expected to bark like dogs, while mermaids have to grow long hair. One spirit, Joao da Mata, likes hats, so a medium expecting him must have a hat ready. All these behaviours and the use of props have to be learnt. The Leacocks' description of mediums learning and practising suggests many parallels with the student teachers described by Lacey (1977). Just as teachers have to learn to 'put on an act' to appear like teachers, so too the novice medium has to learn to put up a convincing performance as a possessed dancer, to become accepted as a genuine medium. Overall, the Leacocks' work offers an account of a teaching and learning centre with many potential insights for studying schools. Instruction and learning go on in many non-school settings. Barbara Heyl's (1979) informant taught new recruits how to be high-earning prostitutes in a classroom-like atmosphere. Dick Hobbs (1988) discusses how young men in London's East End learn to be skilled at the locally recognized criminal activities. Dan Mannix (1951) recounts how he learnt to be a fire-eater and a sword swallower, in an account most ethnographers would kill to have published. Systematic attention to learning in other settings will enrich educational research immeasurably.

Focus on gender, race or sexuality

The importance of gender, race and sexuality not only in their own right is demonstrated in Delamont and Atkinson (1995). Focusing on to gender or race or sexuality can work to make the familiar strange if they are taken for granted in the setting under scrutiny. Using gender to challenge familiarity can mean scrutinizing either women's lives or masculinity. Datnow (1998) focuses on gender in her illuminating analysis of the micropolitics of school reforms, for example. Lori Kendall (2000) focuses on hegemonic masculinity in her study of young people hanging out in an on-line chat room, rather as Fine (1983) did in his work on fantasy gaming. In both cases focusing on gender is revealing in many general ways about how chat rooms and fantasy gaming clubs work. A focus on race, or on sexuality, can work in the same way, as the papers in Fine et al. (1997) or the work of Renold (2000) show.

Conclusions

This chapter has outlined some of the main problems that can impede good fieldwork. Each researcher faces their own personal 'last blue mountain barred with snow', and has to deal with it. Flecker's pilgrims had the right idea, because they set out undeterred by mountains, saying 'surely we are brave'. The good qualitative researcher can emulate the pilgrims and struggle across the 'last blue mountain'.

Key reading

The key reading suggested for this chapter is Nigel Barley's (1983) *The Innocent Anthropologist*.

Chapter 4

Manuscripts in peacock styles
Writing diaries, data and texts

There is one almost infallible way to find honest food at just prices in blue-highway America: count the wall calendars in a café.

No calendar   Same as an interstate pit stop
One calendar   Preprocessed food assembled in New Jersey
Two calendars   Only if fish trophies present
Three calendars   Can't miss on the farm-boy breakfasts
Four calendars   Try the ho made pie too
Five calendars   Keep it under your hat, or they'll franchise.

Once I found a six-calendar café in the Ozarks, which served fried chicken, peach pie, and chocolate malts that left me searching for another ever since. I've never seen a seven-calendar place. But old-time travellers ... have told me the golden legends of seven-calendar cafés.

This quotation from William Least-Heat Moon (1982: 27) is a piece of fine writing, and its relevance to research may not seem immediately obvious. This chapter is about types of writing that need to be done – and those types are rather like the progression to the seven-calendar café. Ethnographers need to do hurried private writing quite unsuitable for outsiders to read, which can be as bad as the food in the 'no-calendar' café, and working papers like the 'three-calendar' place, and superb published work like places where we can eat the 'ho-made pie'.

Peter Woods (1986) has an excellent chapter on writing, which is frequently neglected or skimped in methods textbooks. The reader will be encouraged to learn that Peter Woods finds writing hard and throws away piles of draft as he works. Too many people believe that productive scholars have a 'gift' which makes writing 'easy', when prolific authors like Woods probably force themselves to sit at their desks from 9.00 a.m. to 12.30 p.m. and from 1.30 p.m. to 3.30 p.m. whether anything is being produced or not. Engagingly, Woods also admits that when he is trying to get started on writing something he can be bad-tempered. Equally delightful is Woods's self-portrait, when trying to write, of himself as an ancient Morris Minor 1000 which had to be cranked by hand before it would start. He has to crank himself up before he can write, and is explicit about how he does it, and how it can hurt. In his 1996 book Woods returns to the topic of writing. In the gap between the 1986 and 1996 volumes he had shifted from writing with a pen and giving the draft to a typist to working straight on to a word processor. He explores his shift, and illustrates his exploration with a wonderful range of quotes from academic, creative writers such as the late Iris Murdoch, and popular novelists such as Joanna Trollope. He argues persuasively for keeping the pen as an alternative to the keyboard.

As I came to prepare this new edition of this book the *Guardian* reprinted a short essay on writing from the *New York Times* by Walter Mosley (2000), the author of a series of detective stories set in post Second World War Los Angeles. (He is supposed to be Bill Clinton's favourite author but that should not detract from their merit as novels.) Mosley writes about writing: 'If you want to be a writer, you have to write every day … You don't skip a child's breakfast or forget to wake up in the morning. Sleep comes to you each day, and so does the muse' (p. 12).

Later in the piece he describes writing a novel as 'gathering smoke', and also as 'a kind of guerrilla warfare' because 'there is no vacation'. Academic writing is a little easier because we have data to start from: the image of 'gathering smoke' is harsher than we need. 'Guerrilla warfare', and the idea that we should write as regularly as we feed our children (or in my case a cat who adopted us) or wake up or sleep, are as appropriate for academic production as for novels. The American scholar Philip Jackson has likened writing to running. If you do not run every day, you never become a runner and never get fit. Similarly if you do not write every day, you never become an author. He describes running every morning and then writing every morning, before the real day begins.

Writing may be hard, but it is an essential part of the qualitative research process. There are three main kinds of writing to be done:

1   data;
2   analysis;
3   output.

By data, I mean fieldnotes, interview transcripts or whatever the basic data are. By analysis, I mean the analytic memos and other thought-provoking writing done to record the developing thinking about the data. The output writing is the final product you launch on the world. The first two types of writing are 'input' writing, the third is 'output' writing. The two types are closely related, because what you collect determines what you can publish, and what you want to publish determines what you collect.

Before examining the types of writing, it is important to stress that regular, sustained, detailed written records are central to qualitative research. Patrick Leigh Fermor (1986: 12) makes this point very well. In 1934–5 he was walking from the Hook of Holland to Constantinople. His notebook-cum-diary was lost in Moldavia in 1939, but recovered in 1977. However, when Fermor wanted to use his written record he found that:

> The notebook … has been a great help, but not the unfailing prop it should have been. When I came to a standstill during those long halts, writing stopped too: as I was keeping journal of travel, I wrongly thought there was nothing to record. I was often slow to take it up again when I moved on and, even then, jotted notes sometimes took the place of sustained narrative.

Here Fermor is reporting an exceptionally long gap between 'research' (1934–5) and 'publication' (1984–5). However, if his notebook had been better, he would have felt more secure about his reconstruction. Our data are only as good as our fieldnotes.

Researching on-line, as Lori Kendall (2000) did, involves different forms of writing during data collection. Some scholars who have studied on-line communication have focused on e-mails or newsgroups, and been able to download the text at their own convenience. Kendall gathered data as the participants in the chat room (also known as a 'mud', from the original fantasy gaming abbreviation for a Multi-User Dungeon) actually typed their messages. The participants in Blue Sky 'wrote' to each other 'live', and Kendall participated and read their conversation. She did not have to write fieldnotes because she could print the whole conversation to analyse at her leisure. In some senses her data are more like tape recordings of talk than observational fieldnotes. However, she still had to write herself analytic notes, just as if she had started from fieldnotes. Doing research on-line does not absolve the ethnographer from writing, but it does involve using writing in different ways.

This chapter demonstrates the three types of writing with a concrete example, called 'Bernard Coughing', from the Welsh research on the integration of learning-disabled children into mainstream schools (Upton et al., 1988). This is an incident recorded in my fieldnotes, reflected upon in an analytic memo, and eventually presented in the final published report. Following Bernard and his cough through the stages will illustrate different types of writing. Then the chapter explores what is known about how other qualitative researchers use writing, and how writing figures in non-observational studies.

Types of writing: data

There are few guidelines about what to write in fieldnotes, how to transcribe interviews, what documents are important and how to take notes on them. Researchers rarely show what they actually wrote in the lecture hall or on the games field, but produce an account of what they heard and saw and thought, written much later. Publishing actual fieldnotes has ethical problems (real names and other identifying features are present), may make the researcher look incompetent and, most awkwardly, are almost certainly incomprehensibly full of abbreviations, speed writing and personal shorthand. The three sections of this chapter do include three types of writing (data, analytic memo, polished output) from my own work, but all the names have been changed and identifiers removed.

Researchers use different tools in the field. There is no correct toolkit for fieldwork, only what works. I use a spiral bound reporter's notebook because the pages are quite small, so what has been written is quickly hidden by turning it over. Ballpoint is the easiest pen for me, but it is important to carry spares. In a bag are a file with key documents (e.g. timetables, staff lists, class lists, an A4 pad for more analytic thoughts away from the actual observation site, bus or train timetable and a street map of the area). In some field settings a laptop can be used; in others it would be too intimidating for the informants, in others too dangerous for the researcher.

It is Monday, 7 October 1985 and I am starting fieldwork in an RC comprehensive in an inner-city multi-racial area, focused on the locational integration of children with learning difficulties (those pupils who would have been labelled ESN(M) in the 1970s). In this school, Llandewi, there are nine fourth- and fifth-year pupils in a special class, seven boys and two girls, taught mostly by the head of special needs, Mr Paddock. On my first day with them their first class was cookery with Mrs Bamff, in which they made chocolate loaves. The notes taken at the time, about a particular incident, are reproduced in the form in which they were written down, and then repeated and rewritten as they were expanded afterwards. In the next section some analytic writing for the research team about the incident is presented, and in the following section the form in which the incident appeared in the report to the sponsors is reproduced. The incident can be called 'Bernard Coughing'.

Real time version

10.10
Groups them in one kitchen – show them something.
They are very slow to obey –
She stops everything – reminds them,
Why did she say when told to stop/come round – they must
Vol. Inaud
Mrs B – Not the reason I gave
V. Danger
Mrs B – Yes – Might be an accident about to happen
Pupils not all clear re teasp

Tablesp
Like word for 'spatula'
'spatula boys'
Boy coughs all over dem. of how to put mixt. in tin
Sent away – 'If didn't smoke so many cigs wouldn't have such a bad chest'
   – no sympathy

These notes are impossibly cryptic for anyone but their author. There is about as much as an observer can record in the few minutes available, and they are sufficient to remind her what happened when the time comes to write up the notes later, away from the cookery room. The earliest version can be as cryptic as this, because the researcher is the only person to see them and they only have the function of reminding her what went on. That evening those rough notes, taken in ballpoint in a spiral bound 'shorthand' or 'reporter's' notebook, were rewritten into an expanded form, still for my eyes only, but designed to cover more of what was seen. What was remembered, and taken for granted, is added to the explicit record.

Out-of-the-field version

10.10
Mrs Bamff calls all the children to join her as a group in one of the
   kitchen areas – to show them something. (What is meant by 'drop-
   ping consistency'.)
The children are very slow to stop what they are doing and obey her.
She stops everything – reminds them (of her rules). Asks class why did
   she say that when they are told to stop work and/or to 'come round
   here', they must (obey her immediately).
One pupil volunteers an answer which is inaudible to me.
Mrs Bamff replies 'That's not the reason I gave.'
Another volunteer answers that there might be danger.
Mrs Bamff: Yes – might be an accident about to happen.
Mrs Bamff goes through the recipe so far, and discovers some of the
   pupils are not clear about which spoon is which. That is they do not
   know which of the spoons is the teaspoon, which the dessertspoon
   and which is the tablespoon.
As the recipe calls for teaspoons of some ingredients and tablespoons of
   others (although Mrs Bamff had weighed and measured all the ingredients for them before school), she stops her demonstration to
   explain and demonstrate the different spoons.
Mrs Bamff wants to demonstrate 'dropping consistency' with a wooden
   spoon, and cleaning the mixing bowl with a spatula. She tells them
   the word for 'spatula', saying 'spatula, boys'.
Bernard has an attack of coughing, and coughs all over the demonstration

of how to use the spoon and spatula to put the loaf mixture into the loaf tin.

Mrs Bamff sends him away from the table, saying: 'If you didn't smoke so many ciggies you wouldn't have such a bad chest. I've no sympathy with you.'

This second version has to be produced while the memory is still fresh enough to make sense of the original, cryptic notes. During the course of the day I had learnt Bernard's name, so it was attached to him when the notes were expanded. The incident took perhaps eight to ten minutes in all, from an eighty-minute double period, all of which is recorded in the notebook. The original notes were written in that eight minutes, the expanded version took perhaps twenty minutes, because the record of the whole day is read, and information gathered later (such as Bernard's name) incorporated. There is no intention here to suggest that the original 'real time' or the revised version are 'good' notes. It is possible that all observers regard themselves as poor, lazy or sloppy notetakers. Few researchers produce their originals, or even discuss what they write down. Most researchers are self-taught, and possibly fall into errors. The point of showing this small extract here is to allow the reader to decide that my notes are inadequate and resolve to do better when they go into the field. The out-of-the-field notes are detailed enough to last beyond the period of the fieldwork, so that analysis can be done months later if necessary. Notes alone are not sufficient, of course, and careful researchers keep an out-of-the-field diary and write analytic memos as well. The next section examines analytic memos.

Types of writing: analytical memos

The Welsh integration project depended on the full-time labour of Frances Beasley, who was collecting a range of data, supplemented by a small amount of observation (in five of the nine schools where observation took place) by Sara Delamont, some interviewing and analysis by Graham Upton, and some observation and thinking by Paul Atkinson. As the driving force of the ethnographic work, I wrote two kinds of analytical memos. I circulated analytical memos to the other three at irregular intervals, when there was a point of general interest, and I wrote memos for myself.

Here I have quoted my own thoughts on the experience of watching Bernard cough, and also the memo I circulated in which those thoughts are shared. Clearly, in an individual project the analytical memos are for their author (and perhaps for the supervisor if it is a higher degree project), while in a team effort they are for several readers, and are designed to share developing insights and hypotheses that need testing.

The first analytical memo prepared for the research team started as follows:

WEO integration project

Out-of-the-field report – Sara Delamont

Part One

4.10.85

It has been agreed that Graham Upton and Frances Beasley should have
copies of these reports which will be typed and circulated.

Report One went on to describe the access negotiations and my conversations with Mr Paddock before the observation began. Report Two covered
the day of fieldwork on which Bernard coughed:

WEO report

Part Two

Monday, October 7th, 1985

I spent a whole working day in Llandewi High School. I arrived at 8.45
(too early for most staff) and left at 4.00.
I attended:

(1) double mixed cookery (with 4th and 5th years) [...]

Everyone very helpful and briefed. Research problem is that because Mr
Paddock has set up my day alternating 4J and 1J, it is not easy to
follow my idealized sampling plan (see research planning memos 1
and 2).

It is also hard to 'control' for race and sex when the total size of group is 8.

The target pupil in 4J was not Bernard that day but Aaron, and most of the
account of Mrs Bamff's cookery is focused on him. The incident of 'Bernard
coughing' is only referred to in passing.

During the preparation Aaron claimed that he could not tell the time.
Mrs Bamff showed him carefully on the clock when his cake would be
ready. While adding his whipped egg and chocolate to his flour/fat
mixture Aaron dropped the former into the latter. Mrs Bamff was not at

all cross, but merely mopped up and sorted out the mess.

Mrs Bamff has a relaxed and friendly manner with the pupils. When one boy (Bernard) had a terrible coughing fit she remarked that he smoked too much with no indication that smoking was a breach of school rules. I was reminded of Bob Burgess's account of his Newsom class and their 'truces'.

That is all that appeared in the report to the rest of the project team. In my out-of-the-field diary I wrote about the same incident as follows:

OFD 7/10/85

Everything Paul found in the Aberelwy School in the summer is the same here: just like Bob Burgess's Newsom class – cups of coffee, very little work, a cajoling, joking relationship, and uninhibited pupils. When Bernard coughed all over Mrs Bamff's chocolate loaf mix she shooed him away from the table saying he smoked too much. B was not surprised that she knew he smoked, or that she knew he knew she knew etc. Nor did the others express surprise, shock, delight or any other 'typical' reaction of pupils when a teacher reveals 'guilty knowledge' about a pupil.

Need to think more about the 'special' social relationships that may accompany 'special needs'.

The diary then goes on to discuss race at Llandewi.

The incident of Bernard coughing had now been noted four times: in the field, in the written-up fieldnotes, in the report to colleagues, in my diary. No dazzling sociological insights are recorded, but they remind the author to re-read Burgess (1983) and to think about guilty knowledge, and what levels of meaning might be tied up in 'special'. The eventual 'use' of the incident in the published report appears in the next section. Emerson *et al.* (1995) and Emerson *et al.* (2001) are practical discussions of fieldnotes. Sanjek (1990) collected a series of papers in which anthropologists reflected upon their use of fieldnotes: how they wrote them, what they wrote, why they were especially private, how they moved from fieldnote to other varieties of text. As Jackson (1990) argued, fieldnotes were a liminal variety of text, on the borderline between 'the field' and 'home', between 'data' and 'results', between 'private' and 'public' records. Fieldnotes are not a closed, completed, final text: rather, they are indeterminate, subject to reading, rereading, coding, recording, interpreting, reinterpreting. One of the consequences of the literary turn has been the revisiting, or reopening, of ethnographers' accounts and analyses of their fieldwork. Wolf (1992) for example, revisited her fieldnotes, her journal and a short story she had written doing fieldwork in a Taiwanese village. Reflecting on those materials Wolf realized 'that the field notes, the journals, and the short story represented quite different versions of what had happened' (p. 2).

She recognized that all three texts had 'become data, interesting data that should be analysed and shared with my intellectual community in the usual academic format' (p. 3). The three texts, drawn from fieldwork in the little village of Peihotien, all concern the mental illness (or spirit possession) of a young mother in the early 1960s. Wolf (1992) published a fictional account of this event, selections from the fieldnotes taken at the time and an academic journal article, together in one book, which rapidly became a best-seller, partly because she uses the three texts as a basis for an argument about feminism, postmodernism, orientalism and the future of anthropology.

Other researchers' reports on their writing

Most researchers are protective of their fieldnotes. They are rarely seen by anyone other than their author, and not discussed (Emerson *et al.*, 1995). Scholars are becoming more self-conscious about their writing of data, and Sanjek (1990) has edited a whole volume on fieldnotes. Jean Jackson (1990) has interviewed seventy anthropologists in the USA about their fieldnotes, and says that it is a 'complex, touchy, and disturbing' topic for her informants. She analyses their views in terms of the fieldnotes mediating between three of the binary oppositions that face anthropologists: between public and private, between home and away, and between self and other. The relationship between the fieldnotes (which are private) and the public reality of the research setting and the public writing of eventual articles and books is especially complex. The fieldnotes mediate between the researcher and her respondents and between the scholar and her audience. It is a matter of fascination that public statements are drawn from personal private materials.

The first mediation performed by fieldnotes is that between home and away. Taking the notes in the field is one way of keeping the link to home: to the identity of the researcher back in academic life. Writing notes is what researchers do, so by taking them, one's identity as an outsider, an observer, is reinforced. Donner's (1982) destruction of field data is therefore symbolic of her abandoning her scholarly identity and credibility. Much of Lubeck's (1985) disquiet about her relationship with the African-American women staff of the Headstart centre was crystallized around her use of note-writing to distance herself from them. Her account of this captures all the ambivalences about the role of researcher expressed by Jackson's informants. Wolcott (1981) has discussed how he takes different types of fieldnotes when he does research 'abroad' in alien cultures and when he is studying his 'own' society. It is clear that experienced fieldworkers use their note-taking as an integral part of the role they are playing. For the novice, it is sensible to reflect on how notes are taken, where they are taken, and the ways in which note-taking impacts on the respondents.

Jackson's second theme is the role of the fieldnotes as mediator between the different selves of the scholar. In the fieldnotes one is angry, incompetent, racist, sexist, lazy, purblind, bigoted, naive, frustrated, rude, tired, bored, scared and all the other things that cannot be allowed either to show to the respondents or to appear in the final, polished accounts of the work. They are also the place where one is revealed as insightful, clever, sociologically imaginative, well-read, anti-racist, anti-sexist, eager, cynical and cheerful. See Coffey (1999) for a nuanced account of this ambivalence.

Once the research is over, the notes are a concrete symbol of the work done, and very precious. They are an emblem not only of work done, but also of sacrifices made, risks taken and hardships endured. While educational researchers are unlikely to have starved, frozen, contracted rare diseases or faced down headhunters, the notes are still the proof that one was working in the playground, awake in the dull maths lesson, and alongside the school secretary when she faced the axe-wielding father. It is in the sheer volume of the data that researchers also gain security; in all that mass of material there must be enough for a report/thesis/book. Certainly, educational ethnographers, if they reflect on their data collection at all, tend to report on the size of their haul. Sally Lubeck (1985: 55) said of the research notes she generated: 'Approximately 480 typed pages comprise my fieldnotes and related papers from this time, exclusive of the schedules, maps and flow charts that were done early in the year.'

None of this helps the novice decide what to record, or how to record it. Harry Wolcott (1981) has raised the intriguing question 'Are observational skills "caught" or "taught"?' In a review of attempts at observer training for ethnography, he knows he stresses that too often the question of what to look for is too dominant, and the more important issue how to look is neglected. Parallel to this is the contrast between deciding what to record and how to record.

Among the many possible books which offer practical help on these questions, Lofland and Lofland (1995) have useful chapters on 'logging data' and 'developing analysis', which are clear and level-headed. This can be read in conjunction with a clear autobiographical account, such as Valli's. Linda Valli (1986: 226–8) gives a careful and elaborate account of her uses of writing and her data collection during her study of the office procedures course. Her data were observations and interviews (which she did not tape because she found that taping impeded the rapport). She describes how she kept her information.

> My fieldnotes fell into three main categories. On large note cards I recorded material that was primarily observational in nature. Observations of classroom activities were recorded chronologically and classified under the class name. Observations that were about particular students or Mrs Lewis were also kept chronologically, but were classified under the student's or teacher's name.

> On loose-leaf size paper I kept typed accounts of each interview. These accounts were about ten pages in length, single spaced and were classified under the student's, graduate's or teacher's name.
>
> (p. 227)

Valli seems to have included her analytical memos in with her fieldnotes, for she says:

> The only other type of information I kept in my fieldnotes was insights or inferences I was drawing as the result of the data I was collecting. These second-level constructs, in Schutz's language, were clearly marked off from the observational or interview data. If I were recording the event at the type-writer, I tended to both capitalize my interpretive comments and enclose them in parentheses. If the notes were hand-written, I again used the bracket technique and flagged the comment with a conspicuous star.

I would find it confusing to have my 'data' and my 'analyses' in the same files. When I have an insight about analysis in the field, I record it to prevent myself forgetting it, but as soon as possible it is shifted out of the notebook into the analytical file. I never take any of the analytical material into the field setting – only the reporter's notebook and pens – because it might be lost, or seen by the informants.

Reading Jackson (1990) makes me more confident about my reluctance to show the original notebook to anyone, and the retention of the analytical memos and out-of-the-field diary physically out of the field. Jackson asked her informants to tell her about:

1   their definition of fieldnotes;
2   training – preparation and mentoring, both formal and informal;
3   sharing fieldnotes;
4   confidentiality;
5   disposition of fieldnotes at death;
6   feelings about fieldnotes – especially their actual physical notes;
7   whether anthropologists created their own documents.

If respondents had done more than one project, they were asked to compare and contrast their fieldnotes on different occasions. An interesting project in itself would be to interview school and classroom ethnographers in Britain and the USA on these seven issues to see whether there are differences from 'real' anthropologists as studied by Jackson, and whether the differences between educational ethnographers (Delamont and Atkinson, 1995) begin at the fieldwork stage. Certainly Jackson's key points would make a good starting point for the beginner to focus a reflexive account of her own data collection techniques. Reflexivity in the collection of material, and analysing it as it comes in, not letting it pile up unread, are the two most essential things.

Types of writing: output writing

There are several types of output a researcher may need or want to write, each of which has its own rules. For example:

1   the thesis;
2   the report to sponsors;
3   the journal article reporting findings;
4   the monograph;
5   the confessional/autobiographical piece.

It is important to be clear what you are trying to do and follow the conventions of the genre you are attempting. This means reading examples of the product and looking at how successful or unsuccessful they are. Chapter 12 is all about producing the final stage of the research – the thesis, book, report or article – so in this chapter the focus is upon the writing that has to be done as you go along which is intended as part of the output eventually. It is fatal to leave output writing until the data collection and analysis are completed, and vital to write as you go along. Once you have negotiated your initial access, you can and should start writing the 500–1,000 word section of your 'methods' chapter on 'initial access negotiations'. Every 500 words you draft and file safely is a step towards the final product, but only if these are kept safe. Back up the disks and store the back-ups somewhere well away from the originals. Keep carbon copies. There are tasks to do with writing that can be started early in the research process. Selecting your pseudonyms and using them in your early seminar papers, memos, etc., is good practice ethically, and a task that needs care and so needs time. The methods section, the literature review, the ethical discussion, the acknowledgements and the description of the setting can all be written in draft, and filed away carefully, within days of starting the research.

A sustained example of one form of output writing, the report to sponsors in which the incident of Bernard coughing finally appeared, is given next. It reveals how ideas that were in my head in October 1985 appeared at the end of the research. For the fifth – and final – time, let us return to Mrs Bamff in the cookery lesson at Llandewi. In publications the comment to Bernard was grouped with other examples of teachers being friendly and relaxed with pupils of lower ability. The text stressed that, whatever problems accompanied locational integration of children with learning handicaps, 'the atmosphere in the special classes and units, and in English and Maths lessons for statemented pupils taught by "special needs" staff, was warm, friendly and supportive'.

Burgess (1983, 1988a) conducted a long and detailed ethnographic study in an English comprehensive school. He focused on the 'Newsom Department', a remedial and non-exam grouping for fourth- and fifth-year pupils, with whom he spent time both teaching and observing. His accounts of the atmosphere and behaviour in the Newsom Department captures the feeling of the segregated classes we saw very well. He describes a segregated group of pupils and teachers who have negotiated an uneasy truce, in which teachers expect limited work and ignore breaches of school rules in return for pupils behaving and not disrupting the rest of the school. Burgess found that smoking by pupils was tolerated on trips off campus, endless cups of coffee were made in the classroom and the discourse contained many words and phrases that would never be left unchallenged in 'ordinary' classrooms. The atmosphere of the Newsom Department at Bishop McGregor School, as reported by Burgess, is very similar to that in many of the special classes and units we observed.

In the special classes and units, and the English and Maths lessons for statemented pupils, it was common to find that informality was the prevailing mood. Staff call children 'loverly boy', 'loverly girl', 'love', 'mate' and other informal endearments, or by their Christian names or nick-names. Staff placed emphasis on settling pupils to work, and often ignored chewing, the wearing of coats, and other breaches of rules that were enforced in the wider school. Pupils were also allowed to go to the lavatory during class time, and not told to wait for break or lunchtime.

For example, on our first day's observation at Aberelwy, in Mrs Scudder's class, this informality struck the observer. At 9.15 one girl was unpacking Mrs Scudder's bag after a trip the previous day, one boy was tidying up for her, and a third washing up the coffee cups and checking if there was coffee and 'Coffeemate'. At 9.26 a boy, Douglas, was allowed to leave for the lavatory. At 10.25 Douglas took his book to Mrs Scudder and said 'How do you do number 9, Miss? Do you fill it in or what?' language that would not be tolerated in an 'ordinary' classroom. At 11.15 a boy came into the room with a note. Mrs Scudder dealt with it and said 'Thank you, love'. At 11.35 Douglas came to the observer with his maths book saying 'It's like having another teacher ... can you do maths, mate?' In the observer's experience pupils in ordinary classes rarely approach visitors for help at all. At this point Becky's skirt split, and she and Amy were allowed to retreat behind a screen in one corner to mend it. During the afternoon session, Becky and Amy again sewed Becky's skirt. Douglas left the room for a 'walkabout' and Hugh was sent to retrieve him. At 2.15 Douglas was allowed to tear up the fifth year timetable for the teacher as a treat. At 2.30 Jack invited the observer to have coffee, and makes coffee for the whole group. Again, in the observer's experience these behaviours would not be tolerated or ignored in a mainstream classroom.

Such relaxed and friendly classrooms can inhibit integration, because pupils feel so much more relaxed and comfortable there than in the wider school. Some adolescents may be unwilling to settle into integrated classes if these are more formal, impersonal and strict. In other words the special needs staff can create such a supportive atmosphere for pupils that they are loath to leave it.

At Cynllaith, Mr Wymondham cracked a typical joke. When he was handing out notices about a school trip Chris told the observer he could not go. Mr Wymondham told him to explain why he could not, and Chris grinning says he is going to Tenerife for a month. Mr Wymondham says he has offered to go along as a tutor: '1 hour English with you, and the rest debauchery by myself'! Later that lesson Idris asked how much money they should take on the school trip, and Mr Wymondham said: 'As much as you like and some for me and a tip for the driver. Who's the driver?' 'You, Sir.'

Later still at the close of the lesson, Mr Wymondham told Wynford to tell the observer 'the story about your reading book'. Wynford laughs and tells us that in his junior school, when he was told to bring the page he was reading out to the teacher, he had 'ripped it out of the book'. The whole class laughs, and Mr Wymondham falls about because he thinks it is so funny.

At Llandewi, in a cookery class for the fourth and fifth year statemented pupils, Bernard has a fit of coughing just as all the pupils were gathered round Mrs Bamff's demonstration of 'dropping consistency' and how to fill a greased cake tin for baking. Mrs Bamff sent him away from the table, saying: 'If you didn't smoke so many ciggies you wouldn't have such a bad chest – I've no sympathy for you.'

At Brynhenlog when a group of statemented pupils were doing English and the exercise was about old cars, the boys answering it were allowed to look out of the window. The master pointed to one old car and said it was his – so they all had a good laugh. At St Edeyrn's, in a maths lesson, when a girl gave some measurements that suggested the kitchen of her house was colossal, Mr McGillvray said 'If it's that big, I'll be moving in.'

This was a report for inspectors, advisers, teachers and civil servants, not sociologists. If one were writing an article for a sociological audience the same material would be impregnated with more theory and more references to other relevant literature (see the paper 'The view from the cabbages' in Delamont and Atkinson, 1995).

So far the chapter has demonstrated the three types of writing, with the example of 'Bernard Coughing' moving through its stages from my very rough scribbles in a reporter's notebook, through the expanded version written out by hand on an A4 pad, through the analytical memo written about it, which was typed and shared with Graham Upton, Frances Beasley and Paul Atkinson, and on to the version that appeared in the report to the Welsh Office. In the rest of the chapter some other researchers' discussions of their writing are examined, and the uses of writing in qualitative research other than observation is explored.

One noticeable feature of 'Bernard Coughing' is how the incident becomes embedded in longer and longer texts. The original fieldnote extract occupied eighteen lines, the out-of-the-field one forty-one much longer lines, the analytical memos grow in proportion, and the eventual report embeds Bernard in a four-page account.

Writing about the literature

Conventional higher degree theses and books, and to a lesser extent published papers, have a chapter or section called 'Review of the literature'. However, having such a chapter or section does not absolve the author from referring to the literature elsewhere in the account. That is the conventional pattern and the safest. No one can challenge it. However, if you or your supervisor or the editor dealing with your book or article decide that your book or thesis should not have a conventional structure, and that the literature should be reviewed some other way, that is fine. But you must explain the decision in the introduction. My own PhD (Delamont, 1973) had three small literature reviews, each on a separate topic, each in a different section of the thesis. My introduction said that there were three separate reviews, not one large one, and explained the structure.

Your literature review should:

1   show the reader that you are capable of searching for relevant material, summarizing it, arranging it by some theme and relating it to your own work;
2   show that your study is original or is a principled, conscious replication of a previous one.

The separate 'review of the literature' chapter can be written in a relatively straightforward way. If you are a novice scholar it is safer to write it that way, and leave more elaborated or complex structures to the more experienced. There are some dangers that all authors have to avoid, however experienced they may be.

There are four main dangers. You can leave things out, be out of date, be boring, and be racist or sexist. Try to avoid all these dangers. Leaving things out: remember to ask your supervisor, the library staff, other people, to keep their eyes open for all relevant studies. Out of date: remember to keep reading. You cannot review the literature at the beginning of a research project and leave it. You should keep reading up until the thesis or project is finished. Journals are crucial, so keep an eye on current contents, the latest issues of periodicals, the list of new books on the website of the *Times Literary Supplement* and so on.

The worst danger is to be boring. Try to arrange a literature review by themes, not just in a long list/sequence. Highlight the findings that are relevant to your thesis, article or book. Be critical of the literature. Do not just report it. Generally, a more interesting account comes from integrating issues from several studies, rather than from a summary of one text, followed by an exhaustive summary of the next one. An example of a dull way to organize a review, followed by some more interesting possibilities, follows. The best example of a 'dull' way to organize a review of the literature is that caricatured by Haywood and Wragg (1978: 2):

> More frequent, however, is the uncritical review, the furniture sale catalogue, in which everything merits a one paragraph entry no matter how skilfully it has been conducted. Bloggs (1975) found this, Smith (1976) found that, Jones (1977) found the other, Bloggs, Smith and Jones (1978) found happiness in heaven.

Hart (1998: 172–206) shows in some detail how to write a literature review that lays the foundations for a particular research project. He does not, however, demonstrate any novel or interesting ways to organize the literature. It is sensible to start chronologically, and do a draft review as caricatured by Haywood and Wragg (1978). However, it is then much more impressive for examiners and pleasant for all readers if you do your second draft in one of the following ways.

1   Find two or three standpoints, contrast them, and review the studies according to which standpoint they adopt. The controversy over the presence or absence of institutional racism in English secondary schools is best approached that way.
2   Start with the book or article that seems to you the most important. Highlight that, spend some time on it, justifying its prominence in your review, and then organize the rest of the literature in relation to it (e.g. precursor studies that foreshadow it, precursors that lead away from it, 'successive' studies that have ignored its importance or existence, successor studies that have misrepresented it, and so on).
3   Draw *contrasts* of method, of country of origin, or theory, of gender, of race, of discipline. So, group all the historical work together, then all the geographical. Or group the positivist studies and then shift to the interactionist ones.
4   Work back from your own findings. Select the research which supports or foreshadows your findings and explicitly contrast it with studies that contra-indicate your work.

It is also important to watch out for sexism and racism in your reading, and in your account of the literature. Make sure that you read academic and non-academic work by male and female authors from different races, and works that adopt men's and women's, black and white, perspectives. Scrutinize what you read for sexism and racism, and remember to record any in your notes on it as part of your treatment of the literature as problematic. (It is striking, for example, how homophobic Raymond Chandler's thrillers are, when read in the light of today's heightened consciousness about gay rights.) This leads on to checking your own citations of the literature for race and sex bias: citing mainly male authors or mainly white authors perpetrates academic sexism or racism, and may lead to a badly biased account of the phenomena under investigation.

Women scholars are much more likely to cite work by men *and* women; men frequently fail to cite work by women. This is part of a male tendency to 'forget' the presence of women in their intellectual field in their memoirs, autobiographies and histories of their disciplines. There is a spectacularly blatant example of this in a 1980 life history interview Goffman (1992) gave Verhoeven (1992). Helen Lopata (1995), a contemporary of Goffman's, reflects on the fact that when her male coevals wrote memoirs of their time at Chicago, they completely failed to mention any of the women, who were 15 per cent of the graduate school. She comments that 'While on campus, the women *felt* integrated ... yet the men's memory of the cohort is predominantly male' (p. 382, emphasis mine). A similar conclusion is reached by Eskola (1992: 158) after her study of intellectuals in Finland. Men only mentioned other men as intellectual influences, women mentioned men *and* women. She concludes: 'For men it is interaction with other men that constitutes social capital, while women's social capital is based on relations between the two genders.' Women with doctorates from Chicago, and all women intellectuals in Finland, believe they are part of a mixed, integrated academic world, but their male contemporaries do not 'see', or 'remember' or 'count' them.

It is possible that all literature is by men, or by white people. In that case, you have a finding about the literature. If instead there are studies by men and women, or by black and white authors, then the researcher needs to check whether the men describe the world differently from the women, or the black authors from the white ones. Whether there are differences or not, their existence or absence is worth mentioning in the report. An example of an author who offers a British male 'white' view of educational ethnography by selective mentions of the literature follows.

In 1996 Woods published a 'follow up' (p. vii), to his 1986 methods book which develops his ideas on methods in the light of his own biography, empirical work done since 1986, and the 'discourse of derision' (Ball, 1990) aimed at state schools in England, educational research, teacher training, and universities under the Thatcher and Major governments (Delamont, 1999,

2000a). The book is readable and packed with helpful ideas for novices. But in one way it is no advance at all on the 1986 book. He has not paid any further attention to the bodies of literature he rejected in 1986. There is no mention of any anthropological ethnographers in education (no Spindler, not a single citation to *Anthropology and Education Quarterly*, even though Woods has published in it himself (Woods, 1994), no Ogbu, none of Wolcott's empirical work), and the text still ignores the work of women. Of the women missing from the 1986 book, only Le Compte and Goetz (under her maiden name of Preissle) and Rosalie Wax are cited in the 1996 book. Woods cites the 1971 methods book by John Lofland, rather than the 1984 or 1995 second and third editions by John and Lyn Lofland. Despite Woods's own move into research on primary schools and young children he still ignores the (relevant) scholarship of Guthrie, Heath, Lubeck, McPherson, Sussman and Willes. Also missing are citations to Raphaela Best (1983), V.G. Paley (1984, 1986), Barrie Thorne (1993). Patti Adler is absent, though she has published on children for twenty years. Casanova (1991) on elementary school secretaries is ignored. In the decade between his 1986 and 1996 books, excellent ethnographies were published by American women Woods has ignored, such as Weis (1985, 1990), Fine (1991), Gibson (1988), Metz (1986), and Phillips (1987).

I have illustrated the gender bias and ethnocentrism of Woods's work with a detailed analysis of one chapter. Woods's (1996) book contains a brief summary of symbolic interactionism and the Chicago School (pp. 32–76); this chapter is deeply sexist. First, Woods only mentions male writers from Chicago, and male chroniclers of its history. He ignores the work of Deegan (1988, 1995), who has shown that women were present, both physically and intellectually, in the First Chicago School (1890 to 1930), and in the Second (1946–66). The intellectual and physical labour of women was vital to the ideas and the development of methods in Chicago, and was one of the characteristics that distinguished Chicago sociology from the rival schools at Harvard and Columbia. The original women were driven out, and then excluded from the official history (Deegan, 1988; Delamont, 1992): Woods colludes in that violation by his omission. The Second Chicago School's history, when Blumer, Hughes, Strauss and Goffman were there, is being chronicled today. The same exclusion of women is being fought (Deegan, 1995). Woods, by his failure to cite and celebrate Blanche Geer, Lyn Lofland, Virginia Olesen, and other women symbolic interactionists, is again colluding in the symbolic violence against them.

Woods illustrates the utility of symbolic interactionism with empirical educational examples. Table 4.1 shows the gender and nationality of the authors of the empirical studies Woods has cited (i.e. not the historical, theoretical and methodological texts). The first author of each work cited has been classified by sex and nationality (so Mac an Ghaill is Irish,

Table 4.1   Citations to empirical work in Woods (1996: chapter 2)

	English	Welsh	Scottish	Irish	American	Other	Total
Male	25	2	1	1	4	-	33
Female	11	-	-	-	2	2	15
Unknown	4	-	-	-	3	-	7
Total	40	2	1	1	9	2	55

Patrick is Scottish). Table 4.1 makes the world of exemplary ethnographic studies of education as seen by Woods starkly clear. It is English, and male. British citations outnumber American 44 to 9, but British actually means English. Only one Scot (Patrick) is cited for a study of a gang in Glasgow, only one Irish man (Mac an Ghaill) for his research in England. There are two Welshmen (Beynon and Edwards) but only Beynon has studied a Welsh school. There is only one Australian cited (Sharp) for study done in England. No research in Canada, Australia or New Zealand is cited, and nothing from Europe. So there are no citations to ethnographies of France (MacDonald, Reed Danahay, Anderson Levitt) or Malta (Darmanin). The gender bias is also striking. Men cited outnumber women 33 to 15. In fact the male bias is greater than the simple figures suggest for a few male authors (Mac an Ghaill 1988, 1989, 1994; Willis 1977, 1978; D.H. Hargreaves, 1967; D.H. Hargreaves *et al.*, 1975; A. Hargreaves, 1980, 1984) have citations to several publications and are used for extended or multiple illustration. The only woman to be quoted more than once is Nias (1991).

It is also important to check that one is reading outside the work done by friends, or the supervisor's friends, outside the familiar discipline, and outside one's own country.

In Great Britain, researchers in England frequently ignore educational publications on Wales, Scotland and Northern Ireland, as if England and Britain were synonymous (Delamont, 1999, 2000a). Arnot *et al.* (1999), for example, ignore relevant studies in Wales, Scotland and Northern Ireland on the gender gap in school achievement.

When you write your review of the literature, do a check on your own citation patterns to ensure you write about the whole UK, include male and female authors' works, and do not perpetrate racism.

Conclusions

In Flecker's poem the Principal Jews carry the 'manuscripts in peacock styles' on the golden journey along with swords:

Engraved with storks and apes and crocodiles
And heavy beaten necklaces, for Lords.

As far as qualitative research is concerned, the pen is certainly mightier than even the stork-engraved sword, but only if it is used to write early, and to write often. (Have you made proper notes of the full details of this book? What are you going to write now you have read this chapter?)

Key reading

The key reading suggested for this chapter is Paul Atkinson's (1987) paper, 'Man's best hospital and the mug and muffin: an innocent ethnographer meets American medicine'. It is reprinted in Atkinson (1996).

Chapter 5

Gnawing the nail of hurry

Choosing the topic, setting and problem

> I did not come to South Africa as a neutral observer. I came morally and politically outraged at the brute, unmediated legislation of human inferiority. I was filled with horror by tales of arbitrary banning, detention and imprisonment, forced suicide, and murder, of violent dispossession, banishment and the splitting of families, that are familiar to anyone who reads the newspapers.
>
> (Crapanzano, 1985: 22)

Crapanzano's comment provides one theme for this chapter: the importance of recognizing and recording one's preconceptions (and prejudices) before the fieldwork begins. The second theme, that of eagerness to get started, to get out of the office and the library and to start 'really' doing the research, is reflected in the title. The members of the caravan to Samarkand demand a prompt departure, insisting 'we gnaw the nail of hurry'. The third theme, and the one which is addressed first, is how to choose a research topic, setting and problem to start with. Crapanzano had a clear 'topic' in mind: discovering what the world looks like to the Afrikaners in rural South Africa before the end of apartheid. Flecker's caravan party had a range of objectives – trade, or pilgrimage, or adventure – but all shared a destination, Samarkand, and a route, the golden journey across the desert. The student with a dissertation to produce, or the staff member in higher education being told to do some research, may not be so fortunate. So this chapter deals with three issues: choosing a topic, getting started and documenting not only those two stages but also one's preconceptions, hunches and 'hypotheses' about the fieldwork.

Choosing a topic/setting/problem

The choice of a topic, setting or problem is the best part of the whole exercise for those who have what is sometimes called 'the sociological imagination' (from the book of that name by C. Wright Mills, 1959) or its equivalent in education, geography, or whatever. Some research students, and many people asked to do a short thesis at the end of a taught course, seem to have no ideas at all and ask for suggestions from the supervisor or tutor. It is hard to help such people, both because there are always six or seven projects I wish I were free to start and because it is no use at all 'allocating' or even suggesting topics to other people. I therefore lack any empathy for a person who cannot come up with one or two possible ideas that interest them: it is inconceivable to me that everything they have read has not generated lots of questions. Experience (supervising over fifty MEd theses, a further thirty or so MSc theses and a handful of PhDs and MPhils) has taught me that people who start off on one of my ideas rarely finish them: their motivation is not the same because it was not their topic. Anyone reading this who has to think up a project may feel that a failure to offer a shopping list of desirable projects is a betrayal – but I hope the reasons for this position will be clear by the end of the section.

How to choose a topic

There are three things that have to be borne in mind. A piece of research has to be interesting to the researcher, it has to be feasible, and it has to be ethical. Each of these is examined in turn.

Interest

The topic of a thesis, project or programme must interest the person/people doing it. Fine (1998: x) says he set out on his study of wild fungi collectors 'from a desire to escape a stuffy office'. If it is a single-handed piece of thesis work it will only get done if the student is interested in it, wants to work on it, and can learn to convey that enthusiasm. This is true for the part-timer who has twelve months to do a 20,000-word thesis and the full-timer with three years and 80,000 words to write. A piece of research will occupy lots of 'spare' time, and needs to be more interesting than the garden, TV, concerts, the theatre, seeing friends, bird watching or golf. Sometimes it may have to take precedence over food, sleep, sex and family. If it is not a major intellectual priority at the beginning, it will not get the attention, time and commitment it needs.

Let us take some questions that might be interesting:

Do mermaids talk?

(Shields, 1993a: 79)

Is Foucault's work fertile for feminist use?

(Brodribb, 1992: 45)

What might make introductory science 'hard' or even 'alienating' for students like themselves?

(Tobias, 1990: 15)

Why is Pentecostalism so successful in Brazil?

(Chestnut, 1997)

Who is this Mary Swann?

(Shields, 1993b: 26)

Why is cricket so often taken or promoted as a mirror of England?

(Marqusee, 1994: 26)

What does Kara mean by: 'I read books, but I don't read book-books'?

(Finders, 1997: 92)

Feasibility

There are three kinds of feasibility: 'political', 'academic' and 'management'. By 'political' feasibility, I mean primarily questions of access to the data for the particular researcher. A senior prison psychologist can get access to informants that a part-time literacy tutor in a prison cannot. A black woman can establish herself in some contexts where a white man could not, and so on. Any piece of research using documents, interviews or based on observation involves getting access to archives, or people, or a setting and people, or a location or 'field', or a virtual world on the Net. Some settings have very powerful 'gatekeepers' who control the entry; some groups are hard to find and persuade to take part; some materials are embargoed. Any piece of research should be planned realistically, around the questions: 'Will I get access to that material?' 'Can I find some people who do Y and will talk to me?' 'Who controls entry to Z and how do I get in there?' It is pointless to spend ages planning a project that there is no hope of carrying out – a life history interview with Prince Philip, or partici pant observation of David Copeland or Harold Shipman in captivity, or a re-study of Dorothea Beale's personal papers to challenge Raikes's (1908) eulogy (because the papers were burnt after Raikes worked on them).

Two things follow:

1   maximizing the research potential of settings, populations and archives already available, or under the control of known contacts;
2   applying for access as soon as possible, before the planning is too far advanced, and having alternatives ready if access is denied.

Political feasibility is not the only kind of feasibility to consider. Research must also be academically feasible. Research projects generate data which need analysing and imply theoretical perspectives. It is important not to plan research which will inevitably generate data of types one cannot handle (or learn how to handle) or demand theoretical conceptualizations that are unsympathetic, or lead to findings that one cannot accept emotionally or intellectually. It is sensible to recognize one's own strengths and weaknesses. If you hate being alone, long days in an archive in a strange city are not a good plan. If you are phobic about snakes, it would be silly to plan to do ethnography in the herpetology house at the local zoo, or in the congregations of Southern States Christians in the USA who handle poisonous snakes, or at the visitor centre in Sao Paolo, Brazil, where poisonous snakes are 'milked' for their venom. If you are queasy, participant observation in pathology labs is unlikely to be successful. As computer-based analysis becomes more and more popular and routine, a fear of computers is not a reason to choose a qualitative project. Whatever the researcher is like, it is important to plan the study with her strengths and weaknesses in mind.

The third kind of feasibility turns on whether the proposed research is manageable. Most research ideas are too big. A typical MEd student who needs to do a 20,000-word thesis often plans something that would take six people ten years working as a team to do. Sorting out what is manageable needs discussion with people who have done research before, including the supervisor. The investigator has to be able to reach the setting or population when s/he is awake and alert. So doing an ethnography of a night shelter for alcoholics, or the night shift at a hospital, or in the small hours in a police station is not sensible for anyone with a day job. If the setting is out of doors, will bad weather spoil the research? For example, research on school PE or the British Universities Sports Association (BUSA) cricket tournament or a leisure activity such as beach behaviour, could be seriously disrupted if there is no fine weather in which to see the activity happening. Among the things to think about are:

1   Do not collect more data than you need, or can analyse in the time and space you have.
2   Do not plan to gather data at impossible times or in impossible places.

The third principle which must govern the choice of research is ethics.

Ethics

Burgess (1989b) and Welland and Pugsley (2001) edited collections on this topic. It is important to think about the ethics of any ideas you have. Will it be possible to gather data with a clear conscience, and write it up, and later publish it? Sometimes the researcher discovers that a project has generated ethical dilemmas once it is underway (the population you are studying in all innocence turn out to be running a hot car racket, or dealing crack, or practising euthanasia on the frail elderly), and if so, that has to be handled when it is revealed. Some topics can be seen to have ethical problems long before they are studied, so the researcher needs to be clear about them. Crapanzano (1985) knew that he disagreed with Afrikaner attitudes to race before he began, and had thought about how he would handle the ethics of his fieldwork. Moral dilemmas may not be found where expected, but subsequently crop up elsewhere. Life history interviews with CDT staff do not sound redolent of ethical problems, while an observational study of an abortion advice centre does. It would be possible to discover that the CDT sample included ethical dilemmas, while the abortion clinic research is ethically straightforward. Kendall (2000) makes it clear that she behaved ethically in her study of the Blue Sky on-line forum: 'From the beginning of my participation on Blue Sky, I informed other participants that I was conducting research' (p. 257).

Once there is a research topic or problem which is accessible, ethically sound and can be carried out in the time and space available, it is also necessary to establish whether it is original.

Originality

Most PhD regulations specify that the work has to be original – a requirement which is both exciting and scary. MPhil and shorter master's theses do not have to be original, but most people want to do their own topic, on their own population, in their own choice of setting (or all three at once!). In other words, most social scientists want to do an original, unique, one-off study, even if they are not required to do so. It is hard to discover whether the planned topic is original until a good deal of research has been conducted.

A quick library search will usually reveal whether or not there is a large literature on an issue in the chosen discipline. This was the case for Barbara Tuchman, an American historian, who produced a study of the fourteenth century in Britain and France, focusing on the life of Enguerrand de Courcy (1340–97). De Courcy lived in both countries, and so provided a bridge between them and allowed Tuchman to contrast the cultures. She describes how she decided to centre her research on him, although he had not been discussed by previous specialist historians. Tuchman herself was not a medievalist (she wrote on 1914 and Vietnam as well as 1314) and would have found good professional sources useful for her project. However,

> a compensating advantage [was that] except for a single brief article published in 1939, nothing has been written about him in English, and no formal, reliable biography in French except a doctoral thesis of 1890 that exists only in manuscript.
>
> (Tuchman, 1979: xviii)

Sometimes there appears to be nothing written about the topic at all, not even a French language thesis in manuscript. If so the researcher is lucky in one respect, but will also be intellectually more lonely than if one is working in a scholarly field with colleagues (see Eggleston and Delamont, 1983 and Delamont, Atkinson and Parry, 2000, for a discussion of intellectual isolation).

A study can still be original even if there is a big literature. There may be ample literature which seems to you to 'miss the point', that is, it does not address what you feel are the important or interesting questions. Julia Stanley (1989: 173) says that her reading of the main British school ethnographies had not focused on the question she wanted answered.

> Interesting as these books were, they threw little light on the question I had set out to answer, which was why older teenagers bothered to turn up to class at all – the joys of teacher-baiting were surely an inadequate explanation for most pupils continuing to go to school regularly. Paul Corrigan asked his lads why they bothered, but like so many ethnographers seemed only to be interested in the views of disaffected youths, whose replies are much the same whether they are interviewed ... in Australia, ... in middle America, or ... in North-East England. 'Lads' resent being made to do anything at all, it seems, because their main concern is to establish a reputation for manliness, so the only serious answers they came up with were that education 'keeps you off the streets', or 'helps you find a job', neither of which throws much light on the ideas of teachers in comprehensive schools, or their ability to deliver equal opportunities to a wide range of boys and girls. I decided to join a class of 'ordinary' English youngsters for their last two years of compulsory education, to see for myself what they were getting out of it.

Between the absence of literature (Tuchman) and the ample literature that misses the point (Stanley) may be the particular study or studies which suggest a comparison or contrast to you. Paul Willis's (1977) *Learning to Labour* functioned in this way for Linda Valli who researched young women aiming to be office workers. Valli (1986: 213) had decided to study high school secretarial courses, to see whether American working-class women were aware of the nature of female office work. She realized that she had to ask the students why they had enrolled for a course of office skills, but also she

> had to broaden the question by asking not only why these students were in the program, but what they were learning from their experiences and relationships about the role of women at work, particularly clerical work, and what effect this learning had on their further occupational orientation. I assumed that the primary contexts in which they would learn about themselves as workers would be family, school and work. I did not presume, however, that the messages conveyed through these contexts would be consistent or non-problematic. I was prepared to look for ways in which messages about women workers confirmed or undermined one another and how the students dealt with these messages.

Valli then explains how she formulated her research questions in that setting:

The questions I originally articulated for myself fell under four (what I then called) dimensions: family, gender, school and work. Under the family dimension I wanted to know, for instance, what parents conveyed to these students about their own work and marital experiences and how these messages influenced the students. Under the gender dimension, I was interested in discovering whether or not the students perceived clerical work as women's work, how they perceived sexual subordination, and whether or not they accepted such a world. Under the school dimension, I wanted information regarding tracking mechanisms, the students' participation in the formal and informal aspects of school life, and how school experiences corresponded or failed to correspond with work experience. And, lastly, under the work dimension, I was interested in finding out if the students viewed work as temporary jobs or as careers, how they integrated work roles with roles as wives and mothers, and what work factors attracted or disillusioned them.

As the researcher thinks about what interests her and how feasible the various possibilities are, and checks out the originality of the various projects in her head, the research diary should be started. Forgetting is very, very easy, and so it is essential to record why the BUSA cricket tournament was chosen rather than naturist clubs, or why the archive at Wallingford proved more suitable than the life history interviews in Sheffield, while the decision is still fresh in the mind.

Finding a fieldwork site

The issues which arise when choosing a fieldwork site overlap with the question of access which is the main focus of the next chapter. Here the central concern is sampling in qualitative research. All qualitative researchers tend to refer to Glaser and Strauss's (1967) famous work on theoretical sampling, which is the major intellectual justification for not using statistical sampling. There is a useful discussion of their ideas in Hammersley and Atkinson (1995: 44–53). In ordinary life very few people actually manage to follow Glaser and Strauss in their sampling of settings, or even of people in settings. Rather, they proceed with 'opportunity' sampling and 'snowballing'. Opportunity sampling means what it sounds like: seizing the chances of a setting or respondent when the opportunity arises. Barbara Heyl (1979), for example, was teaching a course on deviance when one of her students offered to introduce her to a 'madam' (a woman who ran the brothel in town). Heyl used that madam as a life history informant, and did her PhD and the subsequent book on the material gathered. Snowballing involves getting each respondent to help you find the next one, so one gay man introduces you to his friends, who in turn help you get hold of their friends, and so on until you have a sufficient number of gay men for your research.

The method you use to get a setting or a group of informants or whatever is not that important. What is crucial about sampling is honesty and reflexivity. The most important things are to record how the sample was drawn, and to think carefully about how the selection/recruitment has affected the data collected from them. Jane Collier (1997: 18–20) describes how she and her husband chose the Andalucian village of Los Olivos: 'When we arrived in Seville, we borrowed an atlas of Andalusian communities to make a list of villages that met our requirements.'

They needed:

> a settlement that had between five hundred and one thousand people, was agricultural, and was located in a mountainous region. And because we feared medical emergencies – we were the parents of a two-month-old baby – we eliminated villages that lacked a resident doctor and regular bus service.

They rented a car and went to visit ten possible sites including Los Olivos which was 'not only the prettiest one we visited but also had the friendliest people'.

A sensitive discussion of how a snowballed sample responded to certain questions in your checklist is much more important than anxiety about whether it represents the population, or even whether Glaser and Strauss would call it a theoretical sample. However, all the theoretical issues that would arise in a proper Glaser and Strauss procedure, and many of the issues that would be relevant in designing a stratified statistical sample are relevant, whatever method you have used. The age, class, gender, race, status, sexual orientation, housing conditions and educational level of informants in a snowballed sample is worth detailed attention and careful thought.

Fine (1996: 15) conducted an ethnography of four restaurants as part of his study of food. He chose four establishments that were relatively 'elite: that is, served good, expensive food', in Minnesota. He did not study 'family', 'fast food' or 'ethnic' restaurants. The four places he was able to sample were:

1   La Pomme de Terre: an haute cuisine French restaurant;
2   The Owl's Nest: an award-winning continental restaurant famous for its fish;
3   Stan's Steak House: a family owned steakhouse in a middle-class area;
4   The Twin Cities Blakemore Hotel: part of a chain, used for business travellers and functions.

Fine was most interested in how these kitchens were similar, and how cooking commercially related to the teaching and learning of catering in the two 'trade schools' he had already studied (Fine 1985, 1992). Fine was interested in the 'real' working lives of cooks who had graduated from the two trade schools (further education colleges, in British terms). He chose four restaurants that had employed someone who had attended the trade schools, had similar (small) number of cooks (eight, of whom three or four worked at the same time), and cooked slightly different menus.

The finding of samples in three projects: on the histories of girls' schools, on social science and science PhD students, (Delamont, Atkinson and Parry, 2000), and on slow learners in comprehensives, illustrates the ways in which research usually proceeds. The work on girls' schools is based on documents; the study of PhD students in social science is an interview-based project; the 'slow learners' used observation in classrooms.

The PhD project needed a principled sampling technique to ensure that key variables were covered. There were four teams involved in the programme, so each group had to find sites where the other three were not already working, or planning to investigate. The Cardiff team needed to find two or three places to study anthropology, two or three to study geography, and one or two for each of town planning, urban studies, development studies and area (e.g. Slavonic and East European) studies. The departments/higher education institutions needed to vary (Oxbridge, redbrick, plateglass, ex-CATs, polys, etc.), the status in their subject needed to vary (i.e. small and/or not known for research excellence versus large and/or famous), and ideally the organizational arrangements and the 'ethos' of the places had to be different too. There were many different ways to proceed – but we started with personal contacts, and places we felt we would get co-operation. It is an excellent idea to use contacts to get started on access negotiations. Therefore we approached for social anthropology the following departments:

1   Southersham, in a redbrick, northern university, where the professor and head of department (Professor Tenderton) had taught both Atkinson and Delamont when they were students and had employed Atkinson on a research project.
2   Kingford, a high-status urban department, where the professor and head of department (Professor Dimsdale) was a member of the ESRC committee that was funding the research. He was a stranger to us, but would find it hard to refuse a piece of research set up and funded by a committee on which he served.
3   Masonbridge, a plateglass campus university where the dean had been at school with one of us and at university with both, and whose most recent edited collection had been suggested to the publishers by one of us.

For human geography we approached the following departments:

1   Tolleshurst: a high-status department where one of the professors (not the head of department) knew one of us from a committee.

2   Hernchester: a redbrick department where one of the professors was a major figure in the politics of social science, knew one of us slightly from committees, and knew colleagues of ours well.
3   Boarbridge: a small department in a provincial town pursuing innovative PhD training funded by ESRC, so again unlikely to refuse us access.
4   Eastchester: a 1960s university with a small staff, where there were no full-time students left after funding cuts so only staff could be interviewed. They felt very strongly about their funding, and were keen to express their views to researchers.

For town planning we approached:

1   Chelmsworth: then a polytechnic which prided itself publicly on high-quality provision for PhD students, so could hardly refuse us access.
2   Portminster: a centre of research excellence where several of the professors were friends of ours and would give us access.
3   Wellferry: a small department in a former CAT, where one of us was a visiting professor and so able to 'cash in' on our 'guest' status to do some interviews.

Those departments were likely to treat our access request seriously because of personal contacts or the politics of social science, and they generated a range of high and low status, urban and rural, northern and southern, large and small sites.

The sampling of texts to do an analysis on the rhetoric of histories of girls' schools is considered next. Two papers (Delamont 1993a, 1993b) on the history of girls' schooling were written, for which I wanted to choose particular texts in a systematic way. Before the analysis of girls' school histories could be conducted, it was necessary to reflect on how the selection of the forty books examined (twenty for each paper) was to be made, from the large but indeterminate universe of such books. The first problem was that the total size of the population is unknown. It is not entirely clear how many histories of particular girls' schools in the United Kingdom have been published to date. Barr (1984) is the most comprehensive list published, but is by no means complete. Barr compiled her handlist from information supplied by twenty-seven librarians in charge of education collections in universities. It lists books about 152 different schools in the UK and Eire, along with sources of information for about as many more which were included in general works on education and biographies. Barr's list is by no means exhaustive, even of books available before 1984, as she admits in her introduction. For example, there is a book on the Croydon Girls' High School (Anon, 1954) published to celebrate its eightieth birthday. There is a copy of it in the main university library at Sussex, but it is not held in the education library or in the twenty-six other education libraries which sent data to Barr, so it does not appear. There are at least fifteen other such school histories I have found in second-hand shops or catalogues which none of the twenty-seven education libraries owned, and so are not in Barr either. Peter Cunningham (1976) of Leeds University has produced an alternative list in his work on sources for local historical research. There are two problems associated with using it as a source to try and define the total number of histories of girls' schools. It is now rather out of date and many schools celebrated centenaries in the 1980s with new volumes. More seriously, it is not necessarily clear from the name of any particular school whether it is mixed, or for boys only, or for girls. Getting hold of all the ambiguously titled volumes to check that would be a major piece of research.

The complications around sampling some texts for detailed analysis does not end with the open-ended nature of the 'population'. A further difficulty is that some schools have had multiple volumes prepared about them, especially if they are over a hundred years old. Bedford High School was celebrated at 50 (Westaway, 1932) and at 75 (Westaway, 1957) and at 100 (Godber and Hutchins, 1982), and Westaway (1945) also wrote a book to commemorate the achievements of alumnae in the 1939–45 war. Thus a list of a hundred volumes could contain multiple books about thirty schools and one book about each of twenty others.

Another problem is that the girls' schools which exist today (which can be traced from the Local Authorities Year Book and the Girls' Public Schools Year Book) are not a guide to the range of schools which have existed since 1850. There are histories of schools which have closed down, gone co-educational, or merged with other schools, which should be in the sample. In Edinburgh, for example, there was once a real school in Dick Place called St Trinnean's that has a book about it (Lee, 1962) although the school closed in 1962. Lansdowne House merged with St George's, leaving separate histories (Hale, 1959; Welsh, 1939) and eventually, generating a joint one (Shepley, 1988). Very small, very new or very private schools will not be listed in the published guide books at all, and their histories are most likely to be missed by libraries. There is a great need for a regularly updated, complete listing of the histories of girls' schools in order to reduce these complications.

In the light of all these difficulties in establishing the total universe of girls' school histories, there was no ideal way to choose a sample for the analysis I wished to conduct. My first paper was based on detailed study of twenty volumes about eleven schools, listed in Table 5.1. All the books are owned by the author, and can be said to represent major dimensions along which girls' schools are distributed. These twenty volumes have been chosen to reflect the following criteria: geographical spread (one Welsh, one from Northern Ireland, two Scottish schools); day and boarding; urban, small town and rural; elite and expensive (Cheltenham) or ordinary (Cardiff and Rugby); denominational (Edgehill founded by Methodists, the two Francis Holland Schools by Anglicans) and non-denominational; much written about and famous (Cheltenham and Bedford) and little known (Rugby, Albyn, Richmond

Lodge); celebrated repeatedly (Bedford, Cheltenham, Park School), or only once. There are books published in the 1930s, 1950s and in the 1980s. There are works about schools which have vanished (Cardiff) and those which remain (Cheltenham). Of the twenty volumes thirteen are listed in Barr (1984). The sample of twenty volumes is representative in most respects. There is no convent or other Roman Catholic school; there is nothing in England north of the Shrewsbury High School, nothing published in the nineteenth century.

The second paper (1993b) took a second set of twenty-seven books for analysis, chosen to contrast histories published before 1939 and after 1945 of the same school, so their treatment of chaperonage, mixing girls of different classes and/or religious denominations, and attitudes to suffrage, could be compared. These are shown in Table 5.2.

These twenty-seven books did not include any institution in Northern Ireland, but there are schools in Scotland, Wales, London, large urban areas in northern and southern England, plus one from a cathedral city and one rural boarding school. With these two sets of school histories, I was confident

Table 5.1   School histories selected

School and place	Date published	Author
Albyn School, Aberdeen	1967	Duthie and Duncan
Bedford High School	1932	Westaway
Bedford High School	1957	Westaway
Bedford High School	1982	Godber and Hutchins
Cardiff High School	1955	Carr
Cardiff High School	1986	Leech
Cheltenham Ladies College	1904	Beale
Cheltenham Ladies College	1953	Clarke
Cheltenham Ladies College	1979	Clarke
Edgehill College, Bideford	1934	Pyke
Edgehill College, Bideford	1957	Pyke
Edgehill College, Bideford	1984	Shaw
Francis Holland School, London	1931	Dunning
Francis Holland School, London	1939	Bell
Francis Holland School, London	1978	Hicklin
Park School, Glasgow	1930	Anon
Park School, Glasgow	1980	Lightwood
Richmond Lodge, Belfast	1968	Robb
Rugby High School	1969	Randall
Shrewsbury High School	1962	Bates and Wells

Table 5.2   Schools with pre-1939 and post-1945 histories

School	No. of volumes
Alice Ottley, Worcester	4
Blackheath High School	2
Clifton High School	2
King Edward VI Birmingham	2
Leeds Girls High School	3
Manchester High School	2
Penrhos College, Colwyn Bay	2
Red Maids	3
St Leonard's (St Andrews)	2
St Mary and St Anne (Abbots Bromley)	4

that I had tried to sample systematically and in an informed way. As this book is being finalized I am drawing another sample of school histories, this time to study their presentation of the problematic years between 1919 and 1945.

Next, sampling in the Welsh Office locational integration project is considered. The choice of academic departments for the PhD projects and of texts for the historical work can be compared with the way the schools were chosen for the Welsh Office research on the integration of learning-handicapped pupils in comprehensive schools. All the schools in four local authorities had completed a questionnaire. Twenty heads of special needs had been interviewed. Ethnography was planned for nine schools chosen for field-work visits during the meetings of the whole research team. A variety of criteria was used to pick observation sites from among those schools which had already been selected for interviews with the head of special needs. Among the criteria used were:

1   The number of statemented pupils had to be great enough to allow eight different children to be observed even if some were absent/excluded on the particular days chosen for observation.
2   The school had to be accessible for daily travel from Cardiff or have a suitable guesthouse near by.
3   The school staff had to be willing to receive the researchers.

We were also concerned to include a variety of schools. Our final nine included one single-sex school, two denominational schools, two schools with many children from ethnic minorities, and one school in a rural area. Additionally, we wanted to ensure that we visited at least one school in each of the four LEAs, and at least one school with each type of provision such as a designated unit, or separate classes, or full integration. We avoided schools where there was no head of special needs in post.

Issues of topic choice, selection of research sites and sampling cannot be separated from access negotiations. In both of the 'live' projects described, once a site had been selected in a purposive way, the next set of sampling decisions could not begin until access had been granted. In the higher education departments, once the staff had agreed, decisions had to be taken about which staff and students were to be sampled as informants. In the integration project, choice of particular pupils to observe had to wait until access to the school had been granted. The access negotiations are briefly described before the sampling of pupils and of observational sites can be understood.

Once the research team had chosen a school as a possibility for fieldwork, one of the observers wrote to the head, and to the head of special needs, asking for a meeting to explain what the fieldwork would involve. This meeting was fixed by telephone, and usually involved only the head of special needs. Head teachers rarely saw the observers personally at this stage, but gave permission for the fieldwork on the telephone. At the meeting to arrange the fieldwork the relevant teacher was asked to suggest four days for visits, one each with first, second, third and fourth year pupils. Timetables were examined, and particular days chosen when pupils had opportunities for integration. So a day on which a pupil was timetabled to be in a special class for all lessons would be avoided, in favour of one on which that pupil joined others for some subjects. The researchers accepted the guidance of the teacher about which classes/children to follow on particular days. The head of special needs then made arrangements with the individual teachers who would be observed and gained their permission for the researcher to observe the lesson.

In some schools the preliminary visit included introductions to other staff, a tour of the buildings and meeting with pupils; in others, these preliminaries were left until the fieldwork began. In either case, on the appointed day the observer would begin the research in a school that had been visited on one previous occasion, with at least one familiar face in the staffroom. The choice of particular children to observe could then begin. There were several problems associated with sampling particular pupils to be research targets. These included attendance, pupils' work styles and locational variations. It was discovered that the statemented pupils often had patchy attendance records, and it was quite common to discover, on arrival at a class for registration, that the previously chosen target pupil was absent. An alternative pupil was always located to be a target, but sometimes this was a boy when a girl should have been the target, or vice versa. In this way it was possible to observe seventy-two pupils, each for half a day.

Pupils' work styles and classroom behaviour were also a problem for the observer. Those pupils who are rowdy and disruptive are more visible and audible to everyone in the room, including the researcher. It is a temptation to focus the observation on those 'colourful' pupils, rather than on quiet, solitary children, even when the latter are the designated targets. It is difficult to write conscientious notes about a solitary child working alone without interacting with either teacher or classmates when other pupils in the class are fighting, shouting, quarrelling or leaping about.

The next sampling issue was finding sites for observation inside these schools. Observational research can throw light upon informal as well as formal and organizational aspects of schools. The data gathered for the Welsh Office project by questionnaires and interviews only provided information on the formal and organizational aspects of the school, and its policies, and on the context in which teachers operate. The observer can also look for informal aspects of school life, such as pupils' behaviour en route to the neighbourhood chip shop at lunchtime when no teachers are present. The ethnographic work was planned to focus both on activities in the school which are teacher controlled and those where pupils are relatively free to choose their associates (such as in the playground). Within each context we were concerned to look both at whether social integration was possible in it, and at whether or not it actually took place there. It was important to see whether any particular school was organized to foster social integration, and whether or not it actually took place. It was possible, for example, for a child to be timetabled to attend a class with non-statemented pupils but to sit apart from them and be socially invisible. It was also possible for a child to be taught only with other statemented pupils, but to spend all his or her 'free' time outside lessons with mainstream children.

This discussion will have made it clear how careful a researcher has to be when sampling. All the stages of thinking up a problem, choosing a sample and gaining access to it, need to be carefully documented, so that the criteria used are explicit, and can be 'written up'. The same is true of the other theme of this chapter, the anxiety to begin.

Anxious to get started

The prospect of actually gathering one's own data ought to generate anxieties as well as anticipations (just like starting a new school, or leaving home for higher education). If you are not eager to get started on your own data collection there is a problem. Fear of starting is normal, and has to be faced. Boredom, or lack of interest, means the research is misconceived. If you are too eager that is also a problem. It is important to make sure you have done enough thinking and pre-planning – fieldwork can only be done once in each setting, and it is important not to mess it up. Wade Davis (1986: 15), who studied the Haitian voodoo system of trances and 'living dead', describes how he got fed up with his doctoral programme at Harvard. He was having coffee with another student when this crystallized: 'both of us had come East to study anthropology, but after two years we had grown tired of just reading about Indians'.

If we are to believe Davis, the café had a map of the world on the wall, and the two men picked research sites by pointing to them on the map. His companion left for an Inuit settlement within a week, Davis set out for the upper Amazon three weeks later. The only preparations had been to get two letters of introduction: Davis even ignored the advice (to take a pith helmet) he was given by a Harvard expert on the Amazonian rainforest. It seems unlikely that he actually set off without jabs, visas, camera, notebooks or mosquito nets, and unfortunate that he apparently had no hypotheses either. Anyone who goes into the field unprepared is likely to come out without data.

Wade Davies was of course writing in a particular 'confessional' style, which is itself a genre. Atkinson (1996) in an essay called 'Urban confessions' has explored how and why the apparently intimate, revealing, naive confessional autobiographical paper is actually a particularly conventional genre. Atkinson analyses confessionals as fairy tales of quests (the researcher searching for data as the woodcutter's son rescues the captive princess) and we should not read them literally. However, we do look to such confessionals to tell us how research is really done, as opposed to how the methods texts state it should be done. When authors offer stories of setting off into dangerous field sites without inoculations or mosquito nets (proving how brave and iconoclastic they are) we must not read them literally. Copying such foolhardiness will not produce decent fieldwork.

Preconceptions and foreshadowed problems

It is very important to think through what your preconceptions are before you begin data collection, and to write them down in the 'out-of-the-field diary' before you forget them or they get swamped by your findings. It is also necessary to plan your early days of data collection around your 'before-you-began' hypotheses or 'foreshadowed problems'. If you go into the field without doing these two things, you are likely to come out each day with very little of use in your notebooks. Whether the data are in documents, or coming out in words, or are your observations, they are meaningless unless you structure them. You cannot structure your data unless you have some ideas about what they might mean. These are only working ideas, of course, and the data probably mean something else entirely, but they will be meaningless if a structure is not imposed. Preconceptions are not a bad thing, as long as they are made explicit in your diary (not to your informants, except as oblique questions) and you test them systematically and are reflexive about them. The danger lies in the preconceptions that are implicit, unacknowledged and unexamined.

There is a difference between team research and an individual project. In a team effort it is necessary to discuss the foreshadowed problems, and share them. The main difference between team ethnographies that ended up with a joint project, such as Strauss et al. (1964), and those which produce an unintegrated collection of individual accounts (e.g. Stake and Easley, 1978) is the pooling of the hypotheses before, during and after the fieldwork. The ORACLE project involved co-ordinating the fieldwork of seven observers, most of them untrained. In Galton and Delamont (1985: 169–70) we discussed this as follows:

> The timetable of the ethnographic research allowed us to use the study of the 9–13 schools, in September 1977, as a pilot study for 1978, when the pupils transferred into the 12–18 and 11–14 schools. Thus, by 1978 we had a fistful of ideas from the 1977 study which we could use as 'fore-shadowed problems' or 'sensitizing concepts' in 1978. Sara Delamont and Maurice Galton were involved in both years, and others only worked in one year, but some of the 1977 lessons were carried forward to 1978.

This was an unusual feature of a school ethnography. We had a chance to think for a year between the Ashburton phase of the research, and the Bridgehampton and Coalthorpe phase. Our account continues:

> We never believed that ethnographers enter the field open-minded. In the 1977 study of the two 9–13 schools we had a short list of 'foreshad-owed problems' derived from our reading of other school studies. These were of two kinds: some vaguely 'theoretical' ideas we had derived from the literature, and some 'common sense' ideas derived more from our 'members' knowledge'. Among the more 'theoretical' ideas we were interested in utilizing Basil Bernstein's (1971, 1974) ideas on classification and framing and visible and invisible pedagogies, the beginnings of labelling, and the notion of 'coping strategies'. More concretely, we asked all observers to look carefully at pupils' 'adjustment' to their new schools, sibling comparisons, staffroom discussions of pupils, bullying and the schools' responses to it, and to compare 'theory' and 'practice' in such areas as curriculum balance, pupil groupings, allocation of teachers to classes and so on. For example, in Local Authority A we had found that allocation of children to bands at Guy Mannering School was more closely related to the primary school attended than ability or heads' reports, and so we asked the observers in Local Authorities B and C to examine band allocation, class allocation and so forth.

This is a fairly typical list of foreshadowed problems. Some are theoretical at a high level of generalization (visible pedagogy), some are middle-range concepts (coping strategy), some are concrete issues (how are new children allocated to classes?). The big problem with all team research is that each observer is bound to have her own agenda, and they may not all be equally explicit for the researcher herself, or in the fieldnotes or in the out-of-the-field diary and analytical memos. As we commented on the ORACLE project, 'How far the observers took any notice of these "foreshadowed" problems is, in retrospect, unclear – because of the diverse nature of the observers.'

When a researcher is single-handed this worry does not apply. For a team leader, regular meetings with the foreshadowed problems always on the agenda is the only way.

Conclusions

In Flecker's poem the Chief Merchant claims to 'gnaw the nail of hurry'. Given the perils of the golden journey, the caravan would be equipped with the correct food, water and other supplies before it began. The equivalent precautions for a researcher are to have thought reflexively about one's sampling, and chosen one's site or population carefully, in the light of the reading already done. The foreshadowed problems are the essential baggage for the golden journey.

Key reading

The key reading for this chapter is Gary Alan Fine's Appendix 'Ethnography in the Kitchen' to his monograph *Kitchens* (1996).

Chapter 6

Sweet to ride forth

Gaining access and recording the process

> When I first attempted to rent a room ... I was taken around and intro-
> duced by a well-known, elderly resident, Eliso. Even so, I was refused by
> several families, who gave feeble excuses. Later Eliso explained apologeti-
> cally that people couldn't be sure, since I was a foreigner, whether I was 'a
> good girl'. This was my first indication that real acceptance would mean
> conformity to their notions of good conduct and that this would deter-
> mine the degree of trust I would have with local families in the area.
>
> (Hirschon, 1989: vii)

Renee Hirschon is describing getting somewhere to live in a particular
neighbourhood between Athens and Piraeus, where many of the refugees
from the 1922 exchange of populations with Turkey settled and their families
still live. Access to her informants was dependent on living in the neighbourhood – because Hirschon is an anthropologist who wanted to do an
ethnography of the community – and as she says, finding a room crystallized
the rules she would have to live by.

This chapter is called 'Sweet to ride forth' because the access negotiations
are the first stage of the research journey: the bit of the process which is still in
sight of 'home' among familiar landmarks. There are three major issues in this
chapter: the insights gained during the access negotiations, the length of time
they can take, and how to undertake them. Before embarking on detailed
discussion three caveats are in order. Access is not negotiated once and then
settled; access to formal organizations can take enormous amounts of time to
achieve; and access negotiations that are not properly recorded are wasted. Each
of these is briefly discussed, before the full spread of the chapter opens out.

Access is not negotiated once and then settled for the whole of the fieldwork. Sally Lubeck (1985: 53–4) was observing a Headstart centre when the

> head teacher resigned to take another position and a new teacher took her
> place. This teacher was obviously uncomfortable about being 'observed'. I
> later learned that no one had told her that I would be there, that she felt
> especially vulnerable anyway, since, she believed the children were 'out of

control' when she came. My note-taking only reinforced her sense of being 'spied upon' in a situation that she was responsible for but did not create.

Even without such a change in personnel, access is a process, not a simple decision. Chapter 7 explores this in more detail.

Access negotiations to formal organizations, particularly those such as schools, which are embedded in larger bureaucracies, take a long time. Linda Valli (1986: 215–17) describes how she was nearly caught out. She planned a year's fieldwork in an American high school, and

> I thought I had the summer months to contact the school office, meet with the teacher, gain some knowledge of the way in which cooperative education was implemented, etc. I discovered late in April, however, that to gain clearance for September I had to have a prospectus of my research proposal approved by a joint school district/academic committee at a meeting scheduled for early May. Since my research proposal was not yet written, I was forced to quickly formulate my ideas.

The district office accepted her proposal, and suggested a school. However, the key official who was to introduce her to Mrs Lewis was elusive:

> Once my prospectus was cleared, I was given the name of a school district official who would process my request. This individual proved to be not only difficult to contact, but, more critical to my work, unwilling to solicit Mrs Lewis until the fall semester actually began. Not wanting to jeopardize my relationship with the school district I decided to accept that timeline. While this delay did no irreparable harm to my research, it did prevent me from participating in an important aspect of the program, home visitations.
>
> During the summer, Mrs Lewis visited the homes of the students to explain to their parents what the cooperative office education program was about and to obtain their approval of their daughters' participation in the program. Mrs Lewis told me in the fall she would have been happy for me to accompany her on these visits had she been aware of my research interest at the time.
>
> (pp. 216–17)

Not only did access take five months, but Linda Valli lost an important source of data. The lessons of this are clear: bureaucracies have their own timetables and are unlikely to be able or willing to adjust them to researchers, and it is crucial for the scholar to have other tasks to occupy themselves with while formal permissions are awaited.

Bearing these caveats in mind, the next section looks at how to go about negotiating access.

How to gain access

It is important to break the access process down into stages, such as:

1   initial approaches – by letter?
2   first impressions – in person;
3   persevering in the face of difficulties;
4   gatekeepers – formal and informal.

Initial approaches

There are three main ways to make the initial approach: in person, by phone and by letter. In practice all three probably have to be used at some stage. For informal or public settings it is likely that the initial contacts will be in person: for formal organizations (unless the researcher is already employed, imprisoned or lurking there) a letter is the commonest approach. If a researcher wants to study an organization that they already work in or belong to, then informal personal meetings are probably the best starting point, but for a stranger, a letter makes a good impression.

The first stage of an access negotiation is often a letter. The first rule is to remember to keep copies of all correspondence, both to protect yourself and for inclusion in the thesis or report. Letters need to be carefully drafted, and shown to relevant helpful people before they are sent. Check that your supervisor approves the text of the letter, and get some comments from other people. Make sure that the letter is legible (type is best if it is any official or bureaucracy you are approaching, handwriting may be better for clubs, and informal groups), has an address they can reply to, and is clear but vague. Examples of good and bad letters are given below. These are hypothetical, and were invented for this book. First, a bad letter, which you must imagine is scrawled in pencil on a piece of paper torn out of a note book.

Letter One

Friday

Ashburton

To whom it may concern
    I have to do some research. I want to study why all the schizophrenics in your hospital are black and why psychiatrists are racially prejudiced.
    Can I come to your hospital next week?
    [Illegible signature]

Second, another bad letter with different faults. This one is typed, on headed paper, and is perfectly readable.

Letter Two

Department of Media Studies
Ashburton Institute of Higher Education
Bridgehampton Road
Ashburton
AS2 3PZ

Professor W.G. Eager-Wright
Department of Psychiatry
The Medical School Ashburton University
Gryll Grange Hospital Site
Ashburton
AS3 2TP

May 29th 2007

Dear Professor Eager-Wright,

I am an MPhil student in Media Studies at the Ashburton Institute, registered to do a thesis on a topic in media studies. I have a grant from the Lucy Wellbeloved Trust for the Scholarship Needs of Distressed Daughters of Clergymen in Rutland which lasts for two years from September 2007 until October 2009. I took my first degree at Bridgehampton University in Communication Studies, getting a first [half page list of all the courses in the degree]. Then I did a PGCE in Coalthorpe at the university and then taught for three years at Melin Court School in Coalthorpe, before I came to Ashburton to do my MPhil.

I am particularly interested in Durkheim's theories about totemism, as developed in his work on classification with Marcel Mauss, and [whole page on theories of totemism].

My MPhil topic is a study of psychiatric nurses' leisure activities with particular reference to their use of TV, radio, newspapers, magazines and other media, and their attitudes to the images of psychiatric disorder in the mass media. [two pages of relevant literature about mass media].

I would like to ask psychiatric nurses in your hospital if they are prepared to keep a leisure activities diary for me, and to take part in a short group interview. I realize that the nursing staff actually come under the Area Health Authority but as it is your hospital I would like your permission before I approach the Area Nursing Officer.

Perhaps I could come and see you to discuss my research, and answer any questions you may have.

Yours sincerely
[legible signature]
Polly Flinders (Mrs) BA

Home address	Work address
Flat 2	As above
The Laurels	
Balaclava Road	
Ashburton	
AS1 8SS	
Ashburton 833922	Ashburton 70000 Ext. 4236

The faults in these two letters are blatant, but here is a brief warning about some common pitfalls anyway.

The first letter has no date, no address and the reader cannot contact the sender because it lacks a legible name. The writer has not bothered to find out who the proper recipient is, and so it may never reach the relevant person. It gives no details at all about the writer, and it states that the findings are already known. The recipient of this would be likely to throw it away, or file it under 'nuisance' letters.

The Polly Flinders letter, while avoiding the faults of the first letter, falls into a trap of a different kind. The poor professor is deluged with details she does not need or want, even if her permission is needed to ask psychiatric nurses to keep diaries (which it probably is not). Letters Three and Four are attempts at sensible access letters which might work.

Letter Three

Monday April 2nd 2007

Department of Cultural Studies
University of Ashburton
AS4 907

Dear Professor Eager-Wright

I am a PhD student in the Department of Cultural Studies, specializing in the problems of 'culture-clash' faced by the various ethnic minority residents of Ashburton (e.g. the Vietnamese refugees, the Sikhs and the Maltese) and the overseas students studying at the university (mainly from Arabic-speaking countries). One aspect of my research concerns cultural differences in understanding mental health issues, and I would like to interview doctors, nurses, and other staff at Gryll Grange Hospital about this issue. My research will presumably need to go before the ethics committee, and your colleagues and staff would want to discuss it in some detail before reaching any decision about participating themselves. Could you, or a colleague designated by you, spare me about twenty minutes to discuss my plans? My supervisor, Dr Randall, suggested that if you were too busy, Dr Dimsdale might be an appropriate person to meet me.

I will telephone your secretary next week to see if it is possible to make an appointment for later this term.

Yours sincerely,

[legible signature]

Jack Horner

This version of the letter might get Jack Horner his appointment, at which he can find out what access procedures he will need to go through. He may or may not get access, but he would probably get his foot in the door, where the original Letter One would not.

Letter Four

May 29th 2007

Department of Media Studies
Ashburton Institute of HE
Bridgehampton Road
Ashburton
AS2 3PZ
Ashburton 700000 Ext. 4236

Dear Dr Blake

I am an MPhil student at the Ashburton Institute. I am studying the leisure activities of psychiatric nurses, particularly their use of mass media (e.g. TV) and their attitudes to the mass media they use. I would like to ask the psychiatric nurses at Gryll Grange Hospital to volunteer to keep diaries of their leisure activities for me, and to join in one of the group discussions I plan to arrange. They would be asked to volunteer, all the research will be confidential and take place outside the hospital in the volunteer's free time. However, I would need a list of relevant staff, and would like to give them each a letter at Gryll Grange Hospital inviting their help.

I am very happy to meet you to discuss my research plan, so I can answer any questions you may have. I look forward to hearing from you.

Yours sincerely,

[legible signature]

Polly Flinders (Ms)

The third and fourth letters are brief, clear, and at the same time vague. It is not a good idea to specify precisely what the researcher hopes to do because it colours the response and sets up a whole set of expectations. A general idea of the research topic is enough at this stage – gatekeepers are unlikely to want to hear about Durkheim's theories – but a very specific request can be easily 'fobbed off'. The recipient of the first letter can too easily say 'none of the psychiatrists here are racially prejudiced' and turn down the request.

It is not a good idea to enclose copies of questionnaires or interview schedules at the initial stage, but they should be ready, so that they can be supplied if requested. Offering them is a hostage to fortune, not being able to produce them makes you look unready. If the questionnaires or interview schedules are submitted in advance, it is very easy for gatekeepers to find many faults with them. Handed over in a meeting, or presented on request, they may be scanned quickly in the light of the good personal impression already made, and accepted without queries. (That depends, of course, on making a good impression on gatekeepers when appearing in person.)

First impressions: in person

It is important to plan how you will present yourself at access meetings. Dress can be crucial. Paul Atkinson (1997a) nearly lost his access to the Edinburgh medical school by going to see a gatekeeper in casual clothes with long hair, thinking it was an informal meeting and his dress did not matter. In my autobiographical account of the St Luke's research (Delamont, 1984a) my late-1960s outfit for visiting schools was described: a coat and matching dress, the coat well down below the knee for meeting the heads of schools, the dress well up the thigh for meeting the pupils. Heads saw a respectable coat (and real leather gloves), the girls saw a miniskirt. Sue Lees (1986) discovered well into her fieldwork that 14-year-old girls had decided she was a lesbian because she wore dungarees, and 14-year-olds in Cardiff refused to believe a young woman was an engineer because 'you've got a handbag' (see Pilcher et al., 1989). All clothing, all hairstyles, all make-up (male and female), jewellery and body piercings and all perfumes, colognes and other body odours convey messages, whether we like it or not. It is important to record what is worn, and why, and to think carefully about what is being conveyed to potential respondents by clothing and other bodily signs. British men have a complex sign system in their ties, but it would be naive to imagine that the language of clothing ends there.

Learning from the access process

In the next section three different researchers' entries to three very different settings – a school, a fantasy games club and a Bedouin settlement – are described. The general lessons about those settings which can be learnt from the negotiations are highlighted. Then the implications of such learning are explored with a Dutch example, and the necessity for good records made clear. The three examples dealt with are representative of entry to a formal, bureaucratic setting, and an anthropological or community study.

Access to formal organizations such as schools

Most accounts of access to schools are remarkably similar, whether the school is in New Zealand or Scotland. The example used here is American, dating from the late 1960s, but is fairly typical. Philip Cusick (1973: 234–7) describes his access process to the American high school he studied as follows.

> This project began officially on September 10. I had been in contact with the school district superintendent who agreed it would be a worthwhile study and said that I should take it to the principal. With that assurance, I sought and obtained an interview with Mr Vincent who was also amenable to the idea. Both men readily understood my wishes to be with the students as they carried on their daily activities and neither displayed the least bit of nervousness about my intent to penetrate the student subculture. Both understood that the focus was to be on the students and their perceptions of the school. The principal then invited me to come into the school 'in a week or so after we start … to give us time to get settled'. He also agreed to notify the teachers that the study would be done.

Cusick makes no comment about this delay, but while many institutions like to get 'organized' before a researcher arrives, acquiescing in that delay means that the observer misses the 'settling down' period. As Ball (1980), Beynon and Atkinson (1984), and Delamont and Galton (1986) have all argued, initial encounters are particularly valuable periods for researchers. In schools, the opening days of a new academic year are especially productive for researchers, because rules are explicitly discussed, procedures explained and justified, social relationships are established, and the negotiations leading to a working partnership are begun. It is only in the first few days of a school year that one can record incidents such as the following from the first metalwork lesson at Waverly school.

> Mr Pewter tells them to pick up their pencils in their right hand (unless they are left-handed) and draw a margin in pencil. He then says: 'each teacher you come across will have their own way of setting out work, and this is my way. You've heard the song My Way but I won't sing it because there's a lady present', (the observer). His way is neat. In the fifth year the pupils can choose their own way of setting out their work. In the fifth year they can think that Mr Pewter's way is OK for this work and not for that work, and choose how to set out what they do. For now, though, they should do it his way. This involves a margin a ruler wide down the left-hand side of the page plus a margin across the top of the page. Then they are to put the date in the square in the top left-hand corner. Then he shows them how he likes lettering done in metalwork, and throws

chalk at Neville because he is not watching. Mr Pewter tells them Neville is lucky it was not the board rubber.

Such lessons are an important part of understanding how a school works, and if a researcher allows her starting dates to be postponed she misses them. Cusick therefore missed something, although he does not seem to have realized it. He goes on:

> Thus far, with neither the principal nor with the superintendent had I discussed the students on which I would concentrate. Certainly in a school of 1100 students one could never establish a relationship with all of them. When the vice-principal suggested that the study be done on the senior class because of two interesting innovations, the humanities program and the impact of the new student lounge, I agreed. He added that 'It was a good class, one with a lot of spirit.'

Again, Cusick appears to be controlled by the authorities. He accepts their ideas about which pupils to study, and does not even comment on the way they steered him to a 'good' year: one which they valued. Alert researchers may agree to study the populations chosen for them, but they need to be clear about who chose their targets and find out why. Cusick next describes how he moved on from the staff to the pupils:

> Having made the decision to study the senior class of the school and having obtained permission of the administrators and teachers to do so, my next step was to approach the students. The vice-principal suggested I introduce myself during the September class meeting. Therefore, on September 15, first period, I went into the auditorium where the class was assembled and after other business was taken care of, I got up and explained briefly that I was from the university and doing a study on the way the students react in school. I made a few comments on going to school for a while and on the questions I would be asking.
>
> I finished, and the president returned, recapped the meeting with an account of the new committee, and the bell rang. When I got up to leave with the crowd, no one even looked at me. Outside everyone seemed to go his way, and I went back to the vice-principal. Not knowing what do next, I asked him to introduce me to some specific students. He took me to Mr Summers, head of the English department. More explanations followed – to him, to the head of the social studies department, to a student teacher, to a music and drama teacher.

Cusick's account is interesting at this point. He states that he had the 'permission' of 'teachers', yet he had not actually met the staff teaching

English, drama, music or social studies before. Luckily for his project, they were amenable to his plans:

> I took pains to assure them that I was focusing on the students, not on teachers, and that I would cooperate with them to the extent of telling them what was important for them to know. I had expected to find them somewhat threatened about my wanting to sit in their classes, but was frankly surprised at their openness and lack of concern for some hidden motive. In fact, at no time during the entire study did any teacher refuse me permission to come into his classes. Three times I got replies that there was not much going on for a while and an invitation to come back when something exciting was occurring; but when I told them I was not concerned about them but about what the students were doing in classes, they readily agreed to let me in.

Cusick was very successful in negotiating access to the classrooms of individual teachers if they all allowed him in; most researchers find one or more staff who refuse access or are deeply uncomfortable at an outsider's presence. At 'The Laurels' one history teacher read aloud to the class whenever I was present, and at St Luke's the head of French refused to have me in her classes (Delamont, 1973). Atkinson (1997a: 134) had the same experience in the medical school.

> Although general permission had been forthcoming from the Department of Clinical Surgery, one consultant, when approached, did explicitly deny me access to his wards on the basis of medical ethics. It was, he told me, contrary to his interpretation of his professional code of conduct to allow me to attend his ward rounds.

Cusick wanted access to students, and the senior staff faced his problem as follows:

> Mr Summers, after discussing my particular need for some senior boys to associate with, asked Mr Tomasco: 'How about Jim, Greg and maybe Rick? That's a good group. Jim's sort of a leader.'
>   Tomasco said, 'Yeah, but all he'd meet would be the football players.'
>   'Well, he has to start somewhere.'
>   Mr Summers told me to wait in his office until after fourth period started. He would send in Jim, Greg, and Rick and I could tell them what I wanted.
>   Soon Jim, Greg, and Rick walked in and introduced themselves. 'Mr Summers sent us in, said you wanted to talk to us.'
>   I explained that I wanted to follow them for a period of time to see what they did in school and they had been recommended as those

who knew their way around. They nodded. I asked them if I could
start the following morning; they agreed to this also.

This is all Cusick tells us about the access negotiations with the senior
pupils. If it was really this easy, the young men seem to have been remarkably incurious, and Cusick very lucky. His account continues:

> I asked what classes they had. As it turned out they all started the day
> with a different class; I was disappointed but realized that this was
> bound to occur and elected to go to the ceramics class with Jim the
> first period, the language class with Greg second period, and the math
> class with both for the third period. They accepted my decision
> without question and we agreed to meet the following morning. They
> left and I went to thank the vice-principal, saying that I would begin
> the following day. I again assured him that I would cause no trouble, but
> he was far less nervous about this than I was.

Cusick felt that his initial negotiations had been successful, because he
summarizes his position as follows:

> Thus, with the permission of the school administrators, some teachers,
> and a few students, I began my fieldwork. With Jim and Greg as my
> initial contacts, I was able to avoid standing around alone, which I quickly
> found gave me a very uncomfortable feeling. At the same time I made
> efforts to enlarge my contacts by meeting other students. When I was
> successful I made it a point to ask if I could accompany them to class. In
> this way, keeping a few basic contacts and constantly enlarging my circle
> of acquaintances, I quickly became known well enough in the class to go
> where I pleased, see what I wanted to see, and carry on my study as I
> wished.

Not all researchers manage to gain access to all areas of a school and to
all pupils with such ease. However, the general procedure, down the hierarchy to the pupils, is reasonably typical. Gaining access to unstructured or
public settings is slightly different.

Access to unstructured/public settings

The example of Cusick's access to a school is fairly typical of getting into a
formal organization. Some settings are not like that at all. Gary Fine's (1983:
243–6) study of playing fantasy games (like 'Dungeons and Dragons') did
not involve any formal organizations. Fantasy games were played either in
private houses or in very loosely structured public spaces, which were easy
for a researcher to infiltrate.

I first learned of fantasy gaming groups through informal conversation with a colleague. Because he knew that I was interested in the sociology of culture, he mentioned that his son was an active war gamer, and had recently been talking about a new type of gaming, similar to war games, which he called roleplay gaming. He mentioned that recently an article had been printed in the *Minneapolis Tribune* about these games ... I had some interest in war games in high school, and I obtained a copy of the article. Although the article was not specific, it did describe the local gaming club and indicated the location of its meetings. I decided that I would attend one Friday evening. At this stage I was not planning on doing research, but was only exploring to see whether the site would be appropriate for research.

Fine had previously done a study of pre-adolescent boys playing baseball (published 1987). Here he is outlining the choice of another research topic, and his discovery that a research site was potentially accessible. He goes on:

A few weeks after the publication of the newspaper article I attended the Golden Brigade club for the first time – at that time not as a sociologist, but as an interested member of the public. It seemed that there was no organization to the group: there was no membership chairman, no one that one had to meet to gain access; one simply walked in and spoke to whoever was organizing a game.

The Golden Brigade club met in a room above a fire station. This seems like a classic site without gatekeepers, formal or informal. Actually, as Fine reports:

Many months later I discovered that the Golden Brigade did have formal officers, but they had little impact, and many peripheral players were unaware that this structure existed. Players accepted me that first evening, and I was invited to play several games of Traveller, then the most popular game. I played that evening, and for the next few weeks, without even having read the game rules, as they were out of stock at the local hobby store. It is an indication of how peripheral the rules are to the game that I (and others) could play without destroying the game. The first night I felt that I could use this group to study cultural dynamics. While I did not commit myself to this project until two months later, I did begin typing field notes after the first meeting.

This is a crucial point. Although Fine had not decided whether or not to conduct a piece of research, he began writing down his observations after his first visit. Cusick (1973) does not report to his readers at what stage he began to write notes on his school, but he probably started, at the latest, after his meeting with the high school principal. When a research setting is unstructured or semi-public the boundaries of the fieldwork may not be clear and it is only too easy to ignore notemaking until the research has 'really started'. Fine writes of how the lack of a bureaucratic structure was both a hindrance and a help to his research:

> Access to the public group posed no difficulties; I was accepted immediately, although as a neophyte gamer (and a poor one at first) I did not have high status. This position suited me since I was still learning the rules. Also, being allowed to ask foolish questions aided my research at several points. However, the lack of structure, while convenient in some regards, posed difficulties once I had committed myself to conducting research in the setting. There was no one from whom I could ask permission, no one seemed to be in change, and the individuals I did ask were unaware of any structure. Thus there was no person from whom I could gain official informed consent. This was complicated by the fact that few gamers attended every week; most attended once or twice a month. The lack of structure was coupled with high turnover, as former members drifted away from the group, sometimes to play in private groups, and other members were recruited. As a result, I had to inform individuals in a piecemeal fashion that I was a sociologist studying fantasy gaming groups. Fortunately, members did not object to my presence. Informing players of my intent continued until the time I left the setting a year after I began to play. Some peripheral players never did learn that I was studying them.

Fine does not seem to have had any difficulties gaining access to the club behind the fire station. If he had wanted to watch rather than play, or if he had been a woman, he might have been regarded with greater suspicion. Hardly any women were involved in fantasy gaming, and few 'spectators' were observed. Any male who was prepared to play could probably have gained acceptance at the Golden Brigade.

Not all 'public' or 'semi-public' settings can be approached so easily. Karp (1980) tried to observe the users of pornographic cinemas and dirty book stalls in New York's Times Square. His clumsy attempts make amusing reading, but the difficulties of watching men engaged in a private, disreputable activity – even in a public space – are not trivial. In 1995 a book of ethnographic studies conducted in Times Square was published (McNamara, 1995). The team had been working on Times Square since 1978, focusing on everything from Afro-American theatre audiences to prostitution. McNamara himself studied the pornographic industry, particularly peep shows. He was either a more skilful, or a less self-deprecating, observer than Karp, as he reports no difficulties in gaining access to the vendors, customers or hustlers. Langley (1997), a woman who wanted to photograph women who worked in a Seattle peep show, had to dance naked herself to gain access, a condition imposed by the women owner-managers. Spencer Cahill (1985) and a team observed behaviour in public lavatories, where 'lurking' may be highly problematic. For this research, the sex of the researcher was crucial: only women could observe behaviour in women's lavatories. When Fine (1987) was studying the Little League base-ball teams, he found that although games were played in public, the normal audience was parents and siblings of players. An unknown, unattached male was regarded with some suspicion at these games. Choosing a public or semi-public setting does not, therefore, remove access problems: it generates different types of access problems.

Fine was not content to study the fantasy games that took place in the public setting of the clubroom at the fire station. He also wanted to study private gaming circles where friends met by invitation. Here again, there was no bureaucracy, but gatekeepers were crucial.

> About two months after I began attending the Golden Brigade I began to feel limited by being refereed by the same people in the same location. Also, I had not developed any close research friendships. Fortunately, I gained access to a private gaming group, consisting of a twenty-eight-year-old ex-navy man, a college freshman, a high school senior, and a junior high school student. This group met at the college student's house on Sunday afternoon to play Chivalry and Sorcery and they were eager to have a fifth member join them. One member of the group had asked to borrow a science fiction book that I owned; I told him I would be happy to lend it to him. I had learned that he and his friends ran a private group, and I asked about it; he courteously invited me to join them. I accepted and the group met sporadically for the next ten months – a major source of data.

Here a personal contact is used to gain access for research purposes. Later Fine joined another private circle:

> I gained access to a second private group in July, and participated for two months in their weekly Empire of the Petal Throne games. I had heard of this game, and I made a special point of contacting Professor Barker, the leader of this group and creator of EPT, asking if I could participate in the group while observing it. He agreed and said that he would have to check with the regular members of his group. The following week he told me that the other members agreed, adding that he hoped I wouldn't be writing a 'psychological profile' of them. After assuring him that this would not be the case, I participated in this group as a full, though novice, member.
>
> Finally, I extended the substantive 'theoretical sampling' (Glaser and Strauss, 1967) by examining fantasy role-playing at conventions. I attended

one national and one regional convention. Access to both of these open events posed no difficulties, and I was readily accepted by the players and organizers.

In the private settings Fine was only asking to join a meeting, not enter the lives of the participants. Access negotiations are more complex if one wishes to gain research access to a private setting such as a family to study their privacy. The next section focuses on such negotiations.

Access to families and communities

Few educational researchers try to get access to families, but the problems are worth a brief examination nevertheless. An extreme example is Abu-Lughod's (1986) access to a Bedouin household. Her story begins in 1978 when she arrived in Cairo

> and awaited my father's arrival. Here the reader might pause. I suspect that few, if any, fathers of anthropologists accompany them to the field to make their initial contacts. But my father had insisted that he had something to do in Egypt and might just as well plan his trip to coincide with mine. I had accepted his offer only reluctantly, glad to have the company but also a bit embarrassed by the idea.

Immediately this account of access sounds different. Not only has an American left the USA for Egypt, but her father has views on her access negotiations. She continues:

> Only after living with the Bedouin for a long time did I begin to comprehend some of what had underlain my father's quiet but firm insistence. As an Arab, although by no means a Bedouin, he knew his own culture and society well enough to know that a young, unmarried woman travelling alone on uncertain business was an anomaly. She would be suspect and would have a hard time persuading people of her respectability.

> (p. 11)

Abu-Lughod (1986: 11) had assumed that as she had lived in Egypt for four years as a girl, plus vacations in Jordan with relatives, she would be able to 'fit in' with the Bedouin. Her father knew, although she did not, that she could not present herself as a lone woman apparently without kin, and be acceptable.

> I had failed to anticipate that people as conservative as the Bedouins, for whom belonging to tribe and family are paramount and the education of

girls novel, would assume that a woman alone must have so alienated her family, especially her male kin, that they no longer cared about her. Worse yet, perhaps she had done something so immoral that they had ostracized her. Any girl valued by her family, especially an unmarried girl whose virginity and reputation were critical to a good match, would not be left unprotected to travel alone at the mercy of anyone who wished to take advantage of her. By accompanying me, my father hoped to lay any such suspicions to rest.

(p. 12)

Abu-Lughod was lucky. Her father was able to negotiate with a Bedouin headman on her behalf and convince him that Abu-Lughod would not disgrace the family by staying among them. Thus was her access arranged. Schools rarely consider whether their honour will be damaged by accepting a researcher in quite those terms, but the role of a senior figure as access negotiator is not unknown. Parry (1987) discusses access to naturist clubs, and her paper has striking parallels with Abu-Lughod's.

The three accounts by Cusick, Fine and Abu-Lughod are all written long after the events described, when the fieldwork had been completed. What does not come across in the passages quoted so far is the ways in which access negotiations do not stop when fieldwork starts (the subject of the next chapter). The remaining theme of this chapter is the lessons to be learnt from access negotiations.

Lessons from access negotiations

A great deal can be learnt during access negotiations, even – or rather especially – when they are going slowly. Dale Eickelman (1985: 19) has recalled that his search for somewhere to live in the old quarter (*madina*) of Boujad in Morocco, while frustrating at the time, was actually informative. He says:

> In retrospect, I obtained a very good idea of the traditional quarter and was informally introduced to a number of merchants and residents. At the time, however, the sheer bleakness of available housing weighed more heavily.

Eickelman had 'trudged through the *madina*', being offered houses with 'caved-in second stories' and one 'vacant' because it was haunted by a *jinn*. His retrospective comment is clearly correct, however miserable the search had been at the time. Pardo (1996: 6–7) studied three neighbourhoods (*quartiere*) in Naples. He found a room in a flat occupied by a widow and a middle-aged couple, after four months of research when the residents 'began to regard me with less suspicion'. He was allowed to have a formal contract 'only when I clearly enjoyed local approval and backing'. The flat was believed to be haunted by the ghosts of the dead former residents, a circumstance that allowed Pardo to learn about religious and magical beliefs among the *popolino* (ordinary working people).

Ilja Maso (1990) has discussed the ways in which negotiating access is part of the data collection process – and often a very revealing one. It is important to keep detailed notes, because things may be said and seen then which are apparently insignificant, but actually matter. During negotiations bargains can be struck and promises made that it is helpful to have 'on record', even in one's own files. Maso reports negotiations with the Netherlands Association for Environmental Information and Education (AERIE), a government-subsidized body one of his students had been funded to evaluate, in a paper that explores the data that are available even when access negotiations are problematic.

The project began inauspiciously. In the Netherlands, as in many other countries, as the end of the financial year approaches agencies rush to spend their budget so there is no surplus to be reclaimed by central government. Faced with an unspent surplus, agencies frequently decide on 'research' as a way to disperse it. In this case the Dutch ministry which funded AERIE had an impending surplus, and decided to evaluate AERIE with that surplus. Maso's department got the contract to do the evaluation, and was drawn into a set of prolonged access negotiations with AERIE.

Maso (1990) records a series of meetings, document preparations, further meetings and confrontations which prevented any data gathering from December (when the contract was awarded) until April. As he demonstrates, most of the issues that troubled the ministry about AERIE (such as poor communication between the centre and the regional officers) were made manifest to the evaluators during the protracted negotiations. As he puts it: 'The researchers concluded from the preliminary negotiations concisely described above that they were dealing with five parties: the Ministry, the Association Board, the management, the national employees and the regional employees.'

Each of these five groups had its own agenda, which meant they adopted different attitudes to the evaluators. And, as Maso stresses, the access negotiations will frequently warn researchers about the likely reception of their findings when they are available. As Maso concludes:

> When one wants to benefit in this way by preliminary negotiations, it is a condition that these negotiations are considered as a primary stage of data gathering and analysis. This implies that the preliminary negotiations must be recorded accurately and that the researchers add their own ideas, attitudes and expectations to this. This mode of operation not only facilitates the analysis of the preliminary negotiations, but also that of the material yet to be gathered.
>
> (Maso, 1990)

Or to be blunt: write it down, it is all part of the data.

Conclusions

A 'pilgrim with a sweet voice' sings that it is 'sweet to ride forth' across the desert in the relative cool of the evening, and 'softly through the silence beat the bells' on the golden journey to Samarkand. Certainly it is during access negotiations that the research site beckons like untrodden sand, waiting for the footprints of the investigator. At the beginning one's perceptions are clearest, and some of the best insights can be gained.

Key reading

The one reading recommended to go with this chapter is Odette Parry's (1987) paper 'Uncovering the ethnographer' about her research on naturists.

Chapter 7

Beauty and bright faith

Early days in the field and how to record them

At first I thought the whole village must have been inside the house. There were, my rapid count informed me, some seventy people of all ages. In the courtyard a long table ... had been set with food and drink of all kinds ... Pakis ... explained that all these people were my relatives ...

People had been waiting a long time to eat, and now they started. I found my plate piled high with all kinds of ceremonial foods ...

Pakis ... was bearing the brunt of the ceremonies since he was translating all the remarks addressed from all sides of the room to me, as well as my numbed and fumbling attempts to reply in the spirit of the event.

Unless you are remarkably unselfconscious it is extremely difficult to take part – let alone take centre stage – in a ceremony when you have no idea what is expected. Nor can you simply watch how others do it ... that will take you so far but ...

(Loizos, 1981: 8–9)

Loizos was visiting his fieldwork site, which was also his father's natal village in Cyprus, for the first time. His arrival was a matter for family celebration, and he was being treated as an honoured member of his Cypriot family. At this feast, toasts were drunk, speeches made, and stories told. Loizos was guest of honour, and also a researcher trying not to blot his copybook before he had even begun. Loizos describes the difficulties of being a stranger in an alien culture, who cannot help but be a centre of attention. Flecker's poem talks of 'the Orient sand' which is warm and deep and 'hides the beauty and bright faith of those who made the Golden Journey to Samarkand' (p. 90). This chapter is about keeping the researcher's beauty and bright faith alive, not sinking into the warm sand, and maximizing the research insight that can be gained while the researcher is still an alien.

Luckily few of us arrive in a setting to face such a public exposure of our incompetence. However, we are likely to be at risk of exposing ourselves as idiotic and stupid, unless the setting is familiar. This chapter looks at early days in strange and in familiar settings, at ones which the scholar thought were familiar and found were not, and at how the original 'access' negotiations have to be tested in practice.

In unfamiliar settings

In the early days of fieldwork the researcher is likely to be ignorant about what is happening. Gary Alan Fine (1983: 246–7) describes some of his problems as a novice fantasy game player.

> Learning the ropes in any setting is crucial for the participant observer. Before I began to play each of the games, I purchased as much of the material for that game as I could and read the rules thoroughly. Even so, I found myself learning new ways to play these games as I participated, because of both the sometimes confusing and ambiguous rules and my inexperience. My character was killed at least three times because of stupid decisions that I could have avoided had I understood the rules better. I overcame my ignorance of the rules in time, but even after a year I was only a passable player (competent enough not to have my characters behave in ways that would kill them and embarrass me).
>
> (p. 246)

Fine did not himself risk physical harm through his incompetence as a newcomer. When Keiser (1979: 94) was researching an urban gang, the Vice Lords, he was at risk of being killed in a gun battle through his inexperience of urban violence. For most researchers, incompetence is most likely to lead to pity or mockery, or at worst being thrown out of the field setting. Fine writes well of the contrasts between the formal rules which he could read in advance and the informal procedures in the club: a newcomer, especially a fieldworker, has to learn both.

> In addition to the background information needed for competent gaming, I also had to learn the structure of each game world, what was considered normative, and what was deviant. Many of these worlds had been evolving over months and years. I recall a player once asking me, 'Guess how many gold pieces I got?' then telling me that he had 27,000 gold pieces. My first reaction was to wonder whether he meant for me to consider this a miraculously high number or a disappointingly small amount. I assumed the former, and was correct. But the question indicates the range of assumptions that one must share.
>
> During the first few encounters in any gaming group one becomes acculturated, learning the language and cant, and beginning to feel comfortable with a new group of people. This applied particularly to my first few experiences playing Empire of the Petal Throne, built on a scenario so complex that it was impossible to digest all at once, and played by long–time gamers.
>
> (Fine, 1983: 247)

Fine was entering a fieldwork site he knew very little about, and this probably explains why he is so sensitive to the things he did not know. If the researcher is going into a familiar setting, or one which they expect to be familiar, the problems are slightly different. Apart from trying to make the familiar strange, as a conscious research strategy, one can still be 'gob-smacked' by unfamiliar things, and asked questions that leave one gaping.

During 1985–6 Frances Beasley and I were gathering ethnographic data on how Welsh comprehensive schools were coping with the integration of children suffering learning disabilities into mainstream classes. Reading the fieldnotes and diaries, some incidents and comments stand out from the routines of everyday school life with which I had become familiar since 1968. My 'old hand' position was challenged by some key events which occurred in these South Wales schools. In one school, Cynllaith, the head of special needs introduced two statemented pupils to the researcher as follows:

> Berwyn is the ugly one. I took him to France last year but I made a mistake, I brought him back. Adair is the good looking one, but you won't get a word out of him.

These boys told the researcher later that: 'We're the duppers – the cabbages.' The teacher's introduction, made in front of the whole class, was said in a joking way, but still shocks as a belittling comment. The boys' self-presentation to us, containing a useful dialect word ('duppers') is equally shocking, as perhaps they intended it to be.

At Llanddewi School in one of the first lessons observed, a group of pupils were trying to do an English exercise which involved classifying nouns as masculine, feminine or neuter. They asked the master for help, because they did not know the meaning of masculine or feminine. Mr Paddock explained, saying: 'If masculine is male, and feminine is female, neuter is ...?'

One boy answers 'Baby, Sir!'

These two incidents were very striking to us, because we were newcomers/outsiders. An experienced teacher of children with learning difficulties would find both 'normal', and so, presumably, would the pupils at these two schools. The research of Evans and Wragg (1969) implies that these were not particularly unusual interactions for very slow learning boys. The early days of fieldwork are often the best time to 'see' situations as an outsider.

Blanche Geer (1964) was one of the first sociological ethnographers to publish an account of those crucial 'first days in the field', in which systematic attention is paid to the processes whereby 'culture shock' is experienced or induced, and during which lines of enquiry suggest themselves to the field-worker. Her paper has been widely quoted, it has been anthologized, students are frequently referred to it; yet few others have discussed the issues so clearly. Some people may be under the impression that Geer's paper exhausts the entire topic.

While Geer focuses attention on 'first' days in the field, it would be misleading to infer that the issue of 'strangeness' is of relevance only during the initial phases of fieldwork. My initial shock at finding 14 to 16-year-olds who claimed not to know what 'masculine' and 'feminine' meant, and apparently thought hard to produce the idea that 'neuter' equalled 'baby', coupled with the public, explicit labelling of Berwyn and Adair, had not prepared me for an incident nine months later. In June 1986 I walked into a classroom in a third school (Derllwyn) and was greeted by a boy, Dafydd, saying excitedly: 'Oh Miss, you should have come to woodwork. Mental Trefor stabbed me with a chisel!' I had spent the previous two periods in girls' needlework (no sexual integration of curricula in this school) and missed this disruptive event. As a researcher I felt very ambivalent about that attendance at needlework. I had lost out on observing a dramatic event, but I could also congratulate myself that the woodwork master could not blame my presence for the violent eruption in his lesson.

These three critical incidents early in the fieldwork periods in three of the South Wales schools served to shock me into recognizing that life among the 'remedial and statemented pupils' was very different from the everyday world of the ORACLE schools (Delamont and Galton, 1986). These comprehensives had in turn been a shock after the calm of St Luke's (1984a), although the sixth year classes in statistics at boys' private schools in Edinburgh had given that fieldwork its own 'control' group. Geer's (1964) paper was about her participant observation among first year undergraduates in liberal arts at Kansas which led to the publication of *Making the Grade* (Becker *et al.*, 1968). She reflects on how her preconceptions about student life had to be re-examined. Similarly Lubeck (1985) was forced, by her early weeks in the Afro-American Headstart pre-school centre, to recognize that she did not understand nursery education although she had been studying it for over a year already.

She was trying to compare two different pre-school settings: one a Headstart centre for poor Afro-American children with Afro-American teachers, the other a middle-class kindergarten. She set out to visit each on alternate days, thus doubling her 'first days' but also allowing constant comparisons. She had already spent four months studying another pre-school in the same town, in the school year before she began the research in Irving Headstart centre and the Harmony kindergarten. The Harmony nursery school turned out to be understandable for Lubeck: two and a half months of observing on alternate days gave her 'enough' data to feel secure in her understandings. The Irving centre, by contrast, was a puzzling place, and she ended up studying it for a whole year. As Lubeck tells her story, it is apparent that her 'first days in the field' at the Irving Headstart centre lasted from early

September at least into November, if not longer. During this period she also changed her data collection style and her relationships with the staff (a point picked up in Chapter 9). Lubeck was worried that what she saw at the Headstart centre was merely a confirmation of white stereotypes about negro behaviour:

> I had been disturbed that what I was seeing during the initial weeks of observation seemed to reinforce stereotypes. For example, while block shelves and house shelves at the preschool were neatly organized according to size, shape or function, at the centre things were frequently simply tossed randomly onto shelves at clean-up time.
>
> (Lubeck, 1985: 53)

She went to talk to a respected ethnographer who helped her confusion by reminding her:

> that a social setting always has an order and that perhaps I still needed to find the order that informed the centre. He reminded me that I needed constantly to strive to be aware of my own cultural values and beliefs, that in a very real sense there are different kinds of knowing. His example was graphic: 'Remember that it might be the white kid who knows his address and phone number, and the black kid who can actually find his way home.'
>
> I was beginning to understand that I had been searching for answers to my questions in terms that made sense to me. But I knew the most important thing that I was to learn all year – that I didn't know anything, and that I needed to begin again.
>
> (p. 53)

Geer similarly records how she had to force herself to look at the liberal arts undergraduate curriculum through the eyes of a new student, not as an experienced staff member.

The early days in a new research milieu is a good time to notice aspects of the setting that may soon 'vanish'. During the ORACLE fieldwork (Delamont and Galton, 1986) I actually lived in Ashburton and in Coalthorpe in digs on a council estate and in a university hall of residence. Both were strange towns to me, which I had barely visited before. Walking around the towns, and the neighbourhoods of the schools, provided useful data about the schools. About Ashburton, we wrote that:

> Guy Mannering (AST) School had gone through a series of metamorphoses from elementary school, through girls' secondary modern school. This was a sequence which could be seen all over the city centre. Thus in one area of the old city the visitor can see St Bridget's

Middle School in a set of Victorian buildings, where notices still hang reading 'St Bridget's Secondary Modern School for Girls', and the twin arches over the gates still bear the legends 'Boys' and 'Girls and Infants' carved in the stone when the building was erected in 1870. Similarly in the very centre of the city there still stands, where Linenmarket Street joins Cheesemonger Row, the original 1770 building which once housed Josiah Martlet and Obadiah Heap's SPCK elementary school. This was an elementary school until at least 1945, and today it is a pre-school playgroup. Guy Mannering, unlike St Bridget's, had been given a new building and been moved from the red brick terraces of Balaclava Road to a site surrounded by new estates, but its previous manifestations were still visible in the school library, its cookery facilities and so forth.

(pp. 9–10)

Access tested and explored

The previous chapter stressed that 'access' is not negotiated once and then established as unproblematic for the whole fieldwork period. Access negotiations are likely to be continuing and may even be continuous and continual. One of the important lessons during one's first days in the field is finding out what the access negotiated in advance and in theory/the abstract means in practice. Frequently, it transpires that either it is possible to do much more than the gatekeepers promised or expected, or that apparent freedoms are actually curtailed. Paul Atkinson's (1997a, 1984a) access to the Edinburgh medical school took over a year to negotiate, and was eventually granted with rather tight specifications about, for example, only watching bedside teaching when the patient had been told he was not a medical student and had given permission to be observed. In theory, of course, this was an extension of the idea that a patient should not be 'taught on' without permission. In practice in a busy hospital, teaching is routinely done on patients who have not formally been asked to consent, and no doctor ever asked a patient or a medical student if they minded Atkinson being present at the bedside teaching sessions (see Atkinson, 1997a, for a full account of this ethnography of bedside teaching). Atkinson found that the initially severe restrictions placed on his access were rarely enforced in practice, certainly as far as patients were concerned. At the opposite extreme, access may be offered without explicit limits, but may turn out to be restricted in practice. Abu-Lughod (1986: 14) is a good example of the reverse problem:

> The Haj and his relatives took seriously their obligation to my father, who had given them the sacred trust of protecting me. Although the Haj understood that I was there to find out about their customs and

traditions (*adat wtaqalid*) and in our initial chat assured me that I must feel free to go anywhere that my study required as long as I informed him of my whereabouts, I soon discovered that my freedom was in fact restricted. Through the subtle cues of tactful but stubborn adults, I came to understand that I was to feel free to go anywhere within the camp but that to step beyond the bounds of the community, particularly alone, was not appropriate.

There were good reasons from the Haj's perspective for this restriction, which, as Abu-Lughod came to appreciate, increased her understanding of life in the Bedouin community she had come to study. First, the Haj had taken responsibility for her as a daughter. She could not therefore behave in ways that would disgrace a real daughter, damaging her own reputation and that of the whole group. Second, if she visited any other group's settlement, obligations of hospitality and guest relationships would be incurred. As a naive outsider she might distort or destroy the social fabric with its complex web of obligations. Third, if she came to any harm, the Haj would be obligated to avenge the insult or even take vengeance on the perpetrator: her blundering could start a blood feud. Even when the 'rules' originally negotiated do not turn out to be less stringent than expected, or more rigid and restrictive, access may still need to be renegotiated.

Fieldwork sometimes starts at the pace of the informants, rather than the eager researcher. Ulin (1996: 4) was observing French wine growers in the Dordogne. He found that 'The early phases of my research, like most field-work, proceeded very slowly.' Ulin was particularly disturbed by the casualness of his informants: it 'took some time to acquire the patience to cope with cancelled or postponed appointments'.

This is a double lesson. First, it is a test of access. Informants may genuinely need to reschedule appointments or have forgotten the arrangements, but they may also be gently testing the investigator's keenness. If you really want to get the data, you will pursue the appointment. Second, it is a source of data on attitudes to time, to arrangements and to priorities. If your appointments are broken but other people's are not, that shows the priority they give your research. If all appointments are routinely disrupted then attitudes to time are different from yours.

Similarly, as the time passes, the people being studied may change their activities, and the researcher may have to negotiate access to the new setting, co-participants or whatever. A group of pupils may have a new subject with a new teacher, medical students move from a chest ward to a kidney unit, pregnant women see a new midwife or gynaecologist, and the researcher who wants to follow them has to renegotiate what is going on.

The writing you do in your notes, and in your reflexive diary, during your first days will be particularly valuable. Write a lot, and keep it safely.

Conclusions

This chapter has celebrated the 'beauty and bright faith' of those who set out on the golden journey.

Key reading

The one recommended text for this chapter is Blanche Geer's (1964) paper 'First days in the field'.

Chapter 8

Spikenard, mastic and terebinth

Varieties of data collected and recorded

We have rose-candy, we have spikenard,
Mastic and terebinth and oil and spice
And such sweet jams meticulously jarred
As God's own Prophet eats in Paradise.

This mysterious-sounding list consists of the goods taken on the golden journey by the grocers. The varieties of data collected by qualitative researchers are not so exotic-sounding, but should provide the collector with as much profit as the sweets, aromatic oils, gum-resin, wood from the turpentine tree, oils, spices and jam carried by the merchants. The chapter is divided into sections on observational data, interview data and documentary data, and within each section a range and spread of different approaches are discussed. Observations, interviews and documents do not sound very exciting, but they make up a typical 'package' for an educational ethnographer.

A concrete example of how some school fieldwork was conducted and the varieties of opportunities available for data collection will illustrate this. In the study of an American high school — or rather the high-status senior pupils in it — done by Cusick (1973: 239), he worked as follows:

In general while in the school, my fieldwork used six major approaches. (1) Attendance at classes: I made it a point to attend the classes that those students whom I knew attended. This ran from calculus to ceramics to automechanics to humanities. (2) Attendance at meetings such as student council, prom committee, drama club, ski club, yearbook and newspaper meetings. (3) Informal interviewing: as I moved through the halls, the lounge, the classes, the cafeteria, I would talk to various students about what they were doing or where they were going. (4) Formal interviewing: towards the end of the study I interviewed twenty-two students and teachers to test my general perceptions. (5) Use of records, such as honour roll, activity lists, club membership lists, past yearbooks, and old newspapers. These were used as background material. And of course, (6) observation. There is no substitute for being on the scene. At the end of each day's fieldwork, I would sit down and type everything that occurred that day. Needless to say, it was a long and painful process before I became reasonably accomplished at the art of remembering and recording events and conversations.

This is a fairly typical list of types and varieties of context where data can (and should) be collected in the field. It is odd, in that Cusick lists two contexts for observation – (1) and (2) – and then gives 'observation' a further category of its own. Observation, formal interviews, informal interviews and documents provide a 'starter' list of methods, each of which is elaborated and explored below.

This chapter is organized so that it begins with documents, moves on to interviewing, and then concentrates on observational research, for me the central plank of qualitative research. The methods are organized in this way to build up to observational data. I am totally convinced that observational data, gathered over a long period of immersion, are superior to any others. The fashion for replacing proper fieldwork with either unstructured interviews or focus groups or the collection of narratives (Atkinson, 1997a; Atkinson and Silverman, 1997) is thoroughly bad. Such data are only interesting or useful to provide foreshadowed problems before observation or extra insight after it. Proper fieldwork is time-consuming, interviewing is a quick fix. Proper fieldwork is like a casserole: it should simmer for a long time at a low heat. Interviewing is a take-away chow mein; it lacks authenticity and does not satisfy for long – 'data to go'.

Documentary data

Hammersley and Atkinson (1995) have a substantial chapter on documents. There may be:

1   published sources about the fieldsite (e.g. school histories, school magazines);
2   mass media sources (local newspapers, student newspapers);
3   public documents inside the institution (notices pinned up, booklets for students or their parents);
4   semi-public documents (minutes of union meetings, records of student clubs);
5   semi-private documents (students' written work designed for one teacher to see);
6   private documents (letters from the head teacher to a parent).
7   documents that the researcher has asked for, such as diaries kept by informants, essays written by students; or autobiographies.

All such sources can be historical or contemporary. Whatever the type of document, the golden rule to remember is that all written records are socially produced. It is clear that if a researcher persuades twenty primary teachers to keep diaries for her, those documents are produced for the researcher. Harder to recognize is that all documents are written in a social context, with some audience in mind, even if the audience is only the author. Just as the good researcher is sceptical of what is said to her, so too documents must be sceptically read and examined in their social context.

Asking informants to write can be a useful research strategy, as long as the potential respondents are literate. Many of the well-known educational texts contain material gathered in written form, such as Lacey's (1970) use of pupil diaries, and Bryan's (1980) of essays. Robert Burgess (1988b), for example, presents an analysis of using teachers' diaries to illuminate both their own practice and his investigation. His paper uses diaries to illuminate both the impact on teachers of having adults in their classes alongside pupils, and the process of 'opening up' teaching to adult gaze. Burgess is careful to treat these diaries as social products.

Many researchers have asked pupils to write essays, as we did for the ORACLE project (Delamont and Galton, 1986). Pupil diaries are less commonly requested, but Lacey (1970) showed how valuable a data source they can be. In the 1980s I requested sixth formers in 'Ledshire' to write, anonymously, any scary stories they were told before their transfer to secondary school. Because the event occurred seven or eight years earlier, the sixth formers feel free in anonymous written texts to reveal stories they heard which are vulgar, sexual or both. At the time of transfer these 'dirty' elements in children's culture are kept hidden from all but the most trusted adults (Bauman, 1982; Fine, 1988; Grugeon, 1988a, 1988b; Measor and Woods, 1983, 1984). In written form, 217 stories were collected in ten minutes, whereas in interviews they would have taken at least ten minutes per story to collect from sixth formers, and to gather them from 11-year-olds would need very intensive fieldwork over some months to establish a high degree of rapport (Delamont, 1991). Subsequently Amanda Coffey, Lesley Pugsley and I collected such stories from undergraduates, and asked them to collect stories from other students for further analyses (see Pugsley et al., 1996a and 1996b).

Documents written for the researcher are much rarer than those produced for other purposes that subsequent scholars can also utilize. Here we can include published material and archives, ephemera and material carefully stored for posterity, mass media and bundles of old letters, the obviously scholarly and the apparently frivolous. Two of the best summaries of the importance of documents for research come from detective stories. In Josephine Tey's (1954: 96) reappraisal of the murder of the princes in the tower, a young historian claims, 'Truth isn't in accounts but in account books,' and explains this as follows:

The real history is written in forms not meant as history. In Wardrobe accounts, in Privy Purse expenses, in personal letters, in estate books. If someone, say, insists that Lady Whoosit never had a child, and you find in the account book the entry: 'for the son born to my lady on Michaelmas Eve: five yards of blue ribbon, fourpence half-penny', it's a reasonably fair deduction that my lady had a son on Michaelmas Eve.

Tony Hillerman's (1971: 122) novel about an investigative journalist details how to use documentary sources. The hero is explaining how a journalist checks out an allegation of corruption.

Let's say somebody tipped me off that you were cheating on your travel expenses ... First I'd check all your expense vouchers for a few months at the city clerk's office. I'd jot down all the dates you were charging the city for using your own car on city business and the places you claimed to have gone. Then I'd look at the city motor-pool records to see if you had a city car checked out on the same days. And I'd go through the billings from the oil companies to see if any of the credit-card slips had your name on them, and the licence numbers on the slips, and the dates, and the places they were signed.

Both these fictional detectives express a proper scepticism, and show a dogged determination to cross-check information. Wherever possible information given orally should be cross-checked with documents, and findings from one written source cross-checked with any others. Any and every possible source can and should be used.

Natalie Zemon Davis (1985: 1–2) writes about how historians proceed:

We look at letters and diaries, autobiographies, memoirs, family histories. We look at literary sources – plays, lyric poems and stories – which, whatever their relation to the real lives of specific people, show us what sentiments and reactions authors considered plausible for a given period.

Davis explains how sparse all these sources are if one wishes to research peasants rather than aristocrats, kings or clerics, and how the literary sources adopt the convention that all rustics are suitable for comedy only. However, there are: 'the records of different court jurisdictions' (p. 3). The research potential of the records kept by the Inquisition, the diocesan courts, the criminal courts, has been revealed in the period since 1945. Davis herself uses all the available documentary sources to explore the story of Martin Guerre (a man who vanished and returned after his wife had lived with an impostor for four years). Her work was filmed in France, and in the USA, as *Sommersby* with the story moved to the American Civil War. Most of us do not get our research filmed with Gerard Depardieu or Richard Gere.

None of these authors convey the joy of unearthing a good set of documents, or even of having a decent library to work in. That is best captured by Barbara Tuchman (1981) in the first part ('The Craft') of her collected papers *Practising History*. She describes the Widener Library at Harvard as: 'my Archimedes' bathtub, my burning bush, my dish of mold where I found my personal penicillin' (p. 15), and of libraries in general that they are: 'food, shelter and even muse' (p. 78). The whole of that section of her book is worth reading for its autobiographical account of doing historical research, and writing it up, and for her passion for finding things out and then communicating them. It is important not to despise any documentary source, because however 'edited', 'censored' or 'trivial', it can lead to fresh questions for the researcher. For example, the letters published in the problem pages of popular magazines can suggest topics for investigation which an adult outsider might never otherwise consider. Delamont (1983) is based on cookery books, women's magazines, wedding etiquette books and menus from hotels. The miseries of school life between 12 and 16 are well captured in this letter to *Woman* (3 July 1989):

> They tease me. Last week I was on the school bus, and some boys in my class stole my bag. Before I could stop them, they'd opened the side pocket and found my tampons. I just burst into tears and got off at the next stop. Now they all laugh and tease me, calling me names like Little Miss Tampon. Please help me. I hate school and sometimes I want to kill myself.

This encapsulates many of the findings of research on being an adolescent girl in general and managing menstruation in particular (Prendergast, 1989). A decade later *Shout* (6 October 2000) published the following on its 'Body Problems' page:

> My friends told me that if you shave the top part of your thighs you can get cancer – is this true, Cathy? I shave there and now I'm worried. This is scaring me so much.

And the following on its 'A Problem Shared' page:

She's Lying About Her Age

> We are really worried about our mate at school. She's started to hang around with her next door neighbour, who's 14 even though she's only 11 and now goes around in a gang of much older people. She's even started going out with a 15 year old boy who thinks she's 14! She's smoking too, although she says it's only a couple a day. We've told her she'd be better going around with us and she agreed, but at the weekend we were going swimming and spotted her with this gang again.

We're scared for her now. She's a good friend and we don't want her to be hurt. What will her boyfriend do when he finds out she's at junior school? Please help.

These letters, too, offer useful ideas for research, about young girls' conceptions of health issues and of peer cultures. Any researcher studying teenage girls would be alerted by this document to a 'hidden' area of their informants' lives. Boys are equally under pressure to shape up as men, as this desperate letter, published on 7 June 1987 in the *TV Times* Problem Page, reveals:

I am a 13-year-old boy at high school, and my problem is name-calling. I do not know why, but other children have started shouting 'gaylord' and 'fruity boy' at me, and I find it very upsetting. Can you please advise me how to cope with the strain?

KK, Antrim, Northern Ireland

Unpicking what lies behind 'Little Miss Tampon', 'gaylord' and 'fruity boy' as taunts would be very revealing about adolescent culture and pre-adolescents in schools (see Renold, 2000). Using mass media sources such as letters to agony aunts is not a new idea. W.I. Thomas (1923), one of the founders of Chicago sociology, used them for his classic *The Unadjusted Girl*. Following up what is meant by 'gaylord' is sound investigative social science with a good pedigree.

Documents of all kinds are, therefore, invaluable as research sources, as long as they are treated with scepticism. Moving on from the written word, the next major category of data is spoken: interview materials and other oral sources.

Oral data

Just as there is a wide variety of documents from the very public to the very private, some designed specifically for the researcher, others not, so too oral data comes in many forms. Researchers may solicit talk from informants, both in formal interviews and meetings and informally in conversations. Much insight also comes from speech heard by researchers which is not solicited by them, but is overheard, or would be happening anyway whether research was going on or not. Some of this will be intended for public consumption, other parts will have been intended for a more restricted audience which may or may not be meant to include the researcher. In a secondary school, for example, a speech by the head to parents and governors is 'public', a homily in assembly is 'public', while a discussion with the secretary is not. A researcher could well hear all three, and use all three, but would be wise to locate each set of words against the context in which they were uttered. Talk, like documents, is produced in a context, and the researcher has to be constantly aware of those contexts. This section begins with oral data deliberately elicited by researchers and then moves on to dealing with talk gathered 'in passing'.

Interviewing in educational research

All the books on how to do qualitative research devote space to interviewing. Spradley (1979) is an excellent instructor if you want to conduct rather formal interviews, have co-operative informants and accept his slightly static concept of subcultures. It is worth reading carefully, even if in the end you decide that you disagree with him. Hammersley and Atkinson (1995) discuss interviewing in a more sensitively reflexive way. Because interviewing is so prominent in most books, little space is given to it here.

There are three main types of interview that qualitative researchers do. First is the 'interview' that is done while observation is going on, when quick questions are put to informants about what is happening. Then there is the more formal interview, perhaps tape recorded, where a check list of questions is covered. Finally, there is the life (or oral) history interview, which may take repeated visits and many hours (or even years).

An example of the first type would be watching a maths lesson in which three different textbooks were in use, and asking the teacher afterwards what determined which children got which books, and how they varied. An example of the second type would be making an appointment with that maths teacher to ask in some detail how she was facing up to her new job as head of department. A life history interview might well take six or more hours in total, usually spread over several separate meetings, and cover many facets of the maths teacher's life. Of course, all the rules about not asking leading questions, phrasing them carefully, handling sensitive topics tactfully and so on are relevant to all three types. Equally important is to write every thing down as soon as possible: what you asked (in the exact words), where, when, how, and who was listening/watching, as well as what the answers were.

The first type of interviewing is unlikely to be tape recorded, while the other two kinds may be. Tape recording or using mini-discs to record sound like wonderful ideas, but transcribing the tapes or mini-discs is unbelievably time-consuming. (At the time of writing, there is no widely available transcribing machine for use with mini-discs, of the kind used for tapes.) Some informants will be inhibited by a recorder, or may refuse to talk at all. Using a tape recorder or mini-discs does not absolve the researcher from making good notes, keeping a diary and reflecting on the social context of the interview.

The guidelines for doing informal interviews with informants as part of a wider observational study are a mixture of careful research techniques and ordinary conversational politeness. The limits upon the possible tone and directness of questioning depends on the closeness of the rapport. An art college lecturer, being observed for the first time, can be asked 'Have you taught here for long?' but not 'Why are you wearing that hideous shirt?'. The same lecturer, known for six months, could be pressed on their clothing in forceful terms, even calling the shirt 'hideous' if that sort of question was normal in the conversation. Informal interviewing in the field setting is the main way that hypotheses can be tested. If a researcher thought that fine art lecturers wore flamboyant clothing while graphics lecturers wore subdued ones, informal questioning of both sets of staff over coffee or lunch would be a wise step to test that insight.

The unstructured interview lasting forty minutes to an hour or more is very frequently used in qualitative research. Spradley (1979), Lofland and Lofland (1995) and Hammersley and Atkinson (1995) all deal with techniques for doing such interviews properly. A variation on the individual interview is the group interview, which can also be built into many qualitative research projects. Woods (1979, 1986) was an early advocate of using group interviews with school pupils to encourage them to reminisce, share experiences and even 'egg each other on' when talking about school. Subsequent school ethnographers have often used a group interview technique for similar reasons. Emma Renold (2000), for example, used group interviews in her study of sexuality among primary school children, as did Haw (1998) in her work on Muslim girls in British schools. A development of the group inter-view which has become very fashionable since 1990 is the focus group. Here the researcher brings a set of questions, or at least topic headings, to the group and leads them through a discussion of these pre-determined subjects. Morgan (1991, 1993) produced the first accessible books popularizing the method, and more recently there is Bloor et al. (2001). Pugsley (1996) used focus groups in her study of sixth formers' views on sex education, and Thomas (1999) collected material on women's romantic and sexual experi-ences on holiday via focus groups.

As the qualitative interview is probably the commonest data collection method in qualitative research, little needs to be said about it here. Life history interviewing is less common, and is therefore discussed in more detail, along with the collection of 'folklore', and the gathering of 'oral history'. There is a long tradition of researchers gathering life histories, and collecting oral evidence on folk cultures, in social science. For most of the twentieth century much of the data related to deviants and criminals (Plummer, 2001), or the elderly survivors of 'proud old lineage' and dying cultures such as the Kwakiutl or the Yanomamo (Spradley, 1969; Donnor, 1982). Mayerhoff (1978), who studied elderly Jews in California with disturbing holocaust memories, is an example of an oral history/life history study. As Mary Metz points out, 'Teachers' life experiences and the cultural and structural demands of their work setting shape their behaviour – with fateful consequences for their students' (Mary Haywood Metz, 1984: 199).

Dunaway and Baum (1996) is a useful collection on oral history as a method, and Gluck and Pattai (1991) a feminist collection. Growth of life history interviewing and oral history can be seen in the collection edited by Ball and Goodson (1985) and in Woods (1985a and 1985b). The collection of oral historical material in general and life histories in particular has been a major element of Renee Saran's (1981, 1982, 1985) study of the Burnham pay negotiating machinery. Other relevant studies include Louis Smith's long-term follow-up of personnel from Kensington Elementary School (Smith *et al.*, 1986, 1987, 1988) and the fate of the institution itself. This trilogy, on the school described in Smith and Keith (1971), is a major contribution to our understanding of educational innovations. John Quicke (1988) reports using life histories to assess sociological and social psychological learning in an MEd course. This is a particularly promising area for collaborative studies. The occupational culture of teachers (Hargreaves, 1980) has been particularly illuminated by a series of studies based on life history interviews with teachers in Yorkshire and the south-east (Sikes *et al.*, 1985) and the range of material gathered in Ball and Goodson (1985) reveals the potential of the life history interview as a method. Researchers wishing to carry out life history or oral history interviews would do well to consult the Sikes *et al.* (1985) volume, and to study Barbara Heyl's (1979) account of the life history of a prostitute which exemplifies the method, as do Helen Hughes's (1961) life history of a heroin addict, Sutton's (1998) life histories from Kalymnos, Pitkin's (1985) oral history of an Italian family and Koromila's (1994) oral biography of a Black Sea Greek.

During the 1990s the most fashionable type of interview with teachers involved collecting 'narratives' from them. Martin Cortazzi (1993) has produced an excellent text book on collecting an analysing such narratives, and his earlier volume (1991) is drawn from the analysis of a collection of primary teachers' narratives (see also Cortazzi, 2001). In the USA the collection edited by Witherall and Noddings (1991) started a fashion for collecting and celebrating the contents of teachers' narratives. Ivor Goodson (1995) raised some cautionary questions about the celebration of narrative which are developed by Atkinson and Silverman (1997). Many feminists have been particularly enthusiastic about gathering narratives, because they give 'voice' to the silenced or unheard. Susan Chase (1995) presents the narratives of women school superintendents from the USA, Petra Munro (1998) those of three women teachers. Fine (1993) is a well-known example, as is the work of Sue Middleton (1993, 1998) from New Zealand. Potts (1997) is a collection of life histories of Australian college lecturers.

Alongside gathering the life histories of participants in educational settings – and those of secretaries, lab technicians, caretakers or cooks might be more novel than more of teachers – is the gathering of the folk culture of informants. Candace Slater has produced three very readable studies of oral culture in Granada (1990), and Brazil (1986, 1994). The 1994 volume *Dance of the Dolphin* deals with folklore about the dolphins of the Amazon, who come to dances disguised as handsome men, and kidnap girls and take them to the enchanted city beneath the waves. Most people like to tell stories, and collecting these can be worthwhile as research. Cortazzi (1991) systematically collected and analysed 'stories' told by primary teachers, and such work could be repeated on the staff of other sectors of the education system.

Moving outwards from folklore gathered in educational settings, the importance of the oral culture(s) of pupils' homes for educational research should also be mentioned. Shirley Brice Heath's (1983) evocation of language use in poor Afro-American and poor white families makes this abundantly clear. The papers in Jordan and Kalcik (1985) and Vaz (1997) reveal the wide range of material that can be collected, all of it with research mileage.

The data gathered by open questioning of informants in educational research has a clear status as data. As long as the respondents know that a researcher is working, what they say to her in answer to direct questions can be regarded as 'on the record'. The ethical status of things informants say which the researcher can hear is much less clear, but data gathered that way may be enormously valuable. In general, if the participants know that I am a researcher, I assume anything said in my vicinity was either meant for me or is 'fair game'. The types of spoken data which can be collected while observing in a field setting are considered in the next section on observation.

Observational data

Actually observing life in educational institutions is my favourite kind of data collection. A pile of documents, a well-written book or a co-operative inter-viewee may excite others, but I would always prefer to sit and watch something. The data gathered by watching and listening over weeks, even months, are for me the sweetest jams and the most aromatic oils and spices. Whenever a research project is under discussion I want to go and look, or send the 'hired hand' (Roth, 1966) or graduate student to go and see for me or with me. One of the disadvantages of having a full-time job is the lack of time for observational data collection and the pressure to work on documents or do interviews.

This section deals with four aspects of gathering observational data: what to look at; how to look; where and when to look and listen; and finally what to record.

What to look at

Novices frequently ask what they should be looking at, and how to record what they see. These are not easy questions to answer, because the answer is 'it depends'. What to look at depends on what the research is about. As it is not possible to observe and record everything going on for any length of time in a useful way, the period of general scanning should be short. Following an initial period of relatively unfocused watching, it is essential to start paying close attention to a selective set of phenomena. Choosing that limited focus is hard, unless the project has been set up with pre-specified objectives. In the Welsh locational integration project, the funding body had pre-specified what we were to concentrate on. For that study we had to look at children with mild learning difficulties when, and if, they were integrated with mainstream pupils. We were not there to look at teachers, or science lessons, or bullying in the playground between mainstream pupils, or staffroom seating patterns, or the work of the lab technicians or dinner ladies.

In the research on medical students at Edinburgh (Atkinson, 1997a) the focus was bedside teaching, rather than lectures, or the lives of patients, or the work of nurses, or the behaviour of hospital porters and cleaners, or the inter-professional interactions of doctors, nurses, occupational therapists, dieticians, radiographers and so on. These are all feasible topics for ethnographic work, but each of them is a full project in its own right. Atkinson focused on bedside teaching, and, quite rightly, observed, recorded and analysed very little of the behaviour and conversation of other actors in the busy university hospitals.

In an ethnographic study of classroom life it is usual to observe the clothing of the participants, the decor of the room, the arrangement of furniture and fittings, the materials used for the lesson, and so on, before any interaction begins. In addition to drawing seating plans and the layout of the room, keeping a record of the time, noting the lesson content, watching the teacher's physical movements, recording verbatim speech as far as practical, it may also be useful to focus on 'object use'. In the ORACLE project on the first weeks of secondary schooling (Delamont and Galton, 1986) one issue we covered was what objects were available to pupils, and how they were used. The children were meeting new teachers in strange rooms, to study unfamiliar subjects, among unknown companions. One way to focus our adult minds on how this experience impinged on the pupils was to concentrate on how they were introduced to the objects in each room. Every teacher gave the new pupils a matching set of rules about the use and abuse of objects in their subject, and these were worth studying for the insights they provided about these teachers, subjects and classrooms. All school work in the six schools involved using objects – textbooks, ruler, pottery kilns or hockey sticks – and all the teachers had their own ideas about how these objects should be used. Sometimes the rules were concerned with familiar things – exercise books or pencils – sometimes novel – bunsen burners or microscopes – and we looked at how both kinds of object were introduced. The observations on the use of the bunsen in introductory science lessons led to a paper (Atkinson, Delamont and Beynon, 1988) in which the nature of the school science lessons was conveyed by the initial encounter with the bunsen burner.

The focus of observation will depend on the researcher's interests, both personal and academic. Metz (1978) was interested in how desegregation of

American junior high schools was working out in practice. She focused upon the behaviour of young adolescents inside the classrooms and in the public spaces of the school. Bossert (1979) was interested in how junior school pupils dealt with tasks in classrooms, so he concentrated on that.

In an important sense it does not matter what the observer looks at, as long as the gaze is focused on some person, object or location in a thoughtful, principled way. A scholar who concentrated on one catering student all day could be doing excellent work as long as this concentration was reflexive, properly documented and had a clear aim. Leila Sussman (1977) was evaluating progressive primary education in the United States, and yet she spent a good deal of time observing in the playgrounds. This might have seemed perverse, but she had the hypothesis that the vacuum left by the removal of teacher authority in the classroom would be filled by pupil-created structures which would be revealed in the playground. Her data on peer group formations and hierarchies were a crucial part of her condemnation of progressive education as it was being implemented in those schools. Observing in the playground was a rational part of her research strategy.

How to observe

Explaining how to look is harder. It is important to stay alert all the time, which can be very difficult. It helps to focus on a particular person, location or object for a period of time, for example watching a specific pupil or student for five minutes, then another one for the same period. Observing systematically is necessary; note and record what is on all the noticeboards not just one; search out and list all the worksheets in use; if one sink is filthy, check the others in the laboratory; if one patient has behaved oddly during bedside teaching keep an eye open for the others to do so too, or not to do so.

Wolcott (1981) is the best paper I know on how to observe, which draws on courses he teaches in ethnographic methods. The discussion begins with a story – about how Agassiz, the famous nineteenth-century biologist, terrorized a young graduate student into observing the same dead fish for two weeks so he learnt really thorough observational techniques. Then Wolcott points out that discussion of observation usually shifts into considerations of field relations, access, ethics or anything other than how and what to watch. In Wolcott's course, he says, there is never time to get down to how to observe. He is sceptical about whether observational techniques of an ethnographic, reflexive kind can be taught. The research done with systematic coding schedules, such as Flanders (1970) described in Croll (1986) is quite different. For those coding schemes the training of observers is all about how and what to observe. Wolcott's attempts to train people to observe frequently reduces them to clones of the trainer, thus losing the reflexivity. Given these reservations, what does Wolcott suggest doing?

Wolcott proposes four strategies for deciding what to look at and how to look. He suggests:

1   observations by broad sweep;
2   observations of nothing in particular;
3   searching for paradoxes;
4   searching for the problem(s) facing the group.

The first strategy is to try and look at everything – as Wolcott (1981: 254) says, 'walls, games, tablecloths, advertisements, rubbish piles, footpaths, picnics, jokes, the Congressional Record, you name it'.

Looking at and recording everything is, of course, impossible. The very impossibility precipitates two good consequences. First, the research has to begin to look selectively; and as long as that process and the choices are made reflexively and recorded, good ethnography will follow. Second, the features of the setting selected will begin to inform the observer about what kind of observer she is. As Wolcott says, you begin to discover your own 'habits' as a researcher. A third useful side benefit of the 'observing everything' strategy is that data gathered at that stage will inform the written account of the setting for a reader who is unfamiliar with it. Before a detailed account of the use of hairdryers in the hairdressing classes at a vocational college, a broad view of the institution, of the hairdressing areas and of the staff, students and customers will be illuminating.

Wolcott's second strategy – looking at 'nothing in particular' – sounds pathetic. In fact, the idea is that when something unusual happens it will jump out from the drab background and force itself upon the researcher. The metaphor here is the observer as a radar scan, watching for the 'blip' that signals a disturbance.

The third and fourth strategies are more obvious. Observing a setting to try and spot paradoxes, or to discover what the participants think is their biggest problem, are well known ploys. Both are good for fighting familiarity. During the ORACLE project we found that children drew more in ordinary lessons than they did in art, and moved more in ordinary classes than they did in PE. Paradoxically, art is the last place where drawing is done, and much of the PE lesson is spent being still. The most famous examples of observers working out what the participants' problems were can be found in the studies of medical students and liberal arts undergraduates by Becker and his collaborators (Becker et al., 1961 and 1968).

Wolcott does have a fifth strategy, which he mentions only briefly at the end of his paper: that is, being trained to observe what the participants in the setting are trained to observe. Among the Kwakiutl he was taught how to spot fish under water, floating logs and deer in the woods. A friend has tried to show him how to spot wigs at twenty-five paces because it mattered in the friend's world. When my mother was dying I learnt the signals that the experienced nurses used to mark each stage in her dying trajectory, because they taught me what to look for. Asking a college lecturer in hairdressing how she knew that the student had put the dryer on too high a heat setting may be data, but it will also be training in how to look.

Where and when to look

Choosing where to look and when to look is also a matter of systematic, principled, reflexive decision-making, This can be illustrated from the Welsh study of locational integration (Upton et al., 1988). This research was on how children with learning difficulties were actually integrated into ordinary schools. Observation was focused on target children with learning difficulties who were followed for half a day through all their activities. In the schools, I would get to the relevant class early in the morning and be introduced to pupils. If there was an assembly I attended it, and then followed the target child to his/her lessons until break. Break was usually spent in the staffroom, meeting the staff who would be seen afterwards. Lessons were then observed until lunchtime. During the lunch hour I usually had a meal with the pupils in the dining hall to see how integration worked there, or followed target children to the neighbourhood chip shop, or in the playground. Alternatively, I would meet staff who were to be seen in the afternoon. Picking up the afternoon's target child at registration, the researcher would again attend up to four lessons before school finished. The policy issue – pupil integration – meant that different contexts within the comprehensives had to be visited.

Observations took place in three types of contexts:

1   those where pupils were free to choose both their activities and their companions (such as the playground);
2   those where large groups of children were relatively free to mingle within broad categories, such as assemblies, lunch sittings and communal singing sessions;
3   those where small groups of pupils were in close proximity, such as lessons.

Doing observation in all three contexts was complicated by sex segregation in some schools, where boys and girls attended separate craft subjects and the observer could only see one sex at work. In these schools, during that project, it was important to spend time in all three types of context and to observe both sexes in gender-segregated classes or areas (e.g. boys' dinner sitting) and in mixed ones (maths lessons).

It is equally as important to observe in the corridors, the yard, the dining hall and the staffroom as it is in classrooms. In many ethnographies in educational settings it would be crucial to spend time in the staffroom, watching and listening. Just as classroom talk (Edwards and Westgate, 1994) is a major source, so too is staffroom talk. Staffrooms are just as important places to observe as classrooms, and the different types of talk that go on there are all varieties of data. Andrew Hargreaves (1984) pointed out how much staffroom talk is what he calls 'contrastive rhetoric': that is, speech which contrasts 'sensible', 'realistic' teachers with 'others' who lack sense and realism. Secondary teachers frequently contrast themselves with the primary sector. Primary teachers have been labelled as 'soft', 'permissive' and 'progressive', people who fail to discipline children or teach them anything systematically. These accusations are made by secondary teachers (Stillman and Maychell, 1984: 96). There is a powerful rhetoric of abuse levelled at primary teachers, which has little relation to facts or evidence and is remarkably resistant to rational argument.

It can, however, also be heard among primary teachers. It is possible to trace from at least 1948 a rhetorical division between those espousing traditional and progressive ideals, and the feelings about these ideals are bitter and vehemently held. However, underneath the simple picture of stable, opposed groups, one made up of sensible teachers and the other of inexperienced teachers and ivory-towered lecturers, the reality is more complex. What counts as 'progressive' and 'traditional' has changed over the last fifty years, and beneath the rhetoric all the evidence suggests that teachers value the 3Rs as much as they ever did. The teacher who ignores basic skills is a creation of 'traditionalists'; very few such teachers have ever been found in real life. But they are very real in the 'contrastive' rhetoric of staffroom talk (Hargreaves, 1984).

Of course, contrastive rhetoric is not limited to teachers: it is found everywhere, especially among older people. A study of cricket lovers, for example, will produce nostalgia for a golden age. As Marqusee (1994: 27) points out, the most famous cricket poem, Francis Thompson's 'At Lords', published in 1898, is nostalgic for 1878 when Thompson skived off from medical school to watch Gloucestershire (with W.G. Grace) play at Old Trafford. (He failed as a medical student, went to London and became a drug addict.) Marqusee (1994: 27–8) writes of cricket's eternal elegy.

> From nearly the beginning, people have said the game is not what it used to be. Standards of technique, sportsmanship, loyalty or patriotism are perennially in decline … This veneration of the game's past, inevitably accompanied by deprecation of its present, may be attributed in part to an association between this past and the individual's own childhood … the mythic power of childhood (or, in the case of most English cricket writers, public-school boyhood) overrides the discipline of history.

Cricket lovers, from former Prime Minister John Major to the humblest amateur on the smallest village green, share the nostalgia, and produce contrastive rhetoric. Herzfeld (1983) reports similar rhetorical talk about the past in rural Crete when all the young women were virgins and immorality was unknown. When gathering data it is wise to be on the lookout for contrastive rhetoric and rosy-trimmed nostalgia (see also Delamont, Atkinson and Parry, 2000: chapter 8). Like the myth that England had no hooligans until today (Pearson, 1983; Delamont, 1999), our informants may *believe* that food tasted better, the summers were hot, and children in non-exam classes were docile and deferential. Your job is to gather their views, but not to be suckered into believing them.

As well as 'contrastive rhetoric', there are many other forms of talk to be heard in faculty common rooms, staff dining clubs and school staffrooms. The astute observer should be alert for folklore, jokes, narrative, atrocity stories, serious educational discussion and barbed comments made to the researcher or about her. Educational institutions are rich in contemporary folklore. Pupils and students (especially medical and nursing students) have rich oral cultures about which we know something; the equivalent folklore of teachers and lecturers, heads and lab technicians has not been tapped. Collecting such folklore is revealing about the occupational cultures of different groups of staff. The only study which included an urban legend circulating through staffrooms is that of Morin (1971) on a panic in Orleans, when a story circulated that the fashionable boutiques were kidnapping young female customers for the white slave trade. Morin found that some teachers had believed this myth, and explicitly used it to warn adolescent girls not to buy fashionable clothes from the boutiques. Staffrooms in British schools certainly allow folklore to develop and spread, and many aspects of colleagues, parents, pupils and educational policy are good subjects for urban legends. Sedgwick (1990) wrote in the *TES* (16 March 1990) about developing urban legends in English schools that summer.

> I'm sure you've come across modern folk myths – those stories the teller insists are true but they didn't happen to him … but a friend swears she knew a family who took Grandma on holiday to France and the old lady died and they put her on a box on the roof of the car to bring her home and the car was stolen while they were in a café just south of Chartres … The School Examinations and the Assessment Council booklets, *A Guide to Teacher Assessment*, have attracted their own folk myths. The best one to come my way says the kids on the front cover, with that handsome moustached young teacher in the specs and the striped shirt, constituted the verucca-smitten rump of an otherwise foot-healthy swimming class.
>
> Another told of two teachers who resigned on first sight of the contents of the boxes, the educational equivalent of a dead grandma. While the National Curriculum ring binders and local management of schools (notwithstanding the head's constant grumbling) had received grudging acquiescence, SEAC's A4 glossies were the last straw.
>
> (Sedgwick, 1990)

Brunvand (1983, 1984) is a good introduction to the collection and analysis of this modern folklore, which can be found in playgrounds (Measor and Woods, 1983, 1984; Delamont and Galton, 1986, 1987; Pugsley *et al.*, 1996a, 1996b) and staffrooms. The material on jokes and the importance of narratives in the talk of all participants in education (for secretaries, caretakers, dinner ladies and parents will have such stories too), is related to the types of information we might call folklore.

In the pupil and student areas of educational institutions a researcher may overhear jokes and insults. These can be very important as keys to understanding the culture of respondents. Fine (1987), for example, reveals a great deal about pre-adolescent boys via a collection of their insults. Such material will probably only become accessible by 'accidental' eavesdropping or after long periods of ethnography, when trust has been established, because, as Bauman says, pupils are often reluctant to discuss 'dirty' stories with adults.

> The free peer group activity of children is by its very nature a privileged realm in which adults are alien intruders, especially so insofar as much of the children's folklore repertoire violates what children understand to be adult standards of decorum.
>
> (Bauman, 1982: 178)

Fine (1988) has written about 'Good children and dirty play', and stresses how 'Dirty play is important in shaping relationships within the group as well as outside' (p. ii). Elizabeth Grugeon (1988a) has made a similar point about the 'vulgar' aspects of small girls' playground games. For the researcher, such 'dirty' talk may be distasteful, or seem trivial and not worth adult notice. It may also be impossible to collect without jeopardizing other fieldwork relationships – for example, the dinner ladies may object if an adult encourages 'smut'. Elsewhere (Delamont, 1989b) the case for paying attention to these stories as part of the ethnographic endeavour has been argued. However seriously or dismissively one regards them, they can be a sensitizing device. The physical features of the school that matter to new pupils might be overlooked by an adult, and so could adolescents' curiosity about the teachers' personal lives. The alert researcher does not neglect the urban legends or other folklore in playground or staffroom.

What to record

The final theme in this section is what and how to record. Generally it is sensible to record as unobtrusively as possible. If everyone is writing on an A4 pad, then an A4 pad is fine for the fieldworker. However, if no one else is writing, then the observer may have to leave writing till afterwards, or keep rushing to the lavatory. Parry (1987) discusses the problems of writing in a notebook when participating in a naturist club, and Hobbs (1988) clearly could not stop in the middle of a pub to write detailed notes. Educational researchers are lucky in that writing is usually possible in the milieu, because participants are frequently writing themselves. As a rule, researchers should write on whatever they can carry easily in the setting, and feel comfortable doing. Knowing what to record comes from experimenting with one's memory. Enough should be written to enable the events to be recalled later – which may be a few key words, or dozens of hastily scribbled lines. A scholar with shorthand would have an advantage; most of us develop our own abbreviations and informal codings. Wherever and whenever possible it is useful to record speech verbatim, to note who is speaking, and to provide rough timings of events. It is not possible to record too much about a person, place or interaction, but it is idiotic to pile up lots of material without reviewing it and beginning to reflect upon it. Ten minutes of good observation well written up is worth an hour's notes lying forgotten in an unopened notebook.

Organizing as you go

The previous section focused upon the varieties of data that can and should be collected. These data have to be analysed and interpreted as you go along. Sometimes researchers fall down on this aspect. Florinda Donner (1982: 6–9) describes how she was working in 'a small town in eastern Venezuela' where she studied the healing practices of three curers. She found herself unable to make any sense of what she learnt from them.

> After transcribing, translating and analysing the numerous tapes and hundreds of pages of notes gathered during the months of fieldwork, I had seriously begun doubting the validity and purpose of my research. My endeavour to organize the data into a meaningful, theoretical framework proved to be futile, in that the material was ridden with inconsistencies and contradictions.
>
> (p. 6)

Donner gave up, went off into the jungle and lived among the Yanomamo instead. Before leaving she watched one of her three curers, Dona Mercedes, burn her fieldnotes. Whatever she felt, that was plain silly.

Conclusions

It may appear that none of the varieties of data discussed in this chapter has the romance of rose-candy, spikenard, mastic, terebinth, oil, spice or the jams eaten by Allah in Paradise. However, at a symbolic level, the data are just as romantic, and at a practical one, they are the trade-goods the researcher sells to earn her living. The value of data depends on their careful collection and storage, and there, too, they are extremely similar to the mastic, spikenard and terebinth of the poem.

Key reading

The one recommended reading for this chapter is Barbara Tuchman's (1981) *Practising History*, especially Part One, 'The Craft'.

Chapter 9

Seek not excess

Maintaining relationships in the field

Initially villagers had some problem with the reasons I declared for wanting to be in their midst, namely, to learn the language and then their customs and the history of the village ... they doubted those were the real reasons ... people believed that the CIA ... was not only deeply involved in the 1967 coup d'etat but was also active in the current affairs of Greece. In 1969 villagers had an initial inclination to wonder if I were a CIA agent.

(Aschenbrenner, 1986: viii)

It is unusual for educational researchers in Britain to be taken for CIA spies, although quite common for American anthropologists, but establishing and maintaining usable relationships in the field is still a problem and a source of data. Flecker's poem includes an old man warning the caravan 'seek not excess', which is a good maxim for this chapter.

The dangers of over-identifying, or 'going native', have already been outlined in Chapter 3. Cusick's (1973) high school ethnography was criticized as an example of the researcher over-identifying with one group of students. Walker (1988), like Cusick, began his study of pupil cultures with a male clique of footballers, but he was careful also to spend time with three other cliques: 'the handballers', 'the Greeks' and the 'three friends' (p. 12). His aim was to 'analyze inter-group relations from each relevant culture perspective' (p. 12). It is harder work to make sure that you do not over-identify with one faction in a setting, but establish some relationship with several. In this chapter the difficulties that can arise in establishing enough rapport to do fieldwork, without over-identifying with one section of the respondents or 'going native', are explored. Throughout the chapter two themes are stressed: the importance of reflecting about one's field relationships, and the need to document them. The chapter starts with some discussion of establishing relationships among teachers and pupils, then moves on to self-presentation in research and possible roles during fieldwork, and thence to the great unmentionable: sex in the field.

Establishing fieldwork relationships

Difficulties in establishing rapport may be due to culture-clash (a Christian among Muslims, a pacifist among soldiers), or personality, or tensions in the field setting, or all three. It is crucial not to take fieldwork problems which are structural personally (i.e. if you are a Turk in Greece or Greek in Cyprus, the problems go back a thousand years, and are not your personal inadequacies). Nor should the individual fieldworker blame herself for problems in the field setting which predated her arrival. Both sorts of tension are useful to generate data, though personally uncomfortable. It is also the case that any skill or qualification that a researcher has will have advantages and disadvantages. To do anthropological fieldwork in Spain, fluent Spanish would seem an essential qualification. Yet Susan Tax Freeman (1979: xxii) found it a mixed blessing:

> I arrived in Vega de Pas with many blank notebooks, my earlier experience in Spain, and a compass. I rented a room in a family home above a busy tavern in the center of town, owned and run by the family, and I arranged to share my meals with them.

She had already done one ethnography in rural Spain (Freeman, 1970), and thought she would be able to do her study of the Pasiegos (transhumant cattle herders in northern Spain) in the same way. However, there were problems she had not expected. Fluent Spanish proved to be a drawback as well as an advantage.

> Conversance in Spanish language and culture ... had its drawbacks. I learned gradually, from encounters with a few incredulous people, that I was not being granted the status of foreigner by *barrio* people, but, rather, was assumed to be Spanish. Therefore I was suspected both of unpleasant motives, such as property assessment for tax collection, and of holding the prejudices against Pasiegos which Spaniards could be expected to hold. When, to counteract this, I advertised my foreignness, I was disbelieved.
>
> (pp. xxiii–xxiv)

Freeman reports that some people were not just suspicious and antagonistic to being interviewed; they actually refused even to exchange greetings. Pasiegos are believed – by other Spaniards – to exhibit *recelo* or 'suspicious reserve'. Freeman found it extremely hard to do fieldwork among a group of people whose behaviour was governed by *recelo*. After eighteen months she had begun to feel that: 'I was finally ready to begin my fieldwork in the *barrios*' (p. xxv).

An observer is likely to be in the way when hard physical labour has to be undertaken, but one is equally obtrusive in classrooms. It is hard to recognize that as a researcher one is a nuisance (at best) and that many people in the setting may actively resent, fear or resist one's presence. Abu-Lughod (1986: 13) reports some of the initial difficulties she had in the Bedouin household which had accepted her for fieldwork.

My Muslim credentials were shaky, as I did not pray and my mother was known to be an American. But most assumed that I shared with them a fundamental identity as a Muslim, and my father's speech was no doubt so sprinkled with religious phrases that they believed in his piety, which in turn rubbed off on me. Many times during my stay I was confronted with the critical importance of the shared Muslim identity in the community's acceptance of me. As always, the old women and the young children bluntly stated what most adults were too polite to say. The hostility they felt toward Europeans (*nasara*, or Christians) came out in the children's violent objections to my listening to English radio broadcasts, an old woman's horror at the thought of drinking out of a teacup a European woman visitor had just used, and comments made about an American friend who came out to visit me (whom they liked very much) that she was good 'for someone of her religion' (*ala dinha*).

It was also clear that I came from a good family and good stock, so the Haj's family could accept me as a member of their household without compromising their social standing.

Abu-Lughod was not being rejected as an individual, but aspects of her structural location, behaviour and dress were offensive to her informants.

Stewart (1991: 3–16) went to Naxos to study folklore about *exotika* (spirits, ghosts, mermaids, the devil, etc.). He described himself as a folklorist, a term understood on Naxos, rather than a scientist or an anthropologist. A scientist would not be interested in *exotika*, and, of course, any Naxos resident who told stories of *exotika* to a scientist would appear 'uneducated', 'backward', 'superstitious' and a 'country bumpkin'. Anthropology only became a university subject in Greece in 1987, so the term was not known. However, a folklorist was a known category, and residents could only gain status by telling a folklorist stories. However, Stewart found that not being a Greek Orthodox believer distanced him from the Naxiotes. One family gave him a hand-carved cross, shaped in a place 'where the cock does not crow', of wood that did not float on water, bearing the Greek Orthodox abbreviation for 'Jesus Christ conquers' on its four points and set with the blue beads that keep off the evil eye (p. 5). If Stewart was going to collect stories of dangerous *exotika*, he needed Jesus's protection. The family did not enquire, because it would never have entered their heads, whether Stewart was a Christian. He was not a Turk or other Muslim, or a Bulgarian Communist, and so was a Christian like them, and in similar danger from bad spirits, ghosts, the evil eye and the devil.

Culture-clash between researcher and informants can be acute, even in a school in an American city, as Sally Lubeck (1985: 55) points out. Her relations with the Afro-American women who taught at the Headstart centre were potentially troubled.

The teachers had had many reasons to mistrust me: I was white, they were black; I was an 'observer', they the observed. Both role differentials have had a history of abuse. What was ultimately of relevance, however, was that we were all women, all working single parents, all struggling daily with the ups and downs of working with small children.

Even when race is not a potential source of misunderstanding, the relationships between teachers and researchers can be strained. Linda Valli (1986: 217–18) describes her interactions with Mrs Lewis, the commercial studies teacher, who

> proved to be an invaluable source and contact … She introduced me to teachers, students and business people, allowed me to sit in on any of her classes, told me how to go about getting documents and permissions I needed, and brought me to meetings with supervisors who eventually gave me access to do field research in their offices. If Mrs Lewis had not established positive and trusting relations with these work supervisors herself, my research would have been severely curtailed.

Valli was lucky, in that Mrs Lewis had seen her as a kindred spirit before they met, and believed that they shared a feminist outlook. With some other teachers, being labelled a feminist would damage the researcher's status severely. Valli explains:

> Unbeknown to me, Mrs Lewis had received a copy of my research prospectus so she could decide whether or not she would participate in the field work. Something in that proposal, probably the focus on women in the work force, or in my mode of self-presentation, indicated to her that I was a feminist. Thus, within a week of our acquaintance, she had characterized the two of us as kindred spirits, as women who were both concerned about women's rights and equality in the workplace. She said that she herself was quite a vociferous spokesperson for the women's movement and that it was very interesting that a person like me managed to hook up with someone like her.
>
> This identification seemed to establish the trust between us that ethnographers invariably indicate is an essential component of good field work.

However, there were hitches in their relationship.

Although Mrs Lewis and I had some common meeting ground (I had also been a high school teacher and, like Mrs Lewis, thought of myself as a pro-union feminist), I did not always agree with her about social issues or educational procedures. Being conscious of my status as a research guest, whose invitation to study the cooperative program could easily be revoked, and being personally less assertive than Mrs Lewis, I began to develop an overly withdrawn presence as a way of coping with potential conflicts that could arise. This silence produced a growing sense of unease in Mrs Lewis who, at one point, in front of a supervisor and in a jesting tone announced that I had not shown her any of my field notes but that that was all right since she could sue me if she did not like what I wrote.

Valli here describes the perennial problem of fieldwork: being always' on trial'. Signithia Fordham (1996: 27) was tested by Afro-American boys in her high school study to see if she was 'really' black, or only an 'Oreo' (a biscuit that is black on the outside but white inside). She had said she wanted to follow them after school, doing whatever they typically did. They visited a well-known sex shop to prove they were 'real men' and to test her.

Many researchers have described how they were very subdued, withdrawn or careful in their setting, for fear of being forced to leave. David Altheide (1980), for example, describes how

partly because of my concern about not stepping on toes, or saying the wrong thing lest the news director terminate the study, I had avoided direct assaults on certain topics, and with particular individuals.

(p. 306)

Valli reports that she overcame the bad patch in her relationship with Mrs Lewis, who was then able to talk about their interactions.

After a time, once Mrs Lewis and I had re-established a more trusting relationship, she told me there had been a period during the year when she had questioned whether or not she had done the right thing in agreeing to the study, saying 'I felt as though it was a very vulnerable position I had put myself in and there had been times in the past when I put myself in a similar position and had been hurt because of it.' Part of this feeling of vulnerability and distrust might have been avoided had I been more verbal and shown Mrs Lewis some of my writing as the year went on. I was, however, afraid to take that risk, knowing she had abso-lute control over the continuation of my research.

(Valli, 1986: 218)

The literature (e.g. Woods, 1986; Hammersley and Atkinson, 1995; Burgess, 1984a) includes useful discussions of the range of strategies researchers have adopted to establish themselves in educational settings. If the researcher is an ex-teacher, the approach used by John Beynon is a serious possibility. Beynon (1983) has written vividly about how he established himself in a tough boys' comprehensive.

My principal means of 'proving myself' was to display to staff that I could 'stand the pace' and that I was not, as Mr Megaphone had first labelled me, 'one of those people who bounce into a school for one afternoon and slum it'. I arrived in Victoria Road before most and made it a point to be amongst the last to leave at about five o'clock. I showed myself able to share their working lifestyle, stuck rigidly to the daily routine, dressed appropriately, was punctual, and gave out occasional 'verbal buck-ups' to those who felt vulnerable about having me in their classes. I carried through my pledge to accompany 1X through all their contacts with teachers during their first half-term in secondary school, even if this meant going swimming, playing soccer and running a cross country each week! My aim here was less to gather data than to build up credibility with Mr Megaphone, who was one of my severest critics and who (being a high-status member of the staffroom) coloured to a considerable extent how I was seen by his colleagues. After one tortuous cross country I was sitting in the staff room at break-time clearly the worse for wear. Mr Megaphone shouted across the room:

'Look at old Beynon there, dripping sweat everywhere! He's just run a few miles and learnt what a PE teacher's life is like!'

On the spur of the moment, I managed to out-quip him and turn the laughter against him:

'It was carrying you on my back did it!' (Laughter)

At that time I had no idea that my near-geriatric jog constituted 'breakthrough'. It's worth quoting Mr Megaphone at length on the matter.

'When you first arrived we all thought "Here's another bloke getting a degree on our backs!" We resented the idea that we were just fodder for research. A lot of them asked themselves the question. "What's in it for me? Nothing!" Bill Tangible's spiel about being honest and not hiding anything didn't go down very well, I'm afraid. As far as we were concerned you were in the way as we had a job to do. After a while, we got used to you, but at first everyone was looking over their shoulders to see what your reaction was. For example, when I clouted King the staff said, "What did John Beynon say about that?" I couldn't care less what you thought – King had to learn not to give a load of cheek and how to behave and I took it upon myself to teach him. Some of them would have let him trample all over them, but not me! The staff felt you were judging them all the time. There was a story going the rounds that you were a "spy from on high" (sent down to Lower School from Upper School by Mr Headmaster). But when they got to know you better and saw you were able to fit into the place without pestering them all the time, that you were not just a seven day wonder, they accepted you. But it was going to the baths and on cross countries that did it because they saw that you meant what you said about following 1X through all their lessons, even if that meant slogging through the mud in Seaview Park. It was that which tipped the scales in your favour.'

(pp. 46–7)

Beynon's joke was clearly a turning point in his relationships with several of the senior male staff who had previously been most hostile to him. A similar incident happened to me when studying 9-year-olds in Ashburton in 1977, at Gryll Grange Middle School. Their maths text, *Oxford Middle School Maths*, included an exercise – taking a traffic census – which meant leaving the school for the verges of the main road. Miss Tweed and Mrs Hind could not take their own children, and there was normally no adult available to escort them and the census was skipped. Because I was there, small parties could be taken out to count the traffic. This allowed for a staffroom joke.

> The traffic survey was interesting – I took two groups down the hill to the major dual-carriageway to count traffic – some did both lanes, some only one. There were so many cars that I'm sure most lost count – lorries and vans were easier, motor cycles rarer – but in one lot we had a boat and in another a caravan. Miss Tweed made fun of the boat in the staffroom at lunchtime – saying that when these expert observers and researchers come they cause problems – who would believe they could take a group out to count traffic and see a boat! I said I was sorry, and joined the laughter.

Abu-Lughod (1986: 21) reports a critical incident which, she felt, established her finally as an acceptable member of the Bedouin culture. Her household was headed by 'the Haj', whose mother was still alive, 'the key figure in the camp'. Abu-Lughod felt that the Haj's mother was ambivalent towards her, until:

> Her brother's funeral finally changed her attitude toward me. When we got word that he had died, I insisted on going with the women in our household to pay condolences. I found the whole scene very moving, with the wailing and 'crying'. When I squatted before the old woman to embrace her and give her my sympathies, I found myself crying. Her grief pained me, and because she had been ill for a while, I feared for her health. With each new arrival the ritualized mourning laments would begin again, and I could not hold back my tears. This funeral had awakened my own grief over the death of my grandmother and a cousin, neither of whom I had mourned properly.
>
> I later heard from others how touched the old woman had been that I had come immediately, like her kinswomen and daughters-in-law, to mourn with her. Others told me that it had meant a great deal to her to know that I genuinely cared and could feel with her the grief over the loss of her only blood brother. From that time on she treated me differently, even weeping as she sang me a few poignant songs about separation just before I left the field.

These critical incidents all shared one characteristic: genuine feelings. The Victoria Road staffroom actually found Beynon's quip funny, the joke made by Miss Tweed, though it seems feeble on the printed page, was a rare humorous comment by a normally dour teacher, and Abu-Lughod says she was genuinely grieving. Establishing rapport with informants is hard work, but sometimes one is lucky and an interest, attribute or action works to ease the process. Maryon McDonald (1987, 1989) found her access and field relations in Brittany were better when she stressed her Scottish and Welsh ancestry and refused the label 'English'. As part Welsh, part Scottish, she was a Celt, and therefore acceptable to Breton language activists and ordinary Bretons. Rosemary McKechnie (1993) used the same strategy in Corsica, another region of France where there is a separatist movement and a feeling of resentment towards the central government in Paris. Onagh O'Brien (1994, 1993) did an ethnography in French Catalonia, a rugby-playing region. Her father had been an Irish rugby international, and men in her village had seen him play in Five Nations internationals. This made O'Brien's access to male informants easier, and when he came to visit her he was greeted as an 'old friend', opening more doors for her. Measor (1985) was equally lucky to discover that one of the teachers she was working with on the life history project grew orchids, a hobby of Measor's own. A shared experience or enthusiasm helps a great deal. John Beynon (1983: 41–2) was able to play the card of having been a teacher himself.

> I was too old to adopt the now-familiar ethnographic persona of 'naive student', and found it best to present myself as a former teacher turned lecturer/researcher. That I had once been a teacher undoubtedly hastened my 'acceptance':

> | | |
> |---|---|
> | *Mr Bunsen:* | Where did you teach in London? |
> | *J.B.:* | South London and then Hertfordshire. |
> | *Mr Piano:* | *(who had been reading the staff noticeboard)* Good Lord, I didn't realize you were one of us! I thought you were one of the 'experts' who'd never taught, but knew all about it. |
> | *J.B.:* | I don't know all about it, but I have taught. |
> | *Mr Piano:* | How long? |
> | *J.B.:* | Ten years, in a grammar and then a comprehensive. |
> | *Mr Piano:* | That's a fair stretch. Well, well, I can start thumping them now! *(Week 2)* |

Novice researchers may be slightly shocked by the hostility to researchers expressed to Beynon by the men at Victoria Road. There is a structurally tense relationship between teachers and educational researchers, just as there is between teachers and what Wolcott (1977) called 'technocrats' (outsiders who want to introduce technical changes into schools). Such hostility must not be taken personally, because it is of long standing and is endemic to the occupational culture of teaching. Hostility to researchers, experts and so on is felt in most staffrooms. When Brian Jackson (1964: 40) asked primary teachers to list those who opposed streaming in primary schools he was told in no uncertain terms that it was non-teachers. Table 9.1 shows the results.

Table 9.1 shows that opponents of streaming are seen as definitely 'alien' to teachers: college lecturers, parents and trendy-lefties. Additionally, a few respondents added HMIs and teachers seeking promotion. Opponents were described as:

Ivory towered lecturers in education

Earnest reformers

Extremists who pay homage to the idea of equal opportunity

The cranks of this world

These sociologists with no practical experience

People looking for research to do. Otherwise there is no feeling on this subject.

I feel that one of the causes of social disorder today is this supposition that all are equal.

(Jackson, 1964: 41–2)

If these were the opponents of streaming, who were the sensible supporters? Of Jackson's sample 73 per cent said that 'very experienced teachers' supported streaming. Here too Jackson received comments that everyone accepted streaming except a few cranks, and that it was the proper concern of teachers and no one else.

That research was conducted forty years ago, when almost all primary schools

Table 9.1   The critics of streaming

	%
People in education who are not practising teachers	61
People with a chip on their shoulder	49
Parents of children in low streams	49
People of left-wing sympathies	36
Lesser-educated people	23
Middle-class parents	18
Inexperienced teachers	16

were streamed and the top stream were coached to pass the 11 + exam. I have left in such an 'old' example to show how deep-seated and long-standing are the differences between school teachers and outsiders (whether media pundits, researchers, or government ministers). Given this structural tension between teachers and researchers, and the additional problems that may occur when there are differences of race (e.g. Lubeck, 1985), religion (e.g. Peshkin, 1986, who was a Jew studying an evangelical Christian school), gender (e.g. King, 1978, in infant schools with all-female staffs), or political views, it is amazing how many ethnographers have managed to do good work among teachers.

So far the discussion has focused examples of establishing and maintaining field relationships with teachers. Researchers who want to focus on pupils have to sustain their social relationships just as carefully. Cusick (1973: 237–9) describes this in his high school study.

> By the middle of October I was known fairly well and felt secure enough in the system to find myself looking forward to each day's observation. A strange phenomenon began to occur about that time. Those with whom I had the closest contact seldom mentioned my role as an observer, although I was with them a large part of the day. Even in January Bob once asked, 'Are you taking notes on what us guys do? Are you writing this stuff down?' At the same time, those who knew me, but with whom I did not associate, frequently asked, 'How long are you going to be here?' 'When are you leaving?' 'How is your study going?' To the end, these people never forgot my official role as an observer. There were a few problems. I found later that Bill and his friends thought I was a policeman looking for narcotics; but they, too, eventually forgot my role. One night I was introduced to Roger's cousin, 'Oh, this is Phil, he's some sort of student teacher or something. Is that right?' I told him it was.

Cusick had become very close to a group of high-status male adolescents who were active in football, and was deliberately neglecting all the other student groups. He is claiming here that his closest friends had forgotten his 'research' role, while more 'distant' students held him to it. He seems to be claiming that the data are better when the respondents have 'forgotten' what the researcher is there for. Lois Weis (1985: 172) reports exactly the opposite from her study of Afro-American adult students in a community college. She enrolled at the college, and

> Like all students I spent entire days on campus, taking classes and examinations. I, like other students, suffered through the crowded elevator, limited number of telephones, cafeteria food and generally poor physical facilities. Students began to see me everywhere and increasingly interacted with me ... Once students became aware of my intentions as a researcher they were more than happy to 'tell their story'. I took classes for four

months before conducting any in-depth interviews.

Cusick's (1973: 237–9) account of his rapport continues:

> Actually, that they forgot my role should not be surprising. We know
> people not according to some abstract term but instead according to
> what they do. To them 'researcher' was a word that meant nothing,
> because I never did anything a researcher would do, such as take notes.
> Every day they saw me do just what they did – go to class, hang
> around the halls, eat in the cafeteria, play cards in the lounge, go to the
> gym, get dressed, and play basketball. In fact, that is why it was easy.
> There was so little that they did that I could not do also. Also, I never
> made the mistake, as I had done in the Catholic school, of helping
> them with their work. I was asked twice and both times just refused,
> and so they stopped asking. Of course, I had my own adjusting to do. I
> never cared about sports, but because the athletes spent a lot of time
> talking football, I had to learn something about the local high school
> competition, and find out who was in competition for the NFL and
> AFL titles.

Cusick here admits that he had to learn about both amateur and professional American football, to fit in with the young men he was studying.
Walker (1988: 14) was luckier when he needed to associate with the footballers in his Australian high school.

> In planning the research I had not foreseen that the culture of the domi-
> nant group I was seeking would be based on rugby football. So it was
> both fortunate and fortuitous that this brand of organized physical
> conflict had been my own preferred sport at school, that I had played it at
> … school, in local club competitions on weekends.

These two studies, done in two different countries fifteen years apart, both
show how, when studying some types of young men, sport may be the key.
There is no published study of young women in school which contains such
passages about using sport to cement the researcher–informant relationships.
Yet there are subgroups of young women in schools who do enjoy PE and
talk about it, especially in single-sex schools. At St Luke's there were some
anti-sporting groups but two large cliques (the boarders and the 'debs and
dollies') valued prowess on the games field highly. Hockey, lacrosse, fencing,
badminton, tennis and gymnastics were all taken seriously by those girls, and
it was useful that I had, thanks to a rather 'posh' PE teacher who came to my
grammar school for a few years, played lacrosse as well as hockey, tennis and
badminton. It would have been particularly baffling to watch lacrosse games
or talk to enthusiasts of the game at St Luke's if I had had no knowledge of it.

The importance of sport and teams for some of the girls was made very clear when Monica told me why Deborah was an isolate. The St Luke's team were in the middle of a badminton match against another school which was running late. Deborah's father arrived to collect her and she left, even though the match was not over. St Luke's lost, and for Monica this 'betrayal' revealed that Deborah was too dependent on her parents, too babyish, and even disloyal to her team-mates.

Despite his initial lack of interest in American football, Cusick (1973: 237–9) is cheerfully confident that he was able to blend into the high school scene alongside the high-status male athletes he concentrated on. He writes:

> So, by dressing and acting as they dressed and acted, and being present as much as possible, I simply became part of the school scene. In fact, when I would occasionally skip to work on my notes, I would be asked, 'Hey, where were you yesterday?'

Fine and Sandstrom (1988) have written a whole book on the ethics and practicalities of doing fieldwork with children and adolescents. Emma Renold's (2000) is a recent British study which involved ethnography on primary school children, paralleling Francis (1998). Cusick (1973: 238–9) reflected on the strengths and weaknesses of his strategy as follows:

> It took only a short time for the limitations of the methodology to become quite clear. Students segregate themselves, and therefore I had to choose a group and stay with it. I just could not associate with everyone. This fact limited the generalizability because it prevented me from observing a whole range of phenomena. On the other hand, I benefited from the intense experience that group membership provided. Since the important student social unit was the group, it was not a limitation, but helped fit the methodology to the intent of the research.

Here Cusick appears to be claiming that it is not possible for one researcher to focus on different groups of pupils in a school. He concentrated on one clique of young men and, to a lesser extent, on the young women who dated them. Other groups were seen only through their eyes. Some subsequent researchers, noticeably Willis (1977), have followed this pattern, while others have worked hard to associate with different student groups (Walker, 1988; Stanley, 1989). Cusick suggests that being in with the in-crowd had advantages for an ethnographer.

> An added advantage of being associated with the athletes was that they seemed to be among the biggest, toughest, most well-known students in the class, and their acceptance precluded a challenge to my presence from other students in the student lavatories, lounge, cafeteria, or classes. Also, since I

entered the system from the top, that is, with the approval and consent of the superintendent, principal, teachers, and high-status students, I feel I was granted access that an entering student would never have gained. At the same time that I came, a boy transferred in from another school. To all appearances he was a pleasant, well-dressed, intelligent person, but it was not until January that I saw him begin to interact regularly with a number of other students. If I had attempted to disguise myself as a student, it may have taken me much longer to gain access into a group, and I may have never gained access into a group as prestigious as the 'athletes'.

In a later volume (Cusick, 1983: 137) reflects on this style of establishing relations in the field.

My preference is always to find a few people of like mind and manner, and make my primary associations with them and rely more on observation and interview for the larger group.

The concentration on Cusick's account is deliberate. It is rich and detailed, and makes a case for his one approach compared to two others: trying to get along with all the cliques as a researcher, or, trying to 'pass' as an actual student, as Weis (1985) did in the adult and community college. Whereas researchers in higher education do sometimes enrol as students – Moffat (1989), for example, lived in a student 'dorm' and took classes at Rutgers – or present themselves in a quasi-student role, this is very rare in schools. Corsaro (1981) is spectacularly unusual in his attempts to participate in pre-school groups as if he were a 4-year-old. In hospital settings researchers have taken menial jobs to gather data (Goffman for *Asylums* (1961), Roth for *Timetables* (1963), but this has not been done to study educational settings. Where the researcher has taken a job in a school, it has traditionally been as a teacher (e.g. Bullivant, 1978) not as a cleaner, groundsman or catering assistant. Whatever role one takes, it is important to think hard about how one is being judged and evaluated, and to make detailed notes on how one is received and how this may be interacting with the data being collected. Peshkin (1986) found that his Christian respondents were constantly trying to convert him; this was annoying, but also revealing about their priorities. As one of the elements in how we are judged in the field is how we present ourselves, that is the subject of the next section.

Self-presentation and self-disclosure in the field

Whether the researcher is trying to associate with teachers and lecturers, or pupils and students, or with dinner ladies, secretaries, lab technicians or the librarians, how one presents oneself is crucial. Attention needs to be paid to dress and hairstyle (and make-up), and to what personal information one gives out. For women in the field the two issues may be closely related. Harriet Rosenberg's

(1988: xiii) self-presentation clearly caused her problem: she looked too young.

> The villagers were a little wary at first, I thought, but hardly 'savage'. I later learned that they were simply puzzling over what a young girl was doing alone in their village. Eventually, someone took me aside and asked me if my mother knew where I was.

Once she had lived in Abries for some time, and

> as my French improved, I'm sure I began to seem more three-dimensional and less like a lost child to the villagers.

The examples of Sue Lees (1986: 11) being labelled a lesbian, and Measor (1985) being attacked as 'selfish' because she did not have children, discussed in Chapter 6, illustrate this. Coffey (1999) explores the topic in some depth. For Abu-Lughod (1986: 16–17):

> The other factor was my unmarried status. Being unmarried not only cast me in the role of daughter, but since I was far older than the unmarried Bedouin girls, it also placed me in an ambiguous position. I wished to be part of the women's world, but I did not have one of the most important defining characteristics of women: children. The gap between the two categories is symbolized by clothing, and when I decided to convert to wearing clothing like theirs I was a quandary. Married women wear black veils and red belts ... whereas unmarried girls wear kerchiefs on their heads and around their waists. I compromised, wearing some women's clothing and some girls' and then tying my kerchief in a non Bedouin way. In the end, they put me in an intermediate category. The only real problem this status caused was that it prevented me from asking certain questions about sexuality – I was assumed to be ignorant, and I had no intention of disabusing people of this view, as I wanted to protect my reputation. But women seemed to talk openly, joking bawdily even in front of children, and so I did not feel that the topic was completely closed.

Margaret Kenna (1992) who has done fieldwork on a tiny Greek island since 1966, reports on how her unmarried status, during her first fieldwork, puzzled the islanders.

> Women, like men, asked me over and over again about my family. When I told them that I was an only child and that I had come to the island to collect information in order to write a thesis and gain the 'highest' of university qualifications, they were puzzled. If I was an only child, they reasoned, I was sole heir to my parents' property and

therefore likely to make a very good marriage; but if my parents had allowed me to travel and live by myself, they either didn't care about my reputation and safety or they weren't going to give me a dowry. It was clear that I had to provide my own and find a husband who would tolerate my 'past'.

(p. 153)

Kenna got a PhD, a lectureship and a husband, so when she returned to the island in 1973 with these trophies, the islanders were vindicated. Later she discovered that her 'anomalous' marital status had, like Abu-Lughod's, caused problems. First, she modelled her dress and behaviour on the ideal of a 'good' girl as described by 'middle-aged and elderly women' (p. 153), i.e. as it had been in the 1920s and 1930s. Young women therefore saw her as an anachronism, and the more the old women praised Kenna's 'modesty', the more alien the young women found her. Second, Kenna discovered that her body posture gave a very strange message. She regularly sat with her legs crossed at the knee: a respectable pose in Britain, the USA and Australia, where she had grown up. However, she discovered, on Nisos only prostitutes sat like that: the posture was believed to prevent conception (because it twisted the womb). So Kenna had been proclaiming that she was an academic researcher, but sitting like a whore. In 1973 Kenna's informants were pleased she had married, but worried that 'After three years of marriage I was still childless; [and] I had lost a great deal of weight which meant, in Greek terms, that married life, particularly its physical side, was not satisfying' (p. 188).

Dress and demeanour are not only a matter for women. Dick Hobbs (1988: 6) tells how he was 'extremely obtrusive' among CID officers because of 'poor image-management'.

> On one occasion I attended a semi-formal non-police function with Simon (a detective), and I dressed in a manner that I considered smart yet comfortable: open-necked shirt, sleeveless Fair Isle sweater, and corduroy trousers. Simon told me I looked like 'a fucking social worker – where's your bike clips and bobble hat?'

To do his research – mostly in pubs – Hobbs equipped himself with 'a formidable array of casual shirts with an assortment of logos on the left breast' (p. 6).

My impression, and to test it one would need to look systematically through all the ethnographies produced, is that male researchers are less likely to discuss in their books what they wore in the field than women, but both sexes ought to pay attention to their dress. Certainly what clothing is worn, and what personal information is made public, should be documented, and systematically recorded in the field diary. Self-presentation will be closely related to the roles played in the setting. The next section deals with some roles that are played in the field.

Roles in the field

Sometimes data collection can be combined with developing a 'helping' relationship with one or more participants in the field setting. For example, when Fine (1983: 244) was studying fantasy games:

> In one of the first Traveller groups in which I participated the referee requested that someone in our party keep a 'starship log' for his records, to enable him to keep track of his fantasy universe. I offered to do this, and developed a system whereby I made a carbon copy for myself, as well as writing additional notes. This continued for a month, and after this scenario was no longer played I continued using the journal note pad for my own records, finding that it was unobtrusive and common enough to prevent comments from others.

Such roles are very tempting. They give the researcher a role in the setting, and something concrete to do. The whole issue of what tasks to perform, whether to help with the work, and so on, has been the subject of much debate in the literature, including vacuous typologies. Hammersley and Atkinson (1995) and Lofland and Lofland (1995) both devote space to sensible discussion of the relevant issues. Being useful in the setting is often attractive, but not always possible. Maryon McDonald (1989: 293) points out:

> Acceptance in a rural milieu is not quite the untrammeled celebration that much anthropology might lead one to believe ... One cannot simply tug the udders of someone's prize cow, or fall on one's knees and weed the beetroot with the rest of them.

Fine was able to play an active role, help an informant and get on with his research. If that is possible, then there is probably no harm in being active. Later in his research, when he had become an 'expert' in the setting, Fine (1983: 244) started to referee games.

> In addition to playing the game, I created my own world (two of them, actually) and refereed approximately half a dozen games of Chivalry and Sorcery. By solving problems that other referees faced I learned how referees dealt with these pressures, in ways that I might not have suspected and probably would not have learned from referees had I not known the questions to ask. Since I know that I didn't use the dice rolls as a referee (indeed, I could not, given the difficulty of creating a fantasy

while on one's feet with eight noisy players clamoring for a response), I assumed that other referees responded to similar situations in similar ways. I could ask others about this using my own experiences as a basis for comparison. Until I had refereed I did not realize how many discretionary powers referees had, and later discovered that, if anything, I was less flexible than most referees.

Fine was an experienced ethnographer, and he was making conscious decisions to take on roles which would enable him to answer particular questions. Fantasy games have players and referees, and it was easier to learn about refereeing by trying the role. As Fine found:

> I learned that refereeing and playing 'felt' different. Playing was exhausting, and even boring at times. By the end of an evening of playing I felt drained. Yet when I refereed I was energetic throughout the entire evening without needing caffeine. Refereeing is energizing, although after the game is over one suddenly feels totally exhausted. Other referees also felt this way, and I might not have discovered this had I merely observed or just played the game.
>
> (p. 250)

Here Fine was learning about fantasy gaming, and establishing and maintaining his field relationships. Dale Eickelman (1985) conducted life history interviews and spent many hours working on a set of nineteenth-century Moroccan documents with a key informant, a judge. This man, Hajj 'Abd ar-Rahman, initially rented the Eickelmans a house. The relationship between landlord and tenants had certain problems which Eickelman records: 'I fortunately vented most, but not all, of my petulance only in my fieldnotes' (p. 20). The judge, or *qadi*, let Eickelman watch him at work, in his courtroom, and interview him at length about the cases. Eickelman speculates that:

> I may have appealed [to him] as a poor man's Boswell and obliquely lent him status. When I put questions to him directly, he seemed pleased to live up to his reputation as a man of learning and speak 'high words', quotations from the *Quran* and classical Arabic literature.
>
> (p. 23)

Later Eickelman was given a pile of nineteenth-century documents about the leading local family, and discovered that the *qadi* had always wanted to work on them and been denied access. The two men set out to work through the archive, meeting every day for up to six hours over three months. This cemented a friendship which continued for another decade. On a later visit to Morocco, Eickelman actually lived in the judge's house as a member of his household.

It is unclear to Eickelman himself how he was able to develop such a close relationship with the *qadi*:

> As one of his sons later said, his father never particularly liked Europeans, and as a speaker of only Arabic and *tashalhit*, he had limited means of communicating with them.
>
> (p. 35)

Eickelman offers some speculations, such as their common interest in the archive. Also:

> I think that he enjoyed such work as an end in itself. With me, even as a non-Muslim, he could at least temporarily pick up the threads of the world of learning ... he could transmit to me ... his own values and sensibilities concerning Islamic learning.
>
> (pp. 35–6)

Here, Eickelman suggests that the *qadi* got benefits from the relationship, especially a disciple rather like the traditional novice scholar in the oral Islamic education system that had largely vanished. The roles which researchers have to play in order to relate successfully to informants are many and various; being an apprentice Islamic scholar paid off for Eickelman.

The final theme of this chapter is a great unmentionable: sexuality.

Sexual relations and fieldwork

One aspect of roles in the field which is rarely discussed is sexuality and sexual relations. Two women anthropologists (Donner, 1982; Cesara, 1982) have confessed in print to sexual relationships in the field, Cesara writing under a pseudonym, Donner in a work that has been attacked as invented and/or plagiarized. Cesara reports her sexual encounter as a part of distancing herself from her 'Canadian' self and immersion in her African field setting. Donner apparently had a violent sexual relationship with Iramomowe, a Yanomamo shaman, while they shared a hallucinogenic drug, immediately before she returned to the white world, as part of her 'leaving' the field. It is not at all clear from the passage whether it is to be read as a 'real' sexual encounter, or hallucinations, or a fantasy, or a metaphor about culture clash. One reviewer (Debra Picchi, 1983) has attacked Donner for reporting the encounter, on the grounds that it will legitimize genocide. The image of a savage Indian raping a white woman would fuel prejudice and give credence to those who want to wipe out the Yanomamo.

Two issues arise from this: whether such relationships should occur, and if they have, whether reporting them is a necessary part of reflexivity. Coffey (1999) devotes a chapter to this topic. A young gay man doing interviews with gay male couples had to learn to repulse passes politely but firmly, and this probably increased his insight into his subject matter, and could be used to teach fieldwork survival skills. As a general rule, intense emotional and sexual relationships are unlikely to increase the researcher's credibility if they are revealed in the reports of the findings, yet a failure to mention them is a distortion.

Conclusions

Hilliard (1987) and Hobbs (1988) both report research in which they had to do a great deal of drinking. Hobbs even says he 'repeatedly woke up the following morning with an incredible hangover, facing the dilemma of whether to bring it up or to write it up' (p. 6).

The relationships that the researcher has to develop with informants in order to gather the data can demand terrible sacrifices.

Key reading

The key reading for this chapter is William A. Corsaro (1981) 'Entering the child's world – research and strategies for field entry and data collection in a preschool setting'.

Chapter 10

Leaving the dim-moon city of delight

Terminating your fieldwork

> Four miles beyond the monastery, at the tip of Cape Dinaretum, Cyprus ends ... In ancient times a temple to Aphrodite crowned the promontory. The Acropolis, as I climbed it, showed nothing but lavender and a summit filmed with bluish, wind-bitten stones. From here you may sometimes glimpse other lands – Turkey, Syria, Lebanon – but today, as on most days, the shrine of Aphrodite marked the end of the world.
>
> (Thubron, 1986: 249)

Colin Thubron ends his walk all round Cyprus at the extreme northern tip of the island beyond the monastery of Apostolos Andreas. The above passage is his leave-taking to the reader, and apparently his exit from the field. In reality of course he must have gone back into the island to get a plane or boat out, but in the account of the trip, the peninsula is a good place to stop. In research, there is rarely such an obvious stopping point as a clifftop above a rough sea. Our field settings, and our data-collection processes, become, like Baghdad, a 'dim-moon city of delight' that we are loath to leave. It is more comfortable to go on repeating our now-familiar processes of data collection than face the harsher world of full-time analysis and writing.

Nigel Barley (1983: 153) states cheerfully that: 'When the alien culture you are studying begins to look normal, it is time to go home.' He was writing about 'real' anthropological fieldwork in the Cameroons, and it may not seem quite so obvious when one is studying one's own society which may have seemed 'normal' all along. Dan Mannix (1951) was a young graduate when he joined the carnival on impulse and learnt sword swallowing and fire-eating. He spent six months with the show, but knew it was time to go when the Fat Lady (Jolly Daisy) pointed out to him that everyone with the carnival was a freak of some kind.

> Look at May, crazy in love with her snakes, and Captain Billy having himself covered with tattooing trying to be an out-an-out freak like me, and even you – a college graduate swallowing swords and eating fire when you knew all along it was liable to kill you.
>
> (p. 218)

Daisy warns Dan that the longer he spends with the carnival

the more of a freak you'll get until pretty soon you can't be happy anywhere but in a carny where there're other freaks for you to be with.

(p. 218)

Daisy then challenges him:

What country do you think you've been living in for the last six months?

Dan, surprised, says the USA, and she retorts:

No, you ain't. The United States stops at the marquee out there … You been living in a world that ain't on any map … this is fairyland. It ain't a real world.

(p. 218)

Mannix begins to remember that his original intention was journalism and starts to reconsider his future; five pages later he leaves carnival life for ever. He had recognized the warning in Jolly Daisy's words. Not all ethnographers are lucky enough to meet a Fat Lady who warns them when they are going native.

Gary Fine (1983: 252) has an excellent account of when it had become his time to leave a fantasy gaming club over a fire station where he had been playing, and researching, games such as 'Dungeons and Dragons' for some months.

One problem at the Golden Brigade club that eventually induced me to cease attending was that with each passing week I was becoming a more and more central and powerful person within the gaming structure. I found myself unable to take a minor role, as new players increasingly came to me for advice about the game, since I was an experienced, veteran player. I found myself teaching the newer members about the game, which meant that I couldn't observe their socialization (although I did learn about my knowledge of the game and my socialization through the way I taught them). I slowly found that a group of younger players gathered around me, having found someone who would pay attention to them, listen to their ideas about gaming, and play with them – things many of the older players were unwilling to do. As I mentioned in chapter 5, character status is often correlated with player status, and I found my characters being given power, which was one of the features I hoped to avoid. Eight months after I began to attend the Golden Brigade club I found that I had reached the point of diminishing analytic returns, and soon stopped attending, focusing instead on private groups.

After a while these groups were discontinued, and at that point it seemed appropriate to leave the field to think, continue reading, interview key individuals in the gaming network, and bring the research to a conclusion.

A particularly telling phrase in Fine's account is 'diminishing analytic returns'. If the fieldwork is not limited by money, or timescales imposed by the funding body, or the natural life of the phenomenon being observed, then the researcher has to watch out for the point when nothing new is being learnt. Fine's is a useful comment, because he shows himself in danger of 'going native', and therefore changed his approach.

While there is no ideal, or normal, or desirable length of time to be in any field setting, it is important to stay long enough to appreciate the depth of the material (if documentary) and the historical rhythm of the location or institution if an observational study. A scout camp may only last a week, but schools, universities, polytechnics and other educational settings can have long histories. The participants in any milieu may have established shared meanings which the researcher has to stay around long enough to discover.

It is important to keep one's eyes and ears open for 'narratives', and for traditions building up, and to be around consistently enough to inquire into them. As Atkinson (1990) has pointed out, and Cortazzi (1993) has also discovered, too often researchers violate the historical continuity of informants' lives by seeking out incidents and events detached from their temporal unfolding, and comparing them without their historical context. As Smith and Geoffrey (1968), Cortazzi (1991), and Walker and Adelman (1976) in their famous 'strawberries' story have shown, researchers who enter a social situation which pre-existed (and which will continue after their exit) need to be specially sensitive to such temporal issues. An example of some humorous traditions building up from the ORACLE research will illustrate this.

Walker and Adelman's (1976) decoding of the joke about strawberries has become well known. In Miss Tweed's class at Gryll Grange, we saw such a joke beginning. One of us recorded how:

> During the break I find out about Horace. During the morning Miss Tweed has referred to 'Horace' on several occasions and each time the children have laughed. She says, for example, 'There's Horace at the window again.' One little girl's (stuffed toy) mouse is called Horace. Everyone giggles when it is mentioned. During the break Miss Tweed tells the girl, Yvette, to tell me why it's called Horace. The girl laughs, and Miss Tweed then explains that when she was writing on the first day Yvette spelt 'horse' as 'Horace' and another child called out: 'Look! There's a Horace outside the window eating the grass.' When she made a mouse in needlework Yvette called it Horace. There is much giggling at this.

Later in the fieldwork, the observer wrote:

> Anyone who mis-spells anything is referred to as Horace. For example, Miss Tweed says, 'It's like that Horace looking through the window' to another girl who has mis-spelt a word in her writing, or 'take it away and alter it – we don't allow anyone else to have a Horace in here.'

A few days later, Miss Tweed explained to the researcher why she was particularly supportive to Yvette:

> She tells me more about the little girl with the Horace joke. Her parents are split up and she now lives with her Gran. She was very nervous when she came in and is more settled now. (Miss Tweed allows her to paint during English lesson.)

Both Maurice Galton and I had to be around in Miss Tweed's class over several weeks to spot this shared meaning developing. Staying around long enough to be incorporated into jokes is one signal of good rapport building up; only a researcher with whom a teacher felt relaxed would be told jokes. A further example of a shared joke was also collected from Gryll Grange in the summer after our cohort had transferred – that is, twelve months into the fieldwork:

> The atmosphere is very relaxed. When she comes back she tells him it's mental arithmetic books. Ian can't find his mental book 'I'll do it in my jotter' he says and everybody laughs. Miss Tweed turns to me and says 'you won't understand this but the teacher who died last year was deaf and the children were always playing him up and coming up and saying "Should I do it in my English book? Maths book? etc." and he would always reply "Do it in your jotter". Then one day a boy came up to his desk side and said "Can I go to the toilet?" and he replied "Do it in your jotter." '

This story was also reported by Cortazzi (1991: 19) and is probably an urban, or contemporary, legend (Brunvand, 1983, 1984) often reported in staffrooms across the UK.

Researchers have to stay in the field long enough to share certain aspects of it with the participants, but not too long. Unfortunately most researchers say very little about the end of fieldwork. Sally Lubeck (1985: 60), for example, merely says: 'I also maintained contact with the pre-school teachers after leaving the setting.'

Research in academic or training institutions which have terms or years may impose their own rhythm on the ethnographer, because as the term ends, so does the fieldwork. This appears to be what happened to Lubeck, though it is not made explicit. Similarly, Linda Valli's (1986) 'methodological appendix', which is thirty-three pages long, says nothing about leaving the field. Walker (1988) discusses his access strategy and the ethics of his fieldwork on four cliques in an Australian secondary school, but does not deal with disengagement. As his data-gathering lasted five years, the reader can assume there was a disengagement, but it is not discussed. Peshkin (1986) records that he spent four semesters in the fundamentalist Christian school (p. 24), and that towards the end of the fieldwork he issued a questionnaire and did systematic interviewing, but does not write about leaving the school or the community. There is no discussion in an educational ethnography of the sensitivity of Fine's (1983).

Atkinson (1997a: 133–4) conducted his fieldwork over two years. In his first year he spent all three terms observing the bedside teaching of internal medicine; in the second year he spent two terms observing surgery teaching. He therefore saw two different cohorts of students during their first clinical year. As each cohort moved on, to a long summer holiday and then into their second clinical year, it was natural for his research to end. Within each subject, Atkinson had to choose which particular ward, doctor and student group to observe, and how long to stay with that setting. He says:

> To achieve even a limited acquaintance with these aspects of the work of a clinical unit, a stay of several weeks was necessary. However, I also found that by a month of daily participation and observation, many of the features of life in the unit which had appeared distinctive were tending to become familiar, and that the freshness of my perceptions of the unit was starting to wear off. When such a sense of the familiar became apparent, I would try to move on to a new unit.

Sometimes a researcher can tell that they have been in a setting long enough when they recognize the lies that respondents told them earlier in the fieldwork. As Rosenberg (1988: xiv) says:

> Many villagers had wonderful senses of humour and were quite capable of pulling a researcher's leg. But it is precisely such tall tales that are the pleasures of fieldwork. They also offer another important lesson: not to believe everything one hears.

When the lies have been exposed by superior knowledge of the setting, and skill in recognizing them has grown, it may be time to move on, but only if the material collected has been written up. Atkinson (1997a: 133) is clear on this point:

> One well recorded and illuminating event was worth more than two half-remembered, and possibly less well reported periods of observation.

Sometimes researchers discuss leaving a field setting because their initial methods have become untenable. Julia Stanley (1989: 174) reports how she gradually withdrew from classroom observation:

> Summer 1985 was a bad time in English schools. Industrial action frayed away at the tempers of staff and students alike, and teachers became uncomfortable about my presence in lessons.

At the same time there were rumours in the staffroom about the content of one of Stanley's case studies of a deviant boy and these, too, strained her relationships with teachers. She records: 'It became increasingly difficult to find classes I could visit without embarrassment.' Stanley therefore spent more time visiting parents, and interviewing pupils, and withdrew from lessons altogether.

The neglect of disengagement in the literature should make us immediately suspicious. It is an important part of reflexive qualitative research to make explicit all stages of the data-gathering process, and packing up is no exception. There is one set of accounts by ethnographers which does deal with the topic, and it is to that we must turn for enlightenment.

Shaffir et al. (1980) edited a collection of papers on *Fieldwork Experience*, and, unusually, had a section on leaving the field, with four papers in it. These all concentrated on how fieldworkers disengage themselves from the setting and their informants, rather than, as Fine's account does, on how they knew it was time to go. Each is a useful paper on disengagement, and as all were commissioned for the volume, they report on projects which had not been published widely elsewhere as well as addressing a neglected topic. Altheide (1980) was doing an ethnography of a Californian TV newsroom, and he admits frankly that:

> another reason for deciding to leave was that I was simply getting bored. Much of the novelty had worn off, and I was anxious to complete the study in order to move on to other projects.
>
> (p. 305)

Altheide spent about a year in the newsroom, and his account of the ending of his research shows the ways he was able to use his intending departure to gather different kinds of data and play different roles. As he says: 'more forthright research strategies could not be proposed until I had made the decision to leave' (pp. 305–6). Among these strategies was expressing his own views more freely and forcefully, and: 'I would openly laugh, spar and goof off with the veterans' (pp. 307–8).

Altheide had been challenged by the news director about his continuing presence and had used this as an excuse to set a leaving date seven months ahead, and to arrange several bits of data collection to fill gaps. These included an official interview with the news director, scheduled periods in some previously unvisited departments, and observation of 'several news-workers who had been able to avoid my scrutiny' (p. 303). The news director's attempt to terminate Altheide's research also confirmed the hypotheses about the former's self-perception of his power in the newsroom that Altheide had formulated.

TV newsrooms continue to exist whether or not a researcher is present. Other 'settings' have rhythms which provide an ending to research. Hilliard (1987) joined an American rugby team on a tour of England and Wales in 1984. The trip lasted for three weeks (of which Hilliard studied the first) and the maximum fieldwork period could only have included a few days either end plus the three weeks of the tour. David Maines (1980) studied post-doctoral fellows in the University of Minnesota, and as this population is 'highly transitory' (p. 226) most of his informants left his fieldsite before he did. His respondents were: 'accustomed to the regular influx and outflow of people each year' (p. 266). The particular nature of that population made leaving the field very easy, Maines says:

> because the researcher and the subjects are involved in the same kinds of processes relating to career stage, mobility, goals and family orientations.
>
> (p. 267)

Maines *et al.* (1980) corresponded with a clutch of eminent ethnographers (Becker, Wax, Gans, Denzin, Strauss, Habenstein, Rains, Spector and Roy) about leaving the field. On the basis of these letters and their own work they suggest that:

> settings that prove most difficult to leave are probably those in which persons are not acquainted with the conventions of research – who, in other words, just accepted the researcher as a person and not as a fieldworker.
>
> (p. 278)

Gans, incidentally, said it was easy for him to leave Levittown because his marriage had broken up, and divorced men always leave the suburbs. Engineering a personal status passage may be an extreme strategy to escape from the field, but informing respondents about impending job change, marriage, divorce, or even thesis submission requirements may ease the exit. Some ethnographers, particularly social anthropologists, never leave their fields. There are many scholars who spend time there over decades, and, in anthropology, there is a sense that the 'field' comes back home and is recreated in the office, computer and lecture hall every day for ever and ever. Kenna (1992) has been studying Nisos since 1966–7, Jane Collier (1997) first lived in Los Olivos in Andalucia in 1963, and has been there regularly for fifteen years. Escaping is not, however, the end of the problems associated with 'leaving the field'.

After the field

Apart from leaving the setting, the researcher has to readjust to 'ordinary' life. This can be difficult. Barley (1986: 187) is interesting on how hard it can be to return to one's previous life:

> While the traveller has been away questioning his most basic assumptions, life has continued sweetly unruffled.

In other words, all his friends, family and colleagues were carrying on the same as always, while he was unsettled, and had been much changed by his months in Cameroon. Betty MacDonald (1948) reports the same feelings when she came out of a TB sanatorium. Barley calls the sense of alienation and dislocation from the once-familiar life 'the ethnographic hangover' (p. 190) which is a useful phrase. He found himself unable to begin the analytic work and the writing which are the essential step to follow fieldwork, saying that:

> My notebooks lay neglected on the desk; I felt a deep revulsion to even touching them which lasted for months.
>
> (p. 198)

This revulsion appears to have swamped Florinda Donner (1982) and Wade Davis (1986) who never produced conventional monographs at all. For most researchers, writing is the way that fieldwork is assimilated and made sense of. Danforth (1989: 305) states that anthropologists: 'respond to their encounter with the other by writing'. For Danforth, and others like him:

> the encounter with ethnographic others is at one level at least a thera-peutic quest for meaning … This therapeutic encounter is not confined to the practice of ethnographic fieldwork; it includes the process of ethnographic writing as well.
>
> (p. 300)

Danforth is clear that writing, and therefore analysing the data, are an essential part of leaving the field. In an educational context, Lois Weis (1985: 173) writes well of her analytic work. She points out:

> while data analysis is an ongoing process in participant observation research … it is during the post-fieldwork stage that the researcher engages in the systematic construction of themes and the analysis and interpretation of data.

That is, the real analytic work cannot begin until the fieldwork ends, but it must not be left in its entirety till then.

The permanent hangover

One unintended consequence of adopting qualitative research methods is that the researcher may become contaminated permanently, and unable to return to their previous perspectives on life. All new experiences are 'turned into' ethnographic research projects, because the research strategies used once become applied to all situations, especially new and/or stressful ones. When I had to go into hospital (for the first time in my life) for major surgery I took a notebook and kept fieldnotes, and eventually wrote a paper about the pollution beliefs of the women on the ward (Delamont, 1987b). This was a useful way to avoid boredom, relieve stress by being professional rather than powerless, and to provide data for a future paper. The survey method does not seem to affect people the same way, because it is not immediately applicable to all social situations. The data gathered during the stay in 'Four Winds' hospital were later used in a collection of papers, all of which were autobiographical pieces by sociologists, although I had not written the notes with publication in mind at the time.

John Beynon (1987) had also kept fieldnotes when in hospital, and the two of us agreed to give seminar papers to a day conference of medical sociologists. When McKeganey and Cunningham-Burley advertised for autobiographical papers for their collection we both decided to offer our seminar papers for possible publication. One of the editors actually queried whether my data were the result of 'true' participant observation, which I found a peculiar query. Being an in-patient for major surgery seems as close to being a full participant in hospital as one can get. My worry about using these data for a published paper was ethical, because my 'fieldwork' was not negotiated as such. The data were certainly the only covert data I have ever collected – I did not tell staff or patients I was writing notes or a diary on my time as a patient. At the time I had not planned to publish anything from the notes, even though there was a precedent. Horobin and Davis (1977) had published an edited collection of autobiographical accounts of illness experiences by sociologists, which contained several papers based on being an in-patient.

There is an ethical problem about the use of those data, but as the notes were written in full view of the other people around, I do not feel guilty about this. I would recommend such notetaking as a coping strategy. Beynon (1987) reports that he kept notes 'to help me pass the time and to avert boredom' (p. 144). This is true of my experience also, but I would place dealing with anxiety higher than avoiding boredom.

Conclusions

The watchman at the gates of Baghdad asked the travellers:

> For what land

Leave you the dim-moon city of delight?

The caravan answer that:

We make the Golden Journey to Samarkand

and pass through the gate into the desert. Meanwhile, their loved ones bemoan their departure. If good field relationships have been established, then leaving the field can be sad and painful, but it not only has to be done, it has to be documented.

Key reading

The key reading to be done associated with this chapter is Peter Loizos's (1981) *The Heart Grown Bitter*, which deals with loss.

Chapter 11

Beauty lives though lilies die

Analysing and theorizing

> There still seem to be too many students and practitioners who believe implicitly that qualitative research can be done in a spirit of 'careless rapture' with no principled or disciplined thought whatsoever. They collect data with little thought for research problems and research design, and they think they will know what to do with the data once those data are collected. When they find that things are not quite so simple, they wail 'I've got all these data …'
>
> (Coffey and Atkinson, 1996: 11)

However well the fieldwork has been done, in the end it is the theoretical and analytical concepts that determine whether the work will be remembered, quoted and associated with their author. Furlong's (1976) research on African-Caribbean girls in a London comprehensive is best known for the concept of the 'interaction set', Willis's (1977) Hammertown study for his theories about 'resistance'. This chapter title, stressing that beauty lives on even if lilies die, emphasizes the enduring importance of analytic work.

The chapter starts with a brief summary of the distinction between the level of analysis needed when the ethnographic data are merely illustrative, i.e. colourful examples added to a statistical study, and that needed for a fully qualitative project. Then there is a short list of key points to be remembered when analysing qualitative data. Finally, the chapter moves into a worked example of coding, and a full discussion of how qualitative data should be analysed.

Analysing ethnographic data for illustrative purposes

When a research project is primarily an ethnographic one, such as Robert Burgess's (1983, 1988a) study of Bishop McGregor School, the analysis of the data is a very important stage in the procedure. Proper analytic procedures, such as those specified in Hammersley and Atkinson (1995: chapter 8), are an important part of ensuring reliability and validity. Researchers read and reread their fieldnotes and diaries, and draw out both recurrent patterns and instances that run contrary to those patterns. Themes and categorizations are extracted during these recurrent readings. In some ethnographies the researcher focuses on the concepts used by the participants themselves: what are sometimes called 'folk' categories. In others, the analyst derives the themes from the social science literature. The aims of both approaches are to produce an account of the culture or institution being studied which would enable the reader to live in it without violating its rules. The account is sometimes called a thick description, and aims to make the familiar strange and the exotic familiar, via the analytic categories or themes.

There are some pieces of research which use qualitative methods as an adjunct or companion piece to quantitative or statistical techniques, and the qualitative material is only needed as illustrative. This was the case with the study of integrating mildly learning-disabled pupils into the ordinary comprehensive school in Wales (Upton *et al.*, 1988). Beasley spent most of the time working on test results, pupil records and a questionnaire to schools, followed by a structured interview. The ethnographic observation was done in a small number of the schools for very short periods. All the schools in four LEAS completed the questionnaire, and the heads of special needs in a large sample of secondary schools were interviewed. The project was not primarily an ethnographic one. As with the ORACLE transfer study (Galton and Delamont, 1985), the observational data were gathered to illustrate and make more vivid the material gathered by questionnaire and interviews. That is why each school was only visited for a few days, rather than the usual ethnographic research period of at least six weeks and often six months or a year. The fieldnotes and diaries produced from the visits to the nine schools were not exhaustively analysed. They were merely read several times, and examples of good practice extracted for the report to the Welsh Office. The database would not justify a more complex analytic procedure of the kind recommended by Hammersley and Atkinson (1995) and Coffey and Atkinson (1996).

The rest of this chapter concentrates on how to do a proper qualitative analysis true to the spirit of a reflexive ethnography. There is a short section of basic rules: key things that must be done and dangers to avoid. Then there is a more detailed discussion with worked examples. Becker (1998) *Tricks of the Trade* is a readable discourse on how to think about analysis. There are several books devoted to analysing qualitative data, especially Anselm Strauss's (1987) successor to Glaser and Strauss (1967), Miles and Huberman (1983), Lofland and Lofland (1995) and Fielding and Fielding (1986). Coffey and Atkinson (1996) is entirely devoted to data analysis and representation, and there is a large handbook on analysis (Bryman and Hardy, 2002) with nine chapters on dealing with qualitative data. There are also excellent books on using the software packages available specially designed for qualitative textual data. The spread of microcomputers, and the enormous improvement in software for dealing with text, means that all the books on analysis rapidly become out of date in their discussions of that topic. Computer-assisted qualitative data analysis is frequently abbreviated to CAQDAS, an ugly but striking and therefore memorable acronym. Computers are used by qualitative researchers to edit and store their texts (such as fieldnotes or transcripts), for annotating them with reflexive memoranda, for displaying data, and, of course, for preparing publications, as well as for 'analysis'. Fielding (2001) contains an account of the hostility and suspicion with which many qualitative researchers viewed computers and text-handling software fifteen years ago. The uses of CAQDAS are discussed later in the chapter. Here I will just point out that there are excellent software packages specially developed to help with the analytic tasks (see Kelle, 1995; Dey, 1993, for details). These go out of date, because the packages are changing all the time. The main body of the chapter returns to these issues after the section on 'Basic rules'.

The basic rules

The most important thing is not to allow material to pile up unanalysed or, even worse, unread. It is vital to read your interview transcripts, or fieldnotes, or the diaries people have written for you, over and over again, and to write analytic memos recording your first thoughts on analysis, and the second, third and fourth thoughts as well.

The analysis of interview data and ethnographic fieldnotes is essentially similar. There are no short cuts, and one must allow plenty of time and energy for the tasks. Remember that the 'analysis' of qualitative data is a process that continues throughout the research: it is not a separate, self-contained phase. The following should always be borne in mind:

- Never let data accumulate without preliminary analysis.
- Index your data as you go; do not allow the data to pile up without knowing what you have collected.
- Generate themes and categories as you go along, and review them frequently. It is better to have too many categories which you recombine later than to have too few.
- Index and code your data densely: do not try to summarize them under just a few themes. Generate as many codes as you can; be 'wild' if you can.
- Sort your data into files (either physically cutting up copies, or 'cutting and pasting' in the word processor). Keep sorting and reviewing your files: in itself that can be a process of discovery.
- Every now and then stop and think. Do not go on mechanically working on the data without reflecting on where you are going and how you are getting there.
- Write analytic memoranda as often as you can. Analytic memos are short notes to yourself (and your supervisor if you are a student) in which you

review what you are doing, why you are doing it, where you are going
next, etc.

- Every time you make a decision, write it down and put it in your
  'methods' file.
- Try to enjoy the work. It should be an intellectually engaging and
  creative exercise, not a chore.
- Read other people's work – for ideas, models, parallels, contrasts,
  metaphors, etc.
- Read the methodological literature properly and think about how it can
  inform your work – do not just read it to justify what you are doing anyway!

The various software packages available make these tasks easier and less
monotonous. However, the data need to be prepared from the outset for
microcomputer analysis, so it is important to look at Fielding (2001) and get
access to a machine and the software as early as possible. If you are scared of
using the micro, or desperately ignorant about them, or cannot find one to
use, or have no one around to help you get started, these problems should be
tackled before collecting large amounts of data and before beginning any
analysis by hand. Go on a course, find a more advanced student or a 'post doc'
to show you what to do, or get one of the books and read it carefully.

CAQDAS leads to more systematic and more transparent analyses than
were generally the case in the 'old days', but mindless use of any software is
much worse than careful, reflexive manual analysis. Fielding (2001) says there
are more than twenty packages designed for qualitative social scientists, and
others which can be used by them. He divides the software packages into
three categories: text retrievers, code-and-retrieve packages, and software that
can build theory. Text retrievers use keywords to find segments of text, either
keywords used in the data or codes the scholar has attached to the text. Code-
and-retrieve packages divide text into chunks, attach labels to those chunks,
and then display all the chunks so labelled. These programmes have mostly
been written by social scientists and usually allow analytic memos to be
displayed (or even attached to chunks). Many of these were produced by sociologists wanting to work in the tradition of Glaser and Strauss (1967).
KWALITAN, for example, was written by a Dutch team explicitly to 'do'
grounded theory. The theory-building software facilitates exploring relationships between categories and hypothesis testing. NUD*IST is probably the
best-known example of a theory-building software.

One reason for finding out about CAQDAS before you have collected
piles of data is that some packages allow you to enter the data straight into
them, while others take them from a word processor. Some require the data to
be strictly formatted, others do not. If you end up using a programme that
only allows the text to occupy a 59-character line (the rest of the line is for
codes), your life will be brighter if you have entered the data in that format
from the start.

Analysing qualitative data step by step

Many researchers, especially students and beginners, are particularly scared of analysis. There is no need to be. As long as the same beliefs and practices that characterize choosing the topic, gaining access, doing the reading, establishing rapport and recording the data are used, analysis is straightforward. It is more important to have thought carefully about it, documented the process, and to have recognized the strengths and weaknesses of what was done than to have followed a 'correct' recipe. There are elaborate discussions of analysis in Strauss (1987), Kelle (1995) and Dey (1993), so in this chapter the focus is upon some simple approaches to some straightforward data. Three extracts from my own data are used: one from fieldnotes, one from a published text, and one from an adolescent's writing. The three extracts are given, and then the stages of coding, generating contrasts and moving to potential generalization are shown.

The three data extracts

The three data extracts are: (a) the story written by a sixth former for me, recalling an 'urban legend' she or he had heard before transfer; (b) an extract from a published history of a girls' school sampled as described in Chapter 5, and (c) a chunk of fieldnotes from the Welsh locational integration project. First, the school 'horror story'.

> Before I went to Prior's End School I was told by a friend that was already there a teacher, Mr Paradine, had raped one pupil (girl) and hadn't been asked to leave because he owned the helicopter that the boys took apart and put together again. They also said Mr Paradine got girls into the book cupboard and touched them up.

The second extract is from an anonymous 'old girl' of Edgehill College, printed in Shaw (1984: 66).

> We tolerated school uniform and, looking back, I think we really enjoyed wearing it. In my view a well cut gym slip is quite a flattering garment. We all wore gym slips and had to change from them for tea every day. This was a rule, and, I think, a good one. On Saturdays, at the beginning of the day, we could wear gym slips with something other than the regulation school blouse under them … We had to wear uniform to church, of course. Blue coats and white dresses in the summer, navy blue coats with blouses and skirts under them in the winter.

The third example is from fieldwork. In 1985, I watched a careers lesson for remedial and ESN(M) pupils in a Welsh comprehensive school, Heol-y-

Crynwyr, taken by the deputy head, Mr Despenser, in the main school building. This is the summary, not the more detailed fieldnotes.

> The lesson is centred round a book about starting work. Frank starts his first job, and does everything wrong: he is late, he hasn't brought his NI card, etc., he is cheeky and does not radiate keenness etc. His boss is angry with him.
>
> The pupils read the story aloud and then discuss it. They all side with Frank, and regard the boss as quite unreasonable for shouting at him. Mr Despenser tries to refocus them on to their responsibilities, such as punctuality and politeness. He asks for their ideas on what happens when a young person starts work, and then disputes all their ideas. Frederick said the worst thing about starting work was that it would 'Be a new place, wouldn't know nobody there'. Mr Despenser said that was irrelevant, and asked what time a shop worker has to start work in the morning.
>
> Claudette said '7.00', and Mr Despenser told her that was too early, shops did not open that early in the morning. She tried to tell him about shops that do, but he ignored her.

One irony of this incident was that the shop at the end of the road outside the school, a newsagent and general store, announced on its door that it was open from 7.00 a.m. to 7.00 p.m.

Analysing these three fragments

In the real world, analysis would not begin until there were a few more chunks of data for each of these projects. Analysis begins early in the data collection process, but not usually after only twenty lines of material are available. However, in this case we will pretend that each fragment is representative of one day's work, that we are back from the field and can start analysing. The first procedure is to read through the data several times, becoming familiar with them. Then it is common to begin coding the material.

Coding and indexing

Coding can be done by hand or using one of the computer programs. Here I shall describe doing an analysis by hand: working on a machine involves the researcher in the same decisions, but is quicker and more versatile. It is useful to try a bit of coding by hand, for one interview, one day's notes, one document, and then try one of the packages to see how much less tedious it is.

Some people make multiple codings on one copy of their data, others prefer making multiple copies of the data, and coding one thing on each copy. Before beginning coding it is very sensible to have a back-up copy of everything: if the coding goes wrong, then it is tragic if the data are destroyed or damaged by the erroneous coding.

There are three main ways to proceed. Multiple codings can be attached to one version of the data with coloured pens, highlighting, symbols, or thin slips of coloured paper sellotaped to the text sticking out over the edge. Alternatively, multiple copies of the data can be made, and physically cut up. Then everything relating to a particular category is filed together (in a box, ring binder or old envelope) labelled with that code. Third, the data can be indexed, and the codings recorded on cards or slips of paper. That method leaves the data untouched except for page and line numbers. Imagine we are coding the first extract, which is one of 217 I have collected. If multiple codings of the same text is our strategy, we could code this once we had decided on our colour-coding system. If all stories with sex in them have a 'green' code, all stories about CDT have 'brown', and all stories about weird or fierce teachers are 'blue', we would mark the text with those three coloured indicators. (Some people mark the top corner of the sheet, some mark the margins of the text, some highlight the actual text.) Then later if we were writing about all CDT stories, we would flip through all the 217 stories looking for 'brown' labels/highlights/marginalia.

Now imagine we are using the multiple copy method. The story has been typed, and there are three or four carbons or xeroxes of it. One goes into a file box marked 'Sex', another into the box labelled 'CDT', and a third into 'Weird teachers'. Other copies stay in the main heap ready for future codes we decide to use. Finally, imagine the indexing system. This story has been called Story 1, is on page 1, and has seven lines. On one index card we write that Story 1, page 1, lines 3 and 7 is about sex, and drop that card into a box labelled 'Sex'. On a fresh card we record that Story 1, page 1, lines 5–6 is about CDT, and put that in the 'CDT' box. Then on a third card, we write that Story 1, page 1 is all about a weird/dangerous teacher, and file that one in the box for 'Weird teacher' stories. Whichever system is used, the 217 stories are coded, and the relevant ones can be easily traced. If we want to count the number of stories with CDT in them we can do so quickly and easily, and if we want to reread just those to do more coding, or write something, or rethink the label, they are identifiable.

If we were using a CAQDAS package, the same basic strategy would apply. We would have word-processed all 217 stories, and would then code them for sex, CDT and weird or fierce teachers. Then we can ask the software to retrieve all the stories where sex has been coded, or all those about CDT. The logic is the same: once coded, the computer will search more systematically and much more quickly than you can.

Many qualitative researchers assemble their argument from small chunks of data pulled out of their context by a coding method of this kind. So, for example, they code all the examples of CDT teaching and write a paper on CDT. Sometimes that strategy destroys the chronological or biographical or narrative sequence of events, and it is necessary to work on the material in its original 'long' form. Atkinson (1996: 123) describes how he had originally treated his ethnography of bedside teaching by cutting the material up into short segments, but then felt a need to re-examine the material to explore the unfolding narrative structure of each consultant's sessions. He concluded:

1   Just as 'data' are not fixed, so there is no one best way of reading them. On the contrary, there is every advantage in canvassing different approaches.
2   There is merit in trying different analytic strategies on the same ethnographic data.
3   We should not fall into analytic approaches that are employed routinely, mechanistically, and uncritically.

(p. 126)

The code of small chunks across different interviews, or fieldnotes taken on different days or in different ways or in different locations is a well known strategy, aided by many CAQDAS packages. Alternative approaches, looking for other ways of drawing out meaning, are also worth considering.

Having outlined three different ways to code or index data, it is important to address the other issue: what to code. Novices frequently ask what they should code. The answer is, in one way, simple: code whatever you are interested in. If the research is 'about' race in schools, then that is what must be coded first. (A memo should be written recording the decision to start coding race, with reasons.) The incident from Heol-y-Crynwyr can be used to demonstrate some coding possibilities which might be useful. First, it could be coded by the actors who appear in it. If we were using the multiple copies method, we could file one copy of the lesson under Mr Despenser, one under Frederick (or perhaps under 'fourth-year boys') and one under Claudette (or 'fourth-year girls'). This would be useful if we ever wrote profiles of particular key actors at the school (as Stanley, 1989, does). Alternatively, this lesson could be coded by its location (in the main school building, not in the separate unit where the statemented pupils spent most of their time). It could be coded as a lesson on 'careers', a lesson using a textbook (rather than worksheets, or equipment, or computers, or 'chalk and talk' or whatever), a class where pupils had to read aloud, or one where they all worked on the same task, or a mixed sex group, or a combined remedial and ESN(M) class. The focus of our analysis might be better served by coding this as a class where the academic material was about males (a boy and a man); or a lesson in which teacher and pupils disagreed about life, the universe and everything; or a lesson taught by a deputy head; or one which went 'wrong'.

All these codings are possible from the edited summary of the lesson printed here. The real notes, with natural language included and rich detail, would provide more scope for coding than the fourteen possibilities given above. Even the short memoir from Shaw (1984) can quickly generate many codings: clothing, days of the week, uniforms, mealtimes, churchgoing, seasons, colours, rules, pleasure, choice, then and now, the cut of clothes, and flattering garments. It would also be relevant to code the date the person writing the memoir was at Edgehill (between 1924 and 1947), and which headmistress(es) were in control at the time.

Reading this discussion should have generated ideas about other things that could be coded. The codes should be relevant to the foreshadowed problems, the developing hypotheses, and the social science agenda in the researcher's head. The suggested codes should, however, have demonstrated some possibilities. The next step is to interrogate the data.

Interrogating the data

The reading, rereading, and coding of the data should lead on to interrogating them. This means exploring systematically what the data are saying. No CAQDAS package can do your *thinking* for you. Software reduces the burden of archiving, ordering and sorting the data: it does not give you theoretical insight, any more than the coloured pencils ever did. If we start with the first extract, we can generate some questions to ask of the other 216 stories collected from the Ledshire sixth formers. Among such questions might be: are there any other rape stories? If so, are the victims all female? If not, what other forms of sexual assault occur? Who are the victims of those? Are there any other stories about staff owning valuable resources/property? Do pupils expect sex-segregated technical curricula?

The one story is rather cryptic, and it would be more productive in a research project to choose a set of ten or twelve stories and code all of them before formulating the questions to be posed on the rest of the material. If the data were only written stories then the interrogation has to be focused on the written texts, and broadened into the literature on school transfer and on rumour, urban legends, humour and atrocity stories (e.g. Bennett, 1983). If the research could be expanded into other methods of data collection then the questions raised by the first batch of stories could be posed to a group of sixth formers in a more systematic fashion.

The second extract from the history of Edgehill allows the investigator to pose a wider range of questions. Time is obviously central, so the database can be interrogated about seasons, days of the week, times of the day and mealtimes. How did dress vary according to the season, the day, the time and the meals? Then there is a whole set of questions to be posed, about choice, rules and regulations. Who made the rules? Who enforced them? To whom did they apply? What happened if they were broken? What informal pressures governed 'choice'? Church provides a further set of questions. Who went? How often? How did they get there? Could anyone be excused? By working all through the recollections of old girls from Edgehill it is possible to produce a systematic portrait of everyday life there in a sociological framework.

The Heol-y-Crynwyr data are different, in that a fieldworker would be able to test any hypotheses during the on-going fieldwork. Here the interrogation of the data leads immediately to practical activity in the school the next day or the next week. For example, if it seemed that the target pupils behaved differently when in their 'home unit' from the main school, then a researcher should ensure that the same pupils are watched carefully in the two settings. It would be important to watch staff in the main building other than Mr Despenser, to see if the careers lesson was problematic because of the setting, the teacher or the content. Ideally, if Mr Despenser taught in the home unit it would be possible to 'eliminate' him as a variable. Alternatively, the researcher could watch Mr Despenser with mainstream pupils, and/or look at 'careers' lessons in the wider school to see if similar difficulties arise when mainstream pupils read about starting work. The possibilities are endless, and the most important thing is to write analytic memos, and record which lines of enquiry are being followed and which left, with reasons.

As long as analytic work is done while fieldwork is in progress it is relatively easy to test insights by direct or indirect questioning of informants. For example, Philip Cusick (1973: 239–40) says that:

> All these notes were compiled into 500 pages in addition to all the records, papers, and so forth collected during the time. The notes, as Becker suggests, were classified and coded according to the event, participants, physical setting, time of occurrences, and reaction of the participants. The events and statements of belief which occurred with greatest frequency were combined into tentative perspectives concerning particular situations. Subsequently each tentative perspective was checked by directly asking the group members or others about its applicability to a particular situation. The perspectives that were verified by the subjects were considered to be a part of the total set of perspectives.

It is important to note here that analysis was going on while he was still in the field and able to test his hypotheses by questioning his informants. The procedures followed were based on those used by Becker *et al.* (1968) in their study of liberal arts undergraduates. Most qualitative researchers probably learn to analyse from a book they admire, as Cusick did. He does not make analysis sound very hard, which could lull the unwary into a false sense of security. Analysis is fascinating, but it is hard work. Linda Valli (1986: 228) makes this point cogently:

> Although I was prepared for the research to be a dialectical process, with data and theory mutually informing and transforming one another, nothing I read quite prepared me for the complexity and uncertainty that accompanied every step of the analysis. I painstakingly reviewed my field notes on three separate occasions, taking notes from the field notes, and

went through four or five major reorganizations before making a final organizational decision.

Valli's emphasis on both 'uncertainty' and 'complexity' is a good one. Her admission that she tried four or five different organizational arrangements of her material is also reassuring to the novice. Her detailed rehearsal of the four abandoned structures (228–30) is well worth reading. The formulation which finally satisfied Valli was 'both the most inclusive of my data and the most comprehensive of the extant theories' (p. 229). Valli's account is a very good one. Just as it is sensible to try on several garments before buying a new outfit, or wear new shoes round the shop before purchase, or cook a fancy dish once or twice before offering it at a dinner party, so too various structures and explanatory frameworks should be used before the final version is offered to the public.

The examples used so far have been documents or fieldnotes. Many qualitative researchers have taped interviews, and before these can be coded or interrogated, they have to be transcribed. Lois Weis (1985: 173–4) records how:

> The first step is to transcribe all taped material. This is a very time-consuming task and takes literally months to complete. While it is helpful to employ someone to transcribe tapes, this is nearly impossible without substantial grant support. It cost me three hundred dollars to have eight tapes transcribed by a secretary ... I transcribed most of my own tapes. Any researcher who does not have substantial support should plan on doing the same.

Transcribing is very time-consuming. One hour of tape-recorded interview will take six hours to transcribe roughly, without any of the linguistic features that are needed for conversational analysis or sociolinguistic work or ethnomethodology (see Edwards and Westgate, 1994). A transcript that began to include hesitations with their timings, phonetics or intonations could take sixty hours to prepare for one hour of taped data. If there is any money to pay a secretary then that will ease the burden, but the researcher will still need to listen to all the tapes when checking the typed transcript. A wise researcher copies the tapes, in case they break, get stolen or eaten by the typist's dog. Mini-discs do not break, but they are desirable objects for thieves. Weis followed Bogdan and Taylor (1975) closely, in searching out what she calls 'core cultural elements' (p. 174) in the field setting. Distilling these core cultural elements is the main purpose of most qualitative researchers. After coding and interrogating it is usual to move to making generalizations or contrasts.

Proceeding to analysis, it would be sensible to read some texts on analysing data. Lofland and Lofland (1995) is good on doing it by hand; a special issue of *Urban Life* (1974) contains autobiographical accounts of analysis as does Bryman and Burgess (1994). Compare Lofland and Lofland with Kelle (1995) and Dey (1993) on using a micro to help with analysis. Tesch (1990) is convinced that using a micro, with one of the specialist programs written for social scientists to handle qualitative data, frees the researcher from the dullest mechanical tasks to concentrate on the thinking.

The main analytic tasks are related to establishing patterns or regularities in the date, and then cross-checking to make sure the data are reliable and valid. In qualitative research these concepts (reliability and validity) are not statistical. There are two main strategies for checking reliability and validity in qualitative material which are regularly espoused; respondent validation and triangulation. Respondent validation means checking with participants to see if they recognize the validity of the analysis being developed, and it forms part of many qualitative studies. If the lesson by Mr Despenser is our example, the ESN(M) adolescents refused to co-operate with teachers who made them read aloud when mixed with the remedial pupils because it showed them up. A respondent validation would include asking staff and pupils a set of ques tions about reading aloud, mixing ESN(M) and remedial, and 'showing up'. Similarly, if the Edgehill memoir had led us to the proposal that pupil dress on Saturdays was intermediate between weekday uniform and Sunday best, we could try to find some living 'old girls' and ask if that was the case. If several of the stories from Ledshire sixth formers included mention of Mr Paradine as sexually predatory, we could ask some local teachers to tell stories of 'local characters' in Ledshire schools and see if it was possible to include him in the conversation. (This would be the most difficult to deal with, both because the original story is known to be a myth, and because the topic is particularly sensitive.) If such an attempt at respondent validation revealed that Mr Paradine did sexually harass pupils, the ethical problem for the researcher becomes acute.

Some researchers believe in having their whole account validated by respondents: that is, giving the whole manuscript (or substantial chunks of it) to some or all of the participants. This can be done as a political act by people who believe that the respondents own the data; it may be part of the bargain struck when access was negotiated; or it may be a validation strategy; or all three at once. Atkinson (1997a), for example, agreed not to publish anything without letting his two main gatekeepers (an ex-dean of the medical school and a professor interested in medical education) vet it beforehand. The response to a manuscript by respondents is always interesting, and can provide valuable new data or confirm hypotheses, but a qualitative researcher cannot assume that the respondents have access to truth. The scholar's account may be more valid than any participants' perspectives, because the scholar has been focusing on the setting rather than living in it. Respondents' knowledge is different from ethnographers' knowledge, but not superior to it.

Systematic collection of respondents' reactions to the researcher's analysis can be one element in a process of triangulation. This is a very powerful strategy for defending qualitative research against sceptics, because it makes sense to those academics more used to experiments and surveys. Triangulation means having two or more 'fixed' or 'sightings' of a finding from different angles. There are three main types of triangulation:

1   between method;
2   between investigators;
3   within method.

Between method triangulation means getting data on something with more than one method. So if our observation of Claudette suggested she knew about shop work, we could ask her in an interview if she had a Saturday job in a shop. *Between investigators* triangulation involves more than one person studying the phenomenon or setting. In the monograph on the ORACLE ethnography (Delamont and Galton, 1986), I only reported things which had been recorded by at least three of the six researchers, except for a few clearly labelled things which were unique. (Only one school had advanced swimming coaching in class time, and only I observed it there, so that is reported as something only seen by me.) *Within method* triangulation involves systematically attempting to get several types of data on something within your method. If, for example, you thought that the pupils who vanished behind the science block at break were either smoking or playing pitch and toss, or both, but when you tried to follow them they vanished, it would be within method triangulation to inspect the area for cigarette butts at the end of the day.

At the analysis stage, triangulation can also be done by scrutinizing the data. When a developing idea has emerged from coding the fieldnotes, the researcher can turn to the files of official documents and the transcripts of the formal interviews and so on to see if there are other data that bear on the same issue. In general, it is sensible to set up triangulation exercises while still in the field setting, which is another reason for not letting the data pile up unanalysed.

Moving to theory and generalization

Once the data are coded and have been interrogated until the researcher is exhausted, it is probably time to move on to generalizing and theorizing. Some scholars see themselves testing or illustrating a theory that already exists. Ann Swidler (1979) set out to see how the types of authority proposed by Weber were implemented in American free schools. Such schools were unlikely to show bureaucratic or paternal authority, and indeed she reveals that low-level charismatic leadership characterized teacher control in such institutions. Other educational ethnographers, such as Weis (1985) and Valli (1986), have been exploring Marxist perspectives. Eickelman (1978) uses

Bourdieu to organize his ideas on Islamic education, and so on. Other scholars espouse the ideas of Strauss (1987) and work up from the data to their generalizations and theorizing. There is no necessary relation between qualitative methods and any particular theory or approach to theorizing. Although most people who adopt interactive or interactionist theories prefer qualitative methods, the reverse is not necessarily the case. Weis (1985) and Valli (1986) are not unusual in being Marxist ethnographers.

Whatever the approach to theorizing, and whether the scholar wishes to work 'down' from grand theory or 'up' from the data, it is important to be scrupulously honest. There is always a temptation to ignore the incidents or comments which do not support the general argument that is developing. Thinking about such 'negative' findings, and interrogating them, may lead to refining the initial theoretical position, or may reveal that the negative incident is a genuinely isolated exception that 'proves' the initial rule. Hammersley and Atkinson (1995) have a useful chapter on the relationship between analysing and theorizing in which they discuss respondent validation and triangulation alongside generalizing and conceptualizing. Here, I have concentrated on using contrast and paradox to organize material, because these are accessible first steps for novices.

Much of the force of qualitative argument comes from drawing our attention to contrasts and highlighting paradoxes to make the audience look afresh at social phenomena. (If they 'know' about an institution their knowledge must be challenged; if they have simplistic stereotypes, the complex reality must be presented.) Take Frances Fitzgerald's (1987: 274) explanation of why everyone at the Rajneeshee ranch in Oregon was apparently so cheerful.

> The most obvious explanation for all of this good humour was that work on the ranch was fun; it was play in the ordinary sense of the word. Where else, after all, could a professor (or a belly dancer for that matter) get to fool around on a bulldozer and build a road? Where else could a young architect design a housing project and then get to bang in the nails? Picking lettuces and digging postholes had undeniable satisfactions if you weren't doing it for a living and if you were doing it with a lot of attractive people your own age … Guru or no guru, the ranch was a year-round summer camp for young, urban professionals.

Here Fitzgerald draws contrasts between our assumptions − that the Bagwan had brainwashed people − and the reality − summer camp. Note the contrasts − professor and belly dancer − and the challenges − lettuce-picking can be fun. Once the paragraph is read, it suddenly makes more sense that the ranch was such a happy place.

A similar paradox, although exactly reversed, can be found in Margaret Gibson's (1987a, 1987b) research on Punjabi high school students in northern California. Gibson reports that they are deviant because they concentrate on academic work even when they are not in the college-preparatory track. The local 'Anglo' students outside the college track do the minimum necessary to get high school graduation certification.

> There is an assumption, shared by Valleysider parents, students and teachers, that the more advanced academic courses are only for college-bound students. Those students who do not expect to go on to a 4-year college see little point, therefore, in taking maths, science, and English classes beyond those required for graduation ... Thus for the last two years of high school, the typical Valleysider student turns his or her attention to part-time jobs and social activities.
>
> (1987a: 307)

The Punjabi students were seen as deviant failures because they did not join in school clubs, dances, class picnics, etc. They are viewed as unassimilated because they take school work seriously. This is a paradox exactly reversing Fitzgerald's. She showed that manual work on the Oregon estate was play for the disciples, while Gibson shows that most Valleysider high school students treat having fun as the most serious part of their lives. Punjabi deviance comes from treating work in school seriously.

This demonstration of a paradox is one typical form of ethnographic analysis. To return to the incident at Heol-y-Crynwyr, at least one paradox is instantly apparent. In theory Mr Despenser is teaching the pupils about the realities of the world of work. In actuality the pupil, Claudette, knows more about shop work than he does, and Frederick has a realistic idea about the loneliness of a new employee. These learning-disabled students are educated in a particularly supportive way, and protected by teachers, yet in reality seem to have a more accurate knowledge of the realities of 'work' than Mr Despenser. He is trying to prepare them for things they have already experienced. So one place to start on analysis would be a search for other such paradoxes: incidents where the teachers know less than the pupils. To make a full contrastive analysis of this incident in a proper qualitative study, it would be necessary to have accounts of the 'careers' teaching from Mr Despenser and all the pupils, and to watch Mr Despenser teach other classes, and the pupils being taught by other staff. However, it would be easy to re-check all the fieldnotes to see if there were any other paradoxes of this kind. We might find spinster virgin teachers telling pregnant teenagers about sex; domestic science staff, still living at home and being cooked for by their mothers, teaching adolescents, already feeding hordes of siblings, about 'family meals'; and so on. Alternatively we might discover that careers lessons were the only subject in which that mismatch turned up, which would be a finding of some significance. Or it might be that lessons for remedial and statemented children were full of that paradox, but those for higher ability pupils were not: another finding.

There is no need to be frightened of analysis: it only needs systematic attention to the data, the wide reading already going on, and a bit of self-confidence.

Key reading

The key reading for this chapter is Amanda Coffey and Paul Atkinson's (1996) *Making Sense of Qualitative Data*.

Chapter 12

For glory or for gain
Producing the thesis or book

> Choose an exotic setting – a South American rain forest is ideal. Read authentic reports and select the choice parts (warfare, endo-cannibalism, infanticide, and drug-induced witchcraft). Don't forget to break ties with your own culture (give away your camera, burn your fieldnotes, shed your clothing, and lose your watch). To top it off, ingest the ashes of a native friend, eat grubs and other disgusting foods, and have sex with a native – a shaman would be ideal. Now serve up the account as factual social science and describe yourself as a young, blonde, female anthropologist from UCLA.
>
> (De Holmes, 1983: 65)

Rebecca De Holmes is launching an accusation of plagiarism with the opening paragraph I have just quoted. Her list of the ingredients which make up a best-seller is too exotic for most educational ethnographers to contemplate, but it captures the main theme of this chapter. How does an author – especially a novice – produce texts which are both interesting enough to 'pass' and yet are also authentic? As the chapter title suggests, there are two main reasons for writing: glory or gain. To achieve either glory or gain the author has to arouse the interest of readers and convince them of the realism, truth or authenticity of the account. There is a rapidly expanding literature on how social scientists establish the authenticity of their accounts (see Atkinson, 1990), but that work has not been summarized here. The emphasis in this chapter is more practical: on organizing the production of different kinds of output. However, all potential authors of ethnographic monographs, theses or articles must recognize that their 'writing up' is part of the same reflexive process that has carried them from the planning stage through the fieldwork and the analysis. As Nigel Barley (1983: 34–5) has argued:

> By the very act of writing the standard monograph on any people, he presents them with an image of themselves that must be coloured by his own prejudices and preconceptions since there is no objective reality about an alien people.

Whether the researcher's motivation is glory, or gain, or merely to get rid of the project and move on to something else, an investigation is only over when it is written up and can be read. This chapter deals with the five main types of output writing already mentioned in Chapter 4.

1   the thesis;
2   the report to sponsors;
3   the journal article (with findings);
4   the monograph;
5   the autobiographical/confessional piece.

The chapter also discusses pseudonyms, non-sexist writing and the mechanisms of producing accounts from team projects.

While all kinds of output writing have certain things in common, they also differ in their conventions. Before examining what is common to all varieties of output writing (such as how to get down to it) the five types of text are briefly distinguished. Before discussing the five types, a general piece of advice is to read Becker's (1986) *Writing for Social Scientists*, the funniest book on the topic you will ever come across. It can be usefully read alongside his 1998 *Tricks of the Trade*. Wolcott (1990), Richardson (1990), Spradley (1979) and Woods (1986) all contain ideas on how to produce written accounts which are worth examining, but reading all those six texts is no substitute for writing your own.

The thesis

The thesis, whether for a master's degree or for a doctorate, is usually the first sustained text its author has tried to produce. Some people manage a thesis and never write again. For the researcher who has to produce a thesis, the first thing to do is discover what the rules about theses are, and the second is to read some theses which have been successfully completed under those rules. If you are a student registered at Tolleshurst University, then you need to study the Tolleshurst regulations; if you are at Harvard, it is the Harvard rules you must pore over. Once you are clear how long the thesis can be, whether it can have footnotes, how it must be word-processed, and so on, it is time to read some other theses by your successful predecessors. Ideally, it is good to be able to read qualitative theses from your own institution, but if there are no such works then use quantitative ones with the most relevant topics. If there are no qualitative ones available in your own institution, then it is important to see one or two qualitative ones from somewhere else, borrowed through inter-library loans or read in another library to get a feel for the style and the standard of the degree you are trying to obtain. Ask your supervisor to recommend a good thesis they supervised or examined for you to read. It can also be informative to read your supervisor's master's and/or doctoral thesis.

Some theses are subsequently published as monographs. If the PhD is also a book, you can compare the thesis with the final monograph and see how they differ. For example, Brown's (1987) book is based on a PhD submitted in Wales, Davies' (1984) work on deviant girls was a Birmingham PhD thesis earlier on, Pilcher (1999) is based on her Cardiff PhD.

Phillips and Pugh (2000) has a good chapter on producing the thesis. Later in this chapter there are some general ideas on how to settle to writing, but as a guide to doing a thesis, the ideas of Wilson (1980) shown in Table 12.1 take some beating, and especially 34 and 35. Most of those tips apply equally to the other forms of writing, too.

Table 12.1   Wilson's fifty research tips

Pin them up somewhere and check them regularly.

 1 Don't panic too often.
 2 Only write on one side of the paper.
 3 Be nice to librarians (especially in inter-library loans).
 4 Remember that your supervisor is busy: if she or he isn't, change your supervisor.
 5 Find out how you work best.
 6 Read your degree regulations.
 7 Always have a couple of areas you can work on at any time.
 8 Read a few theses from the university in your area.
 9 Budget for typing and binding.
10 Plan ahead.
11 Don't think that photocopying is the same as reading.
12 Keep writing structures.
13 Put your external's book in the bibliography.
14 Get a good typist, or word processor, or a good package for your own machine.
15 Don't think it will be absolutely perfect . . .
16 . . . read your supervisor's thesis.
17 Remember that ideas change in three years – what you wrote at the outset may need changing.
18 Write your introduction first: write the reader's last.
19 Put typing conventions on cards for your typist.
20 Don't be afraid to point to your strengths and to the weaknesses of others.
21 Keep full bibliographical details.
22 Have someone to comment on your writing style at an early stage.
23 Set yourself short-term goals . . .
24 . . . and if you aren't meeting them, work out why.

25 Allow plenty of time for writing up.
26 Step back from time to time.
27 Overdo footnotes in the early stages – they are easy to pull out, but difficult to put in.
28 With each piece of work ask if it is worth doing.
29 Don't begrudge some time spent on reading very widely.
30 Find out early on about: length, presentation conventions, submission dates.
31 Talk to people about it.
32 Don't begrudge time spent on thinking.
33 Only write on every other line.
34 Think of it as a meal-ticket.
35 Keep writing.
36 Don't think that reading just one more book will solve all your problems . . .
37 . . . and don't use that as an excuse for not starting writing.
38 Criticize, evaluate, analyse; don't just describe.
39 Buy a book on punctuation.
40 Find a typist who has done your sort of work before.
41 Use your research to make contacts.
42 Using quotations doesn't make the idea any more true . . .
43 . . . and you can usually write it better yourself.
44 Use a card index for references, ideas, etc.
45 Don't be afraid to be imaginative.
46 Make sure your bibliography is comprehensive.
47 Label your diagrams properly.
48 If you set something aside for a while, make some notes about your ideas for its continuation.
49 Organize an efficient filing system.
50 Remember that purple clashes horribly with lots of colours.

The report to sponsors

Sponsors always deserve a report on the research they have paid for, and nearly always demand one as part of the contract. It is wise to discuss the type of report that is wanted with the representative of the sponsor early in the process, and to ask to see an example of a report the sponsor was pleased with. Time spent asking about expectations and researching the conventions is never wasted.

There are some features of a report to sponsors which make it different from other types of text. First, a report often has a 'summary of the main conclusions and recommendations' at the front, so that the policy-makers, local councillors, management team or whoever, do not need to read the whole text. For example, in the report Rhian Ellis and I (1979) did on how local authorities in Wales were dealing with victims of domestic violence, based on research conducted by Rhian, we had a Welsh language and an English language summary of our main findings and the recommendations that followed from them. These were at the front of the report, in very clear, simple language.

It is also quite common to report to sponsors with numbered sections and numbered paragraphs. Thus, there might be a 'Section 3' called 'Sampling schools', with Paragraphs 3.1 to 3.10 each making one point about how the schools were chosen. If a committee is going to be meeting to discuss the report, this device helps them enormously, because everyone can quickly find the point they want to discuss. ('Through you, Madam Chair, may I ask the Director why the violence referred to in Paragraph 7.2 was not discussed at a governors' meeting?')

If the sponsors of the research are academic social scientists, the report can be quite like a thesis or article with references, discussion of theory and so on. If the report is for lay people, 'academic' material is better relegated to notes or appendices, so their lack of interest in Habermas does not prevent them agreeing that there is a need for a playground on the council estate or a wheelchair ramp up to the gallery at the squash club. Similarly, if the audience is mainly of lay people, revelations about the researcher's blunders and incompetencies are better omitted, and a gloss (e.g. 'problems in getting access to the squash club were eventually overcome thanks to the leisure centre warden') is sufficient.

The biggest problem with reports to sponsors noted in the academic literature is of adverse reactions, including attempted censorship, to bad news. In Alison Lurie's (1975) *Nowhere City*, an historian fresh from a PhD at a high-status Boston area university takes a job in Los Angeles. He has been commissioned to research and write the history of a multinational company. As he conducts the research he finds evidence of policies and practices that the current management do not want known. They demand that he write the 'official' history, with a positive spin. He refuses to suppress the 'truth', and resigns. The hero decides to go back to the East Coast and to academic life. In the last decade there has been a parallel case in real life, surrounding the official history of a German car manufacturer whose author has been accused of suppressing evidence about the use of slave labour in the Nazi era. Ed Regis (1987) says, in his history of the Institute of Advanced Study at Princeton, that several official histories of the place have been censored, suppressed or aborted. Maryon McDonald (1987) has written on how her publications about the politics of Breton language teaching produced local fury in Brittany. More recently Anastasia Karakasidou (1997) lost her original publisher's contract with Cambridge University Press who decided that publishing her *Hills of Blood, Fields of Wheat* might endanger their staff (or their sales) in Greece. She got a contract instead with Chicago UP. The research on the integration of learning-handicapped children in South Wales presented exactly this problem. One of the findings of the ethnographic work was that some of the mildly learning-handicapped children only mixed with mainstream pupils when a deviant mainstreamer was sent to the 'remedial and statemented class' as a punishment or sanctuary. The use of special needs class-rooms as 'sin bins' was routine in several of the schools we studied, but the Welsh Office officials and the senior teachers on our steering committee flatly refused to believe that this was happening at all. They certainly would not accept it as a variety of integration. Nor did they like the finding that sex segregationist practices in the schools meant that integration of the state-mented pupils was only with mainstreamers of the same sex. In both cases the reaction of the audience was to attack the accuracy of the research, and ask for the material to be removed from the research report.

It is never pleasant being the bearer of bad news, and it can be equally unpleasant to make recommendations that will cost money. Rhian Ellis and I (1979) recommended that there should be a Welsh-medium refuge for Welsh-speaking battered women in Gwynedd and northern Dyfed; Maurice Galton and I (1976) recommended that students doing the integrated PhD and PGCE course in Chemistry should have an enhanced grant. In neither case did the ministry concerned want to spend extra money, and they were clearly not convinced by the evidence. The more you want to change policy, the more carefully the report will need to be written, in order to be convincing.

A researcher who has not previously written a report for a sponsor would be wise to consult a colleague who regularly gets money from agencies, with a draft version, and ask for help with it.

Published output writing

The next three types of output writing are those designed for publication: the journal article, the book and the autobiographical or confessional paper. Before discussing these in detail there are some general points about getting published. There are two main ways of publishing your research: as a mono-graph (i.e. a book) or as journal articles. Not all theses make books, but every successful thesis ought to have at least one journal article in it. If you want the world to know about your research, then try to publish it. Theses themselves are read by very few people and lie forgotten on library shelves.

Just as you have used your intelligence to do your academic research, so too you should research possible outlets. If you have spent a lot of time and effort collecting data and writing them up, then spend a bit more time and effort preparing the ground for publication. There is a useful collection edited by Mary Fox (1985) on scholarly writing and publishing, with chapters on journal publication, book publication and writing a textbook. The collection is written for women, but the advice is equally useful for men. Some of its content is specifically American, but reading about a slightly alien culture is useful for gaining insight into one's own.

The following sections combine some practical hints on how to publish, and some autobiographical accounts of publications of my own.

The journal article: reporting findings

You should think about the following:

- What specialized journals exist for your area?
- What more general journals are there that might welcome your sort of approach?
- What type of audience are you trying to reach? Fellow academic social scientists? Practitioners? The lay public? There will obviously be different outlets for different readerships, which will call for different styles of writing.
- Are there any special or new outlets? Sometimes new journals appear, which put out calls for papers. They may be less heavily subscribed with papers than old-established journals. Sometimes journals announce special issues and call for papers. If your topic fits, then you may have a better chance of publishing than in general competition.

Once you have done your basic research and identified possible journals, then you will need to prepare your paper(s). There are no guarantees of success, but the following will help.

1   Get the format right. Journals have notes for contributors, published at least once a year (and often on web sites) which specify basic requirements for submissions. Check them and make sure your paper complies with them.
2   Get the length right. Many journal submissions fail because they are far too long. Check the guidelines, look at a run of issues and get your own word-count right.
3   Write each paper about a clearly defined topic or issue. Many submissions fail because they are ill-focused, diffuse and incoherent. Do not write a paper which has several different papers struggling to get out.
4   Get the editor and the referees on your side by submitting a clear, read-able typescript. Scruffy typescripts and faint xeroxes do not add up to successful self-presentation.
5   If the journal has such a section, you may have a chance of getting a small, modest piece published as a 'research note' – especially if you are reporting empirical findings.

It is important to have a clear paragraph early in the paper which states what it is about. Here are three examples of such paragraphs.

During 1995–96, I did a small piece of ethnography in a Year 5 class of a London primary school ... to investigate the gendered culture of the children and how questions around sexuality were involved in the ways gendered identities were put in place. The substantive findings of the project have been published elsewhere ... so the purpose of this paper is to consider some of the methodological and ethical questions that arose.

Epstein (1998: 27)

This chapter explores how private education helps some young people gain the 'edge' over young people educated in the state sector of education.

Roker (1994: 122)

The main questions to be addressed in this article are how did the Scribes learn their trade, and how did they acquire the literacy practices and knowledge they needed to make a living writing letters, filling out forms, drawing up contracts, or producing any other kind of written products that a client requires?

Kalman (2000: 188)

Kalman's study is of the public scribes (*mecanografos*) who sit in the Plaza de Santa Domingo and outside government buildings in Mexico City to prepare documents for members of the public, such as applications for driving licences or to get married. Roker is reporting research on girls in a fee-paying school, Epstein reflecting on her methods.

Because a journal article has to be brief, it can usually only make one point. To organize my thoughts for producing a paper I usually try to find an apt quotation to start from: something which encapsulates the theme of the article/chapter/paper. For example, Galton and Delamont (1985) begins with this quotation from Robert Graves:

Pythian Apollo's Oracle at Delphi was notorious for speaking in riddles. For example, when King Adrastus asked the Pythia who should marry his two daughters he received the typically unhelpful reply – 'Yoke to a two-wheeled chariot the boar and the lion which fight in your palace.'

(Graves, 1960, vol. 2: 15)

The Oracle at Delphi, with its famous snake (Pythia) seemed a good metaphor to play with, so Graves' (1960) *Greek Myths* was fetched and all the index references to Delphi and the Pythia were scanned. King Adrastus came off the page as an example of what I wanted: yoking together two disparate research traditions. The paper continues boldly:

In this paper we attempt to reconstruct how we yoked together the lion of 'systematic' classroom schedules and the boar of ethnography.

(Galton and Delamont, 1985: 164)

As the hook was the Pythia at Delphi, the title for the paper came easily:

Speaking with forked tongue?

Two styles of observation in the ORACLE project.

A precisely similar strategy gave the starting point for Delamont (2002). I was writing about women and science, drawing on the theoretical ideas of Collins and Pinch (1993, 1998) in their two books in the Golem series. Like nearly all sociology of science writing, Collins and Pinch had very little to say about gender. But then I came across a wonderful passage in Lichtenstein and Sinclair (1999: 180) *Rodinsky's Room*:

> The golem is that which has been banished, an atavistic cartoon, a dream companion.
> The ugly shape of something that has gone and cannot be recalled.
> A dark absence whose strange gravitational field sucks in the spectres of anxiety, paranoia, impotence.
> Miss Havisham is a golem.
> So is Mr Rochester's first wife (and her pale avatar, Daphne du Maurier's eponymous *Rebecca*).
> Strange how the English like to gender-bend their golems, turn them into women.
> The cobwebs of English romanticism are wisps of an unbloodied wedding dress, *momento mori* for a mad bride in the attic.

There are twenty possible titles in this passage, and at least five ideas for papers. Once I had found that I was well away. Titles are themselves an important part of making a journal article look interesting. Atkinson (1990: 75–81) offers an analysis of how they are typically constructed. No texts are neutral, so it is important to think about what your title says to its readers.

Articles submitted to journals nearly always come back for redrafting and resubmission. It is almost unheard of for a paper to be accepted and printed without revisions. Kronenfeld (1985) has written about journal publishing and gives sound advice. There are three common responses from a journal: outright rejection, lukewarm invitations to perform major redrafting and resubmit, and warm invitations to rewrite and resubmit. Papers rejected outright may have been sent to the wrong journal. Get some advice from colleagues, make the most obvious changes needed, retype it into the conventions of another journal and try elsewhere. Do not send the same manuscript off to another journal complete with coffee stains (the reviewers'), tear stains (yours) and creases.

If the journal has proposed revisions, make them and resubmit. Most editors are distressed when papers which needed a small amount of redrafting do not reappear. Often it is a good idea to leave the rewriting for a few weeks to get over the shock and distress occasioned by the reviewers' comments, but once they are past, redraft it. Resubmit it in a clean typescript, with a letter saying how the reviewers' helpful and farsighted comments have been incorporated into the new version. If the referees disagree, make it clear that you spotted this, and state which one(s) you followed.

When you resubmit the revised article, as well as the letter praising the referees do a list of bullet points stating how you dealt with each point made by each referee. See Table 12.2.

Table 12.2   Specimen list of revisions for editor

- Referee A said I had not cited Kenna (1992). This article is now discussed in para 3, page 4, and para 7 on page 32.
- Referee B said I had not cited Coffey and Atkinson (1996). Their work is now included in the section on 'Analysis' (p. 12) and in the section on messy texts (p. 15).
- Referee A said Table 2 was not clearly labelled: I have now labelled it very clearly.
- Referee B disliked the poem: Referee C loved it. I have left it in, but defended its inclusion (p. 23).

And so on.

In journal publishing, persistence pays off. The scholar who does her research on the conventions, does the revisions requested and hits the deadlines is more likely to build an impressive CV. Journal articles are rewarding to see in print, and it can be exciting to get offprint requests from all over the world. Even more self-gratifying, however, is to publish a book.

The monograph

In the 1960s and 1970s it was possible to find publishers who would take MPhil and PhD theses and issue them as monographs. Today that is very rare. Publishers are much keener to take books written for undergraduates, or texts which focus on methods or theory, because these are more international and can be sold in several countries. Martin Cortazzi split his PhD thesis into two books, one on methods (1993) and one on the empirical study of teachers' narratives (1991), placed with different publishers. It is unlikely that your thesis will be accepted as a book unless you are able to transform it into one (or more) manuscripts that a publisher can sell to a bigger market than those specialists who would be the true fans of your work.

The general advice on book publishing which follows draws on my experience. First, it is essential to do some research on academic book publishers. Who publishes your area of specialization? Do any publishers have special lists or series in your area? Have any publishers already published similar studies? Once you have identified possible publishers, you will need to have something to send them. The editor will not want to be sent a copy of your precious thesis. They will not give you a contract without a detailed review of what you have got to offer. So, prepare a prospectus which incorporates all the information an editor will want to know. If you follow these guidelines, you will look very professional and will get off on the right foot. In a cleanly typed, neat-looking document, tell the editor the following things about your planned book:

1 Working title.
2 Author's name, nationality and mailing address.
3 Brief synopsis of the book: background, aims, content.
4 Market: who is this book aimed at? Students? Practitioners?
5 What level? A-level? Postgraduate?
6 Style: what degree of difficulty is the text to represent? What level of knowledge will the readership need?
7 Will the book be designed for specific courses or types of course? e.g. does every student in the country have to read a book on this topic?
8 How long will your book be?
9 What chapters will it include? How many are written already? Which are available if the editor wants to see them?
10 When could the full manuscript be delivered? Can it be delivered on disk?
11 Anything about you and your work that would make you an addition to the publisher's list.

Once your prospectus is ready, the next task is to discover to whom to send it.

Fox (1985) contains good advice on how to approach American publishers, which becomes more relevant in the rest of the English-speaking world as there are mergers and takeovers in publishing houses. In Britain many of the academic publishers have academics who act as formal or informal gatekeepers, and it is usually easier to get accepted if the relevant gatekeeper sponsors the proposal. If there is a series with named academic editors (e.g. Monograph Series on Circus Life: Series Editor Professor Pam Eager-Wright) into which your book would fit, an approach to the academic may be the best step. Certainly the publishers will not put a book in the series without the academic's approval, and they probably will not want it at all as a competitor to their series.

It is easy to spot the formal gatekeepers, who edit series and/or are directors of the publishing house. Once they are identified, an introduction to them at a conference, or a polite letter, or a recommendation from your supervisor/head of department/external examiner can usually be arranged. The *informal* gatekeeper, the scholar trusted by a publisher to vet manuscripts and proposals, may be harder to discover. The necessary detective work is child's play to a good ethnographer. Watch the publisher's stand at the big conferences, see who gets greeted warmly and taken to lunch by the editor on duty. Ask around. Look at who has had several titles by that publisher which have become well known or have sold extensively. (You can see that from the list of reprintings in the front of the volume.)

Once the prospectus has reached a publisher, it may or may not be of interest. If it is, a specimen chapter is usually requested, or perhaps the whole book manuscript. This often goes to an academic who will write comments. If you are lucky, and have a good proposal, the result will be a contract. If it is a refusal, try another publisher. Keep trying, thinking how proud your mother will be.

One other type of publication which has become much more common in the past twenty years is the 'confessional' paper.

The confessional genre

Since Hammond (1964) there has been a steady trickle of autobiographical or confessional writing about how sociologists and anthropologists have done their research. Atkinson (1987) has commented on this type of writing as follows:

> The question that I want to raise through this paper, then, is this: why do we (ethnographers in general) so often produce autobiographical accounts of this sort? Susan Sontag (1966) has written on the anthropologist as 'hero'. Just as often the anthropologist or sociologist seems to present him or herself in an anti-heroic light. In effect the resulting self-presentation is an ambivalent mixture of the two. There is the wry tradition whereby we rehearse the second-worst thing that ever happened to us in the field, the very worst being too painful or embarrassing. We paint ourselves in unflattering colours, we are by turns naive, vulnerable and incompetent. Of course, we are meant to present ourselves as 'socially acceptable incompetents' for the purposes of data collection. Yet it appears that we are often genuinely incompetent – lacking street wisdom and credibility: 'the sociologist as schlemiel' is a long-running thread in the genre. By the same token, our struggles with an unfamiliar, even hostile, social environment can invest this character with more praiseworthy qualities.
>
> (p. 192)

The autobiographical account is, as Atkinson's piece goes on to show, carefully judged to present its author in a particular light. The range of educational researchers who have now produced such accounts, collected by Shipman (1976), Burgess (1984b, 1985a, 1985c, 1989b), Walford (1987, 1991, 1994, 1998) and included in Messerschmidt (1982), is considerable. Sociological accounts appear in Hammond (1964), Bell and Newby (1977), Bell and Roberts (1984), Bell and Encel (1978) and McKeganey and Cunningham-Burley (1987). There are also collections by anthropologists about their time abroad (e.g. Nordstrom and Robben, 1995), near to home (MacDonald, 1993; Lareau and Schultz, 1996) and at home (Messerschmidt, 1982 and Jackson, 1987). There have also been best-selling autobiographical accounts by anthropologists at book length (e.g. Bowen, 1954; Barley 1983 and 1986) and more serious contributions to the scholarly literature in auto-biographical form (e.g. Rabinow, 1979). Reed-Danahay (1997) is a useful collection of anthropological papers on autoethnography; Ellis and Bochner (1996) are leading exponents of sociological autoethnography. Coffey (1999) is the best introduction to the complexities of the interpenetration of field-work role, auto-ethnography and confessional writing.

There are three points to be made about this type of output writing here. First, it is mainly produced in response to invitations, and then appears in edited collections, rather than being published in refereed journals or as monographs, especially if the autobiography is about research 'at home'. Second, it is probably better to publish some of the empirical work to establish credibility before going public with confessions of how the data were gathered. Third, reading such accounts is a good way to cheer oneself up when feeling particularly incompetent. Reading this genre, one of the main differences between anthropologists and sociologists is made manifest. As Atkinson (1987) points out:

> Of course, the standard sociologist working in his or her own culture can hardly compete with the average social anthropologist. Our research settings do not normally run the risk of contracting obscure tropical diseases. Our privations and dangers (physical and moral) are not as extreme. The food in the average hospital staff canteen may be grim (it is), but does not compete with weird and wonderful cuisines endured by 'proper' anthropologists. Perhaps the ethnographer, like myself – especially one with a kosher training as an anthropologist – has an inferiority complex. 'Look,' our accounts say, 'I've had to suffer too; you just can't begin to understand all I had to get through to get those data.' We offset the manifest arrogance and exploitation of social investigation by self-deprecation. The anti-hero, or even the clown, is valuable camouflage. The result is a highly ambiguous 'trickster' figure, inscribed in these artful autobiographical revelations. Our mirror of 'true confessions' is equally a mask of self-regard.
>
> (p. 192)

A self-deprecating comment by Harriet Rosenberg (1988) about doing historical and ethnographic research as an American anthropologist in an Alpine village in France illustrates the power of the 'hero' myth in the anthropological autobiography.

> I loved living in France and was amused when my anthropologist colleagues who worked in more exotic locales asked about my time in the bush. I would bravely attempt to match their stories of hardship by pointing out that 'my village' was more than twenty-four hours away from the nearest three-star restaurant.
>
> (Rosenberg, 1988: xi)

These then are the five main types of output writing that scholars typically produced from 1945 to 1980. The last twenty years have seen new forms of scholarly writing emerge. The chapter has not yet discussed the current fashion for alternative forms of representation, such as producing a journal article in the form of a poem or a play. The next section deals with this fashion, or liberation. Then three practical issues around how academic texts are written are discussed: team writing, pseudonyms and non-sexist writing. These are three issues not addressed in Becker (1986) or the other books recommended in this chapter. Finally there is a section on how to settle to writing.

The power of the author – fashion or liberation?

Since the first edition of this book, a crisis has hit academic writing, which has been liberating for many scholars because it has widened the range of styles in which academic material can be published. The crisis of representation is dated from the publication of Clifford and Marcus's (1986) *Writing Culture*. This produced or signalled to a mass academic audience the crisis of confidence in the text. Previously the text, typically the monograph, recorded the central process of fieldwork and was the most important product of qualitative research: by their texts shall they be known. After Clifford and Marcus qualitative research took what is variously called the linguistic turn, or the interpretative turn, or the rhetorical turn – with its accompanying legitimation crisis, described by Atkinson (1990, 1992).

In the Clifford and Marcus volume the authors became self-consciously reflexive about how anthropologists 'wrote up' their 'findings' for publication: that is, how the texts of the discipline were constructed. Recognizing that all disciplines are, at one level, rhetorical, in that all arguments have to be framed to convince, or try to convince, the reader, the contributors to Clifford and Marcus began the task of reflecting critically upon the ways in which anthropology had been and was being written. Clifford and Marcus (1986) is now seen as the landmark volume, but there had been precursors such as Boon

(1982), Edmondson (1984) and Fabian (1983). Since the Clifford and Marcus book there has been a steady growth in analysis of all aspects of sociological and anthropological texts from fieldnotes (Sanjek, 1990; Emerson *et al.*, 1995) to publications (Atkinson, 1990, 1992, 1996). The contribution of Richardson (1990) who explained her authorial strategies for reaching diverse audiences, of Wolcott (1990, 1994), the feminist responses to Clifford and Marcus such as Behar and Gordon (1995) and the British anthropological reaction (James *et al.*, 1997) are all examples of the expansion here.

Canons of truth and method were challenged, not least through the critical examination of textual practices. For instance, 'The erosion of classic norms in anthropology (objectivism, complicity with colonialism, social life structured by fixed rituals and customs, ethnographies as monuments to a culture) was complete' (Denzin and Lincoln, 1994: 10). The crisis put in hazard not only the products of the ethnographers' work, but the moral and intellectual authority of ethnographers themselves. The 'crisis' was not founded merely in ethnographers' growing self-consciousness concerning their own literary work and its conventional forms. More fundamentally, it grew out of the growing contestation of ethnographers' (especially mainstream Western ethnographers) implicit claims to a privileged and totalizing gaze. It leads to increasingly urgent claims to legitimacy on the part of 'indigenous' ethnographers, and for increasingly complex relationships between ethnographers' selves, the selves of 'others' and the texts they both engage in (cf Reed-Danahay, 1997; Walford 1994, 1998). In the 1990s it became more acceptable for researchers to publish their results in apparently unacademic forms: as poems, plays, short stories, dialogues and so on. Sociologists of science had been playing with these forms earlier (see Mulkay, 1985) but they were rare in educational research (Eisner, 1997). *Qualitative Studies in Education* carries a good deal of alternative writing, while the *British Journal of Psychology of Education* does not. Alternative textual forms can be good for conveying strong emotions such as pain. Bluebond-Langer's (1978) data on terminally ill children are done as plays, a PhD student's recollection of her viva as a poem (Coffey and Atkinson, 1996: 129–30). Dialogues are useful for displaying the different sides in an argument (e.g. Mulkay, 1985). I used this device to illustrate my own ambivalences about postmodernism (Delamont, 2000b), with a dialogue that *starts* as follows:

Where do I stand?
    Reflecting on where I stand for this conference I have concluded 'it depends', and I have used the freedom available to us to write a dialogue 'about' postmodernism between Sara the Educational Ethnographer and Sara the Feminist Historian. To avoid confusion I have labelled the ethnographer Eowyn (the warrior maiden of *The Lord of the Rings*) and the feminist historian Sophonsiba (for the pioneer Chicago sociologist).

The dialogue

It is 1999: the scene is the rooftop restaurant above the Gallery of Modern Art in Glasgow in the old stock exchange. Two young scholars – Eowyn, an educational ethnographer, and Sophonsiba, an historian – are discussing postmodernism over the blackened catfish and bitter lemon tart.

Eowyn:	I'm going to BERA this year – there's a debate about the present and future of educational ethnography with people from *QSE* speaking.
Sophonsiba:	Is that the journal with all the poems and playlets and polyvocality and stuff in?
Eowyn:	Yes – it's the place where all the Denzin 'sixth and seventh moment' stuff gets aired – totally unlike any other educational journal – off the wall stuff. Are you going to BERA?

(p. 50)

In this play or dialogue the strengths and weaknesses of postmodernist theory for feminist scholarship are set out, allowing the two 'me's' to argue through the issues. You may love or hate this freedom to play with texts, and publish poems, plays or short stories. My advice would be, if you plan to write and publish alternative texts, to ensure you also produce some very orthodox papers if only to prove you *can* do so. Referees and members of appointing panels are often conservative and may be distressed by lots of poems.

In the next section the power which is given to the member of a team of researchers who does the 'writing up' is discussed, using experiences from ORACLE and subsequent projects.

Teams and writing

One of the many invisible aspects of qualitative work has been the division of labour when a team of researchers is involved. In many projects a team gather the data, but only one person produces the public account, yet this process and its consequences have not been explored in print. I have produced the published account of two team-based ethnographic projects, ORACLE (Delamont and Galton, 1986) and the locational integration research (Upton *et al.*, 1988). Here I have reflected on the former. For the two main publications based on the analysis of the ethnographic material from the six transfer schools, Delamont began by reading all the observers' notes and diaries several times, indexing them to locate examples of significant events, and then preparing drafts which were discussed with some of the permanent members of the research team (Galton, Simon, Croll and Willcocks) at meetings in Leicester. There were several reasons why this was practical, but the consequences have to be understood. Three of the observers used to gather ethnographic accounts (Tann, Lea and Greig) were part-time workers, paid by the hour to gather data. Their contracts did not include writing time, and they had all left the project when the relevant volumes came to be prepared for Routledge. They could not be expected to write up that material. Willcocks and Galton were permanent team members, but when the analysis and writing up fell due, they were fully engaged on preparing earlier ORACLE volumes and other chapters of the book on transfer. Delamont had the experience with 'soft' data, the spare writing capacity, and so she prepared the three chapters of Galton and Willcocks (1983) which depend on the ethnographic data, and the text of Delamont and Galton (1986).

This has several consequences. First there were genuine differences among the team over stylistics. Delamont preferred pseudonyms for teachers, pupils and schools, other team members preferred 'Pupil 312', 'Teacher Maths 12' and 'School 3C'. While this may seem trivial, it actually reveals differences about the 'scientific' status of ethnography, the 'read-ability' of the research and so forth which go deeper than a dispute over which nomenclature to use. Susan Krieger (1979: 175–8) is one of the few authors to write about this. In a study of a radio station in California, Krieger says she wanted to produce a text with a coherent narrative, and so had: 'the problem of developing characters who would be capable of carrying its narrative'. To make her characters live for the reader, she decided they had to 'have':

> their own personal, or 'real' names, as well as names indicating something of their relationship with the station.

Delamont felt like this about the ORACLE school ethnography; some other members of the team did not.

Perhaps more serious is the issue of power. Because I wrote the accounts of the ethnography, my version of reality is the one which is offered, and other members of the team can only query it, but do not have the same access to the data, or time to construct an alternative. The account of everyday life in the schools is probably more sociological, more conscious of sexism, and more grounded in other ethnographic work than it would be if it had been written by anyone else involved with the project.

It seemed important to mitigate the effects of this power that had been given to me as far as possible. The main strategy adopted was to make sure that whenever any point was made, it could be illustrated and/or substanti-ated by extracts from at least three observers' notes. It also seemed important to use at least one extract from every one of the six researchers and to make sure that all six schools were represented in the account, including the two not studied in person by me. This would probably have been impossible if I had not some acquaintance with the two 11–14 schools from occasional teaching practice supervision. We decided that we would not identify particular researchers as authors of individual extracts or comments.

Maurice Galton and I are convinced that ours was the only practical way of handling the writing of the ORACLE ethnography, but we are acutely aware that there are no clear ground rules for handling such a decision. Should the 'hired-hand' ethnographer have complete control of her own fieldnotes? And who, if anyone, should veto the account – researchers, or researched? We are not quite sure. These issues need further discussion in public.

Actually producing your text

The first thing to do is to go back and read Chapter 4, paying particular attention to the maxims 'Write early and write often' and 'Don't get it right, get it written', and the wisdom of Philip Jackson and Walter Mosley. The only way to get the thesis, book or article written is to write drafts regularly: ideally to write every single day, keep the writing safe, and keep going until it is fun. People vary in the media they use: some use pencil, others go straight to their PC. Some use a fountain pen, others a laptop. That does not matter. You need to experiment until you find the best times of day, the best media, the best audience for you, and then write. If you write best at 5.00 a.m. with Cajun music, wrapped up in a sleeping bag, then write every day at 5.00 a.m., and use headphones so the Cajun music does not disturb anyone else. I write best from 2.00 p.m. till about 9.00 p.m., and I like speech as my background noise: radio commentary on test cricket is ideal, and if there is no 'real' test match, the cassettes of John Arlott are fine. Great authors reading *Beowulf*, Homer or Tolkien are also good for me. I can only write longhand on scrap paper: a clean pad is paralysing for me. I need to know that what I am writing is 'only a draft', 'does not matter' and can been thrown away. Thus I will myself into a false sense of security.

Do not fall for the myth that you will write when it is clear in your head. Good evidence from research on productive scholars and doctoral students who finished their theses shows that is a fatal myth. Scholars who write, write drafts to sort out the ideas in their heads. Copy them. Get down a draft, redraft it until it says what you want it to say, and then polish it so it is well written using the ideas in Table 12.3, which shows twenty rules for good writing published in the *Guardian* (9 January 1999).

This chapter ends with three issues that rarely crop up in most writing about qualitative research: how to choose pseudonyms, how to avoid sexism and racism in writing, and what name(s) you yourself should use.

Table 12.3   Twenty rules for good writing

1   Verbs has to agree with their subjects.
2   Prepositions are not words to end sentences with.
3   And don't start a sentence with a conjunctive.
4   It is wrong to ever split an infinitive.
5   Avoid clichés like the plague.
6   Also, always avoid annoying alliteration.
7   Be more or less specific.
8   Parenthetical remarks (however relevant) are (usually) unnecessary.
9   No sentence fragments.
10   Contractions aren't necessary and shouldn't be used.
11   One should never generalize.
12   Don't use no double negatives.
13   Eschew ampersands & abbreviations, etc.
14   Eliminate commas, that are, not necessary.
15   Never use a big word when a diminutive one would suffice.
16   Kill all exclamation marks!!!
17   Use words correctly, irregardless of how others use them.
18   Use the apostrophe in it's proper place and omit it when its not needed.
19   Puns are for children, not groan readers.
20   Proofread carefully to see if you any words out.

Pseudonyms

The choice of pseudonyms for your town, suburb, village or neighbourhood, for the schools or colleges or hospitals, for all the teachers, aides, secretaries, caretakers, lectures, dinner ladies and other adults, and for all the students or pupils, is an important matter. Once chosen, they should protect the identity of all your informants from outsiders for ever. It is as Lumley, Hightown, Beachside and Bishop MacGregor that we should remember schools, and as Miss Floral and Mr Fawlty that we should remember teachers.

In this section there is a discussion of how British ethnographers have chosen their pseudonyms in the past, and some ideas for choosing yours in the future. The choice of pseudonyms may need to be discussed with the funding body, or with the informants. Coffield *et al.* (1986) encouraged their respondents (unemployed young people in the north-east of England) to choose their own pseudonyms, and this might be a useful research strategy as well as solving the problem of choosing plausible names. However, young people may choose names they will later regret, names that do not actually disguise them, or even the names of their real classmates or family. Letting people choose their own is not necessarily the best solution.

In the Welsh Office research (Upton *et al.*, 1988) the HMI in charge of the project objected to my original choice of pseudonyms for the schools, because they did not sound Welsh. I had deliberately picked English-sounding names to help the disguise of the schools, but was over-ruled and was forced to choose a new set of Welsh pseudonyms. Table 12.4 shows the two sets of names. The procedure had been to give each school a letter from A to H, and then pick a name beginning with that letter. My first choices had been taken from John Buchan; the second set were invented by scrambling the Welsh names of local railway stations with house names from the property pages of the daily paper, and then asking a Welsh speaker to check they made sense. In such a strategy it is important that schools should not be in their real alphabetical order when you assign the A to H you need for their pseudonyms.

The subsequent research on school pupils' scary stories about transfer to secondary school collected in one county in the south-east of England needed a set of names for towns and schools which sounded like one county's places. Patricia Wentworth's many Miss Silver novels are mostly set in 'Ledshire', a county with a coastline and resorts, a cathedral city, several other towns and multiple villages. A ready-made set of names for places had already been created by Wentworth, and could easily be 'borrowed'. She created 'Ledshire', with the towns of Ledlington, Ledbury, Ledchester, Westhaven, Birleton and Marbury, plus villages called Tallingford, Deeping, Hazledon Heath, Rillington, Milstead, Slepham Halt, Brookenden, Whincliffe, Prior's End, Embank, Paynings, Merefields and Rowberry Common. Much easier to borrow those than create from scratch. Brookenden Comprehensive sounds perfectly plausible, as does Ledlington High School.

These names appear in the publications on urban legends (Pugsley *et al.*,

Table 12.4   Two sets of pseudonyms

English pseudonyms	Welsh pseudonyms
Artinswell	Aberelwy
Burminster	Brynhenlog
Clipperstone	Cynllaith
Sharway Down	Derllwyn
Earisfield	St Edeyrn's
Fosse	Ffynnon Frenhines
Gorston Hall	Gwaelod y Garth
Hanham	Heol-y-Crynwyr
Rushford	Llanddewi

1996a, 1996b; Delamont, 1989b, 1991) and have been recycled for the
fictional episodes in Coffey and Delamont (2000). For the PhD research
(Delamont, Atkinson and Parry, 2000) we drew on Ngaio Marsh and
Marjorie Allingham for the universities' and the lecturers' names. The
students' pseudonyms came from American detective stories by Emma
Lathen and R.B. Dominic which produced names unlikely to be held by
anyone in a UK university in the 1990s. So at Gossingham, Dr Harcourt
and Dr d'Hiver supervised Mick Jesiliko and Nathan Landry, and at
Chelmsworth Prof. Scoop-Drury supervised Loel Stosser and Verena
Anson. The students' names are *not* realistic, but do protect the informants.
Students who were part of the research have not recognized themselves
behind their exotic pseudonyms.

The many British school ethnographers who have been publishing
research since Jackson (1964) have shown too little imagination in their
choices. In the first edition an analysis of 44 researchers' pseudonyms for 98
schools (mainly in England) was presented. This analysis was expanded and
elaborated in Delamont and Atkinson (1995: 71–8). In 2000 a further 13
authors, and new publications by 5 others, were added to the analysis,
increasing the number of school pseudonyms from 98 to 190. The majority of
the additional names came from the work of Stephen Ball and his colleagues
(Gewirtz *et al.*, 1995: 192–4), who generated 49 school pseudonyms. With the
larger number of pseudonyms it is possible to produce a more complex cate-
gorization than the one in the first edition.

I have divided the pseudonyms into six categories: five I am reasonably
confident about, and one which is less clear-cut. The five categories are
urban and industrial; rural and natural world; literary and mythological; religious; and jokes and popular culture. The sixth category, establishment and
local worthies, contains some pseudonyms I am sure invoke a worthy
(Gladstone) and some I am less sure about (Duncan, Emmet, Wrighton).
Table 12.5 shows the literary and mythological, religious, and jokes and
popular culture pseudonyms. Table 12.6 shows the urban/industrial and the
rural/natural pseudonyms. Table 12.7 is the establishment and local
worthies' names. In each of these tables, the pseudonyms which I regard as
problematically placed are indicated with (?). Flatley, for example, could be
in the popular culture category if the Irish dancer from *Riverdance* is being
invoked.

Some names have been used by more than one researcher. Greenfields
has now been used by four scholars (Abraham, Jordan and Lacey, Nias, and
Turner) Greenhill by three, Ashton, Gladstone, Hutton and St Joseph's by
two each. Hutton is a 'new' pseudonym, not found in 1990. It is not clear
whether the authors meant the Yorkshire cricketers (Len and Richard) or
the journalist and intellectual critic of the New Right (Will). There are 8
jokey/popular culture names (assuming Torville is invoking the ice dancer).
There are 11 literary and mythological names, most of which are my

Table 12.5   Pseudonyms in UK ethnographies I

Literary and mythological	Religious	Jokes and popular culture
Casterbridge	Bishop McGregor	Camberwick Green
Gryll Grange	Cardinal Heenan	Grasshopper
Guy Mannering	Carey	John Noakes
Kenilworth	Christchurch	Ladybird
Lady Bracknell	Corpus Christi	Suchard
The Laurels	Fulfilling Prophets	Torville
Maid Marion	Hulme House	Trumpton
Melin Court	Jericho	Yellow View
Phoenix	¡Reverend Smith	
Robin Hood	Sacred Heart	
Waverley	St Bernadette	
	St Birinus	
	St Faith's	
	St Helena	
	St Ignatious	
	St Joseph (x2)	
	St Luke	
	St Michael	
	Trinity	

choices (see Delamont and Galton, 1986). There are 19 religious names, assuming 'Carey' is invoking the Archbishop of Canterbury. There are 45 'urban and industrial' names, and 63 'rural and natural world' names, shown in Table 12.6. Table 12.7 shows 42 names that I have called 'Establishment and local worthies'. Some of the names in this table are clearly invoking establishment places (Blenheim, Windsor), and some establishment people (Gladstone, Nelson, and Victoria). Gewirtz *et al.* (1995) have put a series of feminist heroines into the list: Elizabeth (Garrett) Anderson, Florence Nightingale, (Harriet) Martineau, Pankhurst, and Nancy Astor. These names are all used deliberately for single-sex girls' schools with high achievements. Some of the pseudonyms sound as if they are invoking local worthies (Rowland Hutty, Gammer Wiggins). Those pseudonyms that seem problematic are indicated with (?), and Table 12.7 has more of these than any other table.

In 1992 there were 22 pseudonyms invoking urban and industrial images, and 32 invoking the rural and the natural. In 2001 there are 45 and 61 respectively. The comments made in 1992 about the biases still stand. Researchers frequently choose rural or natural world pseudonyms for schools even though their fieldsites were urban or suburban. Rural schools have been neglected by British researchers in real life, but the pseudonyms invoke the world of Vaughan Williams, Butterfield, Constable and *The Country Diary of an Edwardian Lady*. There are large numbers of trees (alder, apple, ash, beech, cherry, elm, holly, maple, oak), there are flowers and plants (furze, gorse,

Table 12.6   Pseudonyms in UK ethnographies II

Urban/industrial		Rural/natural world	
Albert Park	Hightown	Alder	King's Marsh
Alma Road	Hinsley Mill	Applegate	Lavender Way
Ballyhightown	Inner City	Ashfield	Linton Bray
Branstown	Langley	Ashton (x2)	Lockmere
Burns Road	Livery	Beachside (?)	Lowfield
Burnley Road	Long Estate	Beechgrove	Lowmeadow
Carbridge Road	Lowerside	Broadmere	Maindene
Carlton Hill	Lumley	Cherry Dale	Mapledene Lane
Castle Gate	Municipal	Coombe	Marshbrook
Castle Town	New Town	Cranfield	Marshfield
Cato Park	Northwark Park	Crawford Park	Meadowsfield
Chester	Old Town	Deefords	Millbridge
City Road	Panstation	Deerpark	Millrace
Crescent	Port Primary	Edenfield	Mill Lane
Cross Street	Randleside	Egdon Park	Moorside
Dockside	Sageton	Elmfield	Oakbank
Downtown	Shottsford Road	Elm Park	Oak Farm
East Avenue	Smith Street	Furzedown	Oak Park
Flightpath	Spa Town High	Gorse	Orchard
Girthwaite	Stokingham SFC	Greenfields (x4)	Overbury
Hammertown	Township	Greenhill (x3)	Parkside
Handworth	Victoria Road	Greenhouse	Penchurch
Highmills		Greenside	Rainford
		Heathbrook	Riverdale
		High Rock	Riverway
		Hilledge	Rivendell
		Hillside	Rosemont
		Hillview	Seaton Park
		Hollytop	Sedgemoor
		Honey Bell	South Moleberry
			Stonegrove
			Upper Norton
			Warren Park

lavender, rose, sedge), there are large open spaces (field, dale, park, heath, down, marsh, bray, meadow, dene, moor), there are watery places (beach, bridge, brook, ford, lock, marsh, mere, mill, race, rain, river), picturesque landscape features (coombe, church, dell, grove, hill, rock, stone), country landscape (farm, field, gate, orchard), animals (deer, mole, warren). Overall, then, the commonest pseudonyms for schools invoke the rural and natural. Perhaps most striking is the air of 'Middle Earth' about these names. 'Riverdale', 'Greenhill' and 'Applegate' sound pure Tolkien, and 'Rivendell' *is* pure Tolkien. The hobbits could live in Overbury, Hilledge and Upper Norton; Gandalf might ride over Egdon Park or Furzedown; Galadriel might prophesy about King's Marsh or Maindene, and Tom Bombadil could easily

Table 12.7 Pseudonyms in UK ethnographies III

Establishment and local worthies	
Angrave (?)	Madeley (?)
Arthur Lucas	Manston (?)
Blenheim	Martineau
Carlby (?)	Maxwell
Cunningham (?)	Milner
Ducan (?)	Milton
Elizabeth Anderson	Nancy Astor
Emmet (?)	Nelson
Fenton (?)	Pankhurst
Flatley (?)	Parnell
Fletcher (?)	Parsons
Florence Nightingale	Princess Elizabeth
Gammer Wiggins	Ramsay McDonald
Gladstone (x2)	Redmond (?)
Goddard	Rowland Hutty
Harrod	Simpson
Heliwell	Thomas High
Hutton (x2)	Victoria
Ingham	Warburton (?)
John Ruskin	Windsor
John Manvers	Wrighton (?)

sing about Lowfield, Broadmere or Linton Bray. Are sociologists of education looking for the lost Entwives? In contrast, the urban names are brass bands, steel bands, Lowry and *Coronation Street*. They are descriptive of urban space (Old Town, East Avenue, Smith Street), of manual labour (car, dock, hammer, port, station), of towns, neighbourhoods and council estates which could exist (Branstown, Burnley Road, Northwark, Flightpath, Spatown, Carbridge, Handworth). The urban and literary names are equally evocative of familiar books – Ashton is the coal-mining community studied by Dennis *et al.* (1959) for *Coal is our Life*. Lowfield sounds like Lowood, the poorly disguised Clergy Daughters School at Cowan Bridge where the Brontës were so unhappy, immortalized in *Jane Eyre*. Such names are not neutral. Delamont and Atkinson (1995) contains a chapter elaborating these arguments.

There are two implications for the naming of schools in future ethnographic monographs and texts, apart from the recommendation that Tolkien is not the best source of imagery for contemporary schooling (exactly who are the trolls, orcs and goblins in the local comprehensive?). A scrutiny of the popular school suggests the sociology of education needs to be re-infused with the arguments raised by Raymond Williams (1975) in *The Country and the City*, and face up to urban schooling. At a practical level, it would be helpful if more attention is paid to school pseudonyms in future to avoid duplication. Having two Ashtons and three Greenhills is thoroughly confusing. Equity register the stage names of actors; it would be sensible if there were attempts to avoid duplicating school pseudonyms. BERA and the BSA could hold a list of names already used in published work, to which supervisors of higher degrees could refer students, and leaders of research teams direct the fieldworkers. Then a new author, or anyone disguising any school, could consult the list and choose a fresh, newly minted name rather than adopting the tired label Greenhill again.

Non-sexist writing and anti-racist writing

Do make sure that you do not use sexist language in your publications or thesis. Publishers and journals do not like it, and neither do many social scientists. Train yourself to write in a non-sexist way. The British Sociological Association guidelines on non-sexist writing are available from the BSA, and the BPS/APA have guidelines too. Some general rules follow. In particular, do not use male nouns and pronouns to refer to males and females, do not call 'the researcher' 'he' if it was a woman, and so on. Do not say things like: 'John Smith, a busy architect, and his pretty blonde wife' or 'Highlanders went to America taking their wives and children' or 'I studied a group of motorbike boys and their giggling girlfriends' or 'the men and girls'. If you are unsure whether something is sexist or not, ask one of the women around – they will soon spot any sexist writing. (Yes, that is a sexist sentence!) In general, rephrasing sexist comments will make your writing more precise.

Just as most journals and book publications have codes of non-sexist writing, so, too, they will not publish racist writing. Again the BSA has a code, and the APA guidelines address the issue. In one way, avoiding racism in your writing is a little harder than avoiding sexism, because the preferred term changes faster. Books and articles about African-Americans that used 'Negro' or 'Black' when those were the preferred terms now 'sound' patronizing or racist. In 1975, for example, Aschenbrenner published *Lifelines: Black Families in Chicago* and the subtitle was unremarkable. In 1967 Elliot Liebow had published *Tally's Corner: A Study of Negro Streetcorner Men*, again without criticism. (In 1967 racists used 'nigger' 'nigra', 'coloured' and other terms – 'Black' and 'Negro' were acceptable names.) The appropriate term for the dialect of American English spoken by African-Americans originally described by William Labov in 1961 as Non-Standard Negro English (NNE) has evolved through Black English Vernacular (BEV) and African American English (AAE) to Ebonics (see Fordham 1996) in forty years. The grammar and accent is the same, but the linguistic label has changed as fast as the words used by the native speakers of Ebonics.

Similar changes have occurred in the preferred terms for Spanish-speaking Americans and for the peoples we grew up calling 'Red' Indians:

who have been Indians, North American Indians, Native Americans and First Americans, and what we studied in primary school as Eskimo who are now Inuit or again First Americans or First Canadians. Similar changes have occurred in France, with labels for French people whose origins were in Tunisia, Algeria or Morocco; and in Great Britain. Are Dion Dublin and Dwight Yorke 'West Indians', 'Black British' or 'Afro-Caribbeans'?

Choosing your name

Before you publish it is important to think what name you are going to use on your publications. There are three issues here, one of which is important only for women. First, you need to decide whether you are going to publish under your own name or a pseudonym. Professional authors sometimes use different pseudonyms for their various types of book – Ruth Rendell also publishes as Barbara Vine, the serious novelist Julian Barnes writes detective stories as Dan Kavanagh (his wife's surname is Kavanagh), the poet C.D. Lewis wrote detective stories as Nicholas Blake. Academics who write popular books often keep their persona apart – a detective story series about modern Spain by David Seraphim is actually by a professor of Spanish from an old university; Michelle Spring is the pseudonym of a published sociologist; Amanda Cross is Carolyn Heilbron, a literary scholar at Columbia. If you think you might want to publish westerns, or science fiction, or romantic novels, it is sensible to plan a pseudonym for them so they do not damage your serious career. Occasionally a scholar decides to publish academic work under a pseudonym. In educational research the best-known example is 'James Patrick', author of *A Glasgow Gang Observed*. He felt that publishing under a pseudonym would be safer: it would protect him from revenge attacks by the gang.

Second, you need to think about what form of your name you are going to use. Sometimes you will only be able to use initials, but when you have the choice will you be Michael, Mike, Mick or 'M'? Just as the pseudonyms you give your respondents label them, so too your name labels you. Mairtin Mac an Ghaill is telling his readers he is Irish and proud of it. Autumn Battlesister is telling her readers she is a feminist. If you choose a diminutive (Phil, Mick, Susie, Popsie) it may embarrass you when you are 50.

Third, there is an issue for women. If a woman scholar changes her surname on marriage, divorce, remarriage, divorce ... she damages her career. Tescione (1998) reviews the literature on gender and citation patterns, showing how, if women change the names under which they publish, it damages their careers. In a small piece of research Tescione found that men averaged only two variations of their names (Paul Atkinson and Paul A. Atkinson) while women averaged five (and *one* woman had *eight* variations). The women used nicknames, changed surnames because of marriage or divorce, and used initials intermittently. Tescione gives an example (pp. 40–41), which I have paralleled here. Let us imagine a PhD student called Tamsin Victoria Swann, known to her friends as Tammy. She publishes two articles as T. Swann and Tamsin Swann on her own, one as Tammy Swann, and one with her supervisor and another student as third author (Adams, Mitchell and Swann). That article will not appear in most searches under Swann because only the first author's surname appears in most bibliographic lists. Tamsin then gets married, takes her husband's surname (Fishwick), and publishes her first book as Tamsin Fishwick. Then she discovers there is another T. Fishwick in her field, as well as her new husband who is R. Fishwick, so Tamsin starts to use her middle name, Victoria, and publishes a couple of things as T.V. Fishwick, and one as Tamsin V. Fishwick. Then she has a baby, and she and her husband decide little Bruno should be called Bruno Swann Fishwick. Tamsin begins to publish as T. Swann Fishwick, T. Swann-Fishwick, T.V. Swann Fishwick, Tamsin V.S. Fishwick, and Tamsin Swann-Fishwick. Fifteen years later, divorced, she reverts to Swann, and publishes as Tamsin Swann again. Only when a new PhD student complains that a computer search has not thrown up 'most' of her publications does Tamsin realize what she has done to her own career. All her 'Fishwick' publications are 'invisible'.

Tescione (1998: 41) says firmly:

> Every author should publish under one standard name only, and hyphen-ation should be avoided. If a woman employs her birth name professionally, then she should standardize it early in her career.

Tescione also suggests that when applying for jobs, women should list all their names prominently on their CV, in case anyone on the appointing committee does a citation search on them. This may seem paranoid or absurd. However, there are several women researchers in Britain whose work is published under several names and therefore they may not be as well known as they deserve to be. The late Deanne Boydell (a founder of classroom research) started publication as Bealing, and Madeleine Arnot as MacDonald.

Conclusions

Publishing is one of the most exciting things a scholar can do, and like many other activities the more you do, the better you will get. Remember the following maxims with which Paul Atkinson and I berate our graduate students:

1   Write early and write often.
2   Don't get it right, get it written.

Key reading

The key reading is Paul Atkinson's (1990) *The Ethnographic Imagination*.

Chapter 13

Always a little further
The conclusions

I probably never would have become America's leading fire-eater if Flamo the Great hadn't happened to explode that night in front of Krinko's Great Combined Carnival Side Shows.

(Mannix, 1951: 5)

These are the opening words of Dan Mannix's book about his time with an American carnival. It may appear strange to begin the final chapter of a book with the opening words of another one, but there are two themes embedded in it which make the choice less strange. The first theme of the chapter is indeed endings: how to finish a piece of academic work and conclude scholarly writing. The second theme reflects the title of the chapter which is called 'Always a little further' because that possibility should both inform your thoughts as you conclude your study, and be made explicit in the conclusions of any thesis or book you produce from it. So in the first section, the possible ways to end are considered, and in the second, how to whet your readers' appetites for your next golden journey.

Happy endings

In fairy stories, the conventional sentence of closure is 'and they all lived happily ever after', but life is not like that, and it would be a peculiar piece of qualitative research which ended with that stock conclusion. Equally impossible, although a splendid piece of writing, is the ending produced by a 6-year-old called Nate for Anne Dyson (1990): 'And they died and it was over, the dinosaur season.' It is important for a piece of writing not to fizzle out; it should end, as Nate's story does. Some examples of endings follow. First, Dan Mannix's life with the carnival ended when he decided to change career. He left his carnival partner in Chicago:

and started east in my car. In my inside pocket was the letter from Collier's asking for a series of articles based on carnival life. And on the seat beside me was a secondhand typewriter I'd purchased from the carnival manager.

(1951: 223)

Before analysing ways in which writing can end, it is fun to compare some endings, the sources of which are revealed after all the extracts.

A   A woman in her seventies expressed it thus: 'Our "refugeeness" is disappearing, the old people are dying and whatever one might describe, it is only like a small patch of cloth. We experienced it, but it's like a fairy story to our children.'

B   After that, Rachel and I entered a long, silent passage and for the next month we were as strangers to the sunlight.

C   I found it hard to say to him that after many wars the refugees had not gone home, and that partition had become a commonplace 'solution' to both super-power and regional conflicts, Poland, Ireland, Germany, Korea, Vietnam, were all testaments to this. I was sad for him, for his innocence and hope.

D   Today we see no eagles soaring over the mountains of Abries ... we have no more eagles.

E   If this project should be deemed successful and be well received by the academic community, and the interested general reader, then hopefully this combination of fieldwork, anthropology, and historiography will spark other similar studies in the future.

F   If the portrait of British schooling that results is not a uniformly optimistic one, this is because the comprehensive dream is such an exalted one it is not surprising that it exceeds the grasp of some schools, some teachers and some pupils on some occasions.

G   And although the pilgrims leave the cavern by the way they entered, they see Adonis rising with the spring breeze of flutes and cymbals, and feel the frailness of their feet on the shell of the earth.

H   Then I knew that the prophecy had been true, and that their prophet had not failed them. The long-looked for revelation had come. Greenmantle had appeared at last to an awaiting people.

I   While this critical conception of school knowledge cannot, of course, in and of itself transform either education or society, it is surely 'an essential first step' in generating more emancipatory practices.

These are obviously endings from a variety of texts. Endings A and D both leave the last word to an informant. Ending D is from Harriet Rosenberg's (1988: 211) ethnography of an Alpine village changed from a farming community to a ski-ing resort; A is from Hirschon's (1989: 248) ethnography of a Greek refugee community. It is quite a common strategy in academic writing, and in good journalism. Fitzgerald (1987: 119) lets a gay man summarize the impact of AIDS on San Francisco gay life:

As he was leaving, he asked me for a date. A date! I was shocked. He was, I gathered, looking for commitment. He was looking for a lifelong partnership.

This contrasts the cheerful promiscuity of the pre-AIDS Castro district, with the next generation's desire for fidelity. Walker (1988: 170) uses the same device when we leave his Australian young men:

> On this point let Mosey have the last word. As we were discussing the writing of this book:
> *Mosey (laughing):* A thought just come to me. Are you gurna be comin' to my house in twenty-five years' time sayin' 'How's mid-life crisis goin'?'

The closing paragraph of Walker's book shows a second common strategy: looking forward to the next project. Ending B, from Wade Davis (1986: 263), is so enigmatic it is unclear whether research is going ahead, or life itself is ending. Endings G and H are written in a similarly enigmatic and prophetic style, and seem similar. Yet H is the thunderous conclusion to John Buchan's (1916: 271) *Greenmantle*, and G from Colin Thubron's (1968: 185) travel book about the Lebanon.

In complete contrast are the conclusions which are indisputably academic; E, F and I. These are from Salmone (1986: 206) about Greek refugees, Delamont and Galton (1986: 242–3) and Valli (1986: 209–10). They are apparently very different from the others, yet Salmone is on the same subject as Hirschon, and both closely related to extract C from Loizos (1981: 187) about Cypriot refugees. The Loizos example is partially similar to the Hirschon, but one of the informants has not really had the last word, the superior wisdom of the outsider actually completes the book. In style he is closer to the Delamont and Galton extract, with a generalized comment about the state of schooling. The endings of the other books to which regular reference has been made are most commonly of that pattern, for example:

> Of course there are other contexts of medical education. I have concentrated on only one. But it is one which is of particular importance, making as it does the medical student's first initiation into the clinical culture which lies at the heart of the profession of medicine.
> (Atkinson, 1997a: 122)

> Over the next few years, the public have been given an opportunity to participate in the debate about what state secondary schools should be doing, and they should seize it. Only by doing so will they really be able to judge which schools are delivering the goods – effectively, efficiently and economically.
> (Stanley, 1989: 170)

It is clear from this that there is no uniform way to conclude an ethno-graphic work. The readers can judge which style is preferable for their own publications.

The next project

Qualitative methods are addictive. The ending of each project is likely to overlap with the start of the successor. This volume has looked back to my St Luke's work (done in 1969–71) and the ORACLE project (1976–81), as well as forward. Flecker's pilgrims kept pressing on because they hoped to discover: … a prophet who can understand Why men were born … Whatever one searches for, every project should bear within it the seeds of the next one.

Key reading

The key reading for this chapter is yours. By now you should have written a paper of your own.

Bibliography

Abbott, A. (1999) *Department and Discipline*, Chicago: University of Chicago Press.

Abbott, E. and Beckinridge, S. (1916) *Truancy and Non-Attendance in the Chicago Schools*, Chicago: University of Chicago Press.

Abi-Nader, J. (1990) 'A house for my mother', *Anthropology and Education Quarterly*, 21, 1, 41–58.

Abu-Lughod, L. (1986) *Veiled Sentiments: Honor and Poetry in a Bedouin Society*, Berkeley: University of California Press.

Adkins, L. (1995) *Gendered Work*, Buckingham: Open University Press.

Adler, P. and Adler, P. (1998) *Peer Power*, New Brunswick, NJ: Rutgers University Press.

Aggleton, P. (1987) *Rebels Without a Cause*, London: Falmer Press.

Altheide, D.L. (1980) 'Leaving the newsroom', in W.B. Shaffir, R.A. Stebbins, and A. Turowetz (eds) *Fieldwork Experience: Qualitative Approaches to Social Research*, New York: St Martin's Press.

Angus, L.B. (1988) *Continuity and Change in Catholic Schooling*, London: Falmer Press.

Anon (1930) *The Park School, Glasgow, 1880–1930*, Glasgow and Edinburgh: William Hedge.

——(1954) *Croydon High School '80th' Birthday Book*, Croydon: Croydon High School.

Arnot, M., David, M. and Weiner, G. (1999) *Closing the Gender Gap*, Cambridge: Polity.

Aschenbrenner, S. (1975) *Lifelines*, New York: Holt, Rinehart and Winston.

——(1986) *Life in a Changing Greek Village*, Dubuque, IA: Kendall/Hunt.

Ashmore, M., Myers, G. and Potter, J. (1995) 'Discourse, rhetoric and reflexivity', in S. Jasanoff, G.A. Markle, J.C. Petersen and T. Pinch (eds) *Handbook of Science and Technology Studies*, Thousand Oaks, CA: Sage.

Atkinson, P.A. (1981) *The Clinical Experience*, Farnborough: Gower.

——(1984a) 'Wards and deeds', in R.G. Burgess (ed.) *The Research Process in Educational Settings*, London: Falmer Press.

——(1984b) 'Training for certainty', *Social Science and Medicine*, 19, 949–56.

——(1987) 'Man's best hospital and the mug and muffin: an innocent ethnographer meets American medicine', in N.P. McKeganey and S. Cunningham-Burley (eds) *Enter the Sociologist*, Aldershot: Avebury.

——(1989) 'Goffman's poetics', *Human Studies*, 12, 59–76.

——(1990) *The Ethnographic Imagination*, London: Routledge.

——(1992) *Understanding Ethnographic Texts*, Newbury Park, CA: Sage.

——(1996) *Sociological Readings and Re-Readings*, Aldershot: Ashgate.

——(1997a) *The Clinical Experience* (2nd edition), Aldershot: Ashgate.

——(1997b) 'Narrative turn or blind alley?', *Qualitative Health Research*, 7, 3, 325–44.

Atkinson, P.A. and Delamont, S. (1980) 'The two traditions in educational ethnography: sociology and anthropology compared', *British Journal of Sociology of Education*, 1, 2, 139–52.

Atkinson, P.A. and Silverman, D. (1997) 'Kundera's *Immortality*: the interview society and the invention of the self', *Qualitative Inquiry*, 3, 304–25.

Atkinson, P.A., Delamont, S. and Beynon, J. (1988) 'In the beginning was the bunsen', *Qualitative Studies in Education*, 1, 4, 315–28.

Atkinson, P.A., Delamont, S. and Hammersley, M. (1988) 'Qualitative research traditions', *Review of Educational Research*, 58, 2, 231–50.

Atkinson, P.A., Coffey, A. and Delamont, S. (1999) 'Ethnography: post, past and present', *Journal of Contemporary Ethnography*, 28, 5, 460–71.

Atkinson, P.A., Coffey, A., Delamont, S., Lofland, J. and Lofland, L. (eds) (2001) *Handbook of Ethnography*, London: Sage.

Au, K. H.-P. (1980) 'Participation structures in a reading lesson with Hawaiian children', *Anthropology and Education Quarterly*, 11, 2, 91–115.

Ball, S. (1980) 'Initial encounters', in P. Woods (ed.) *Pupil Strategies*, London: Croom Helm.

——(1990) *Politics and Policy Making in Education*, London: Routledge.

Ball, S.J. and Goodson, I.F. (eds) (1985) *Teachers' Lives and Careers*, London: Falmer Press.

Barley, N. (1983) *The Innocent Anthropologist*, Harmondsworth: Penguin.

——(1986) *A Plague of Caterpillars*, Harmondsworth: Penguin.

Barr, B. (1984) *Histories of Girls Schools and Related Biographical Material*, Leicester: University of Leicester School of Education.

Bates, H. and Wells, A.A.M. (1962) *A History of Shrewsbury High School 1885–1960*, Shrewsbury: Wilding.

Bauman, R. (1982) 'Ethnography of children's folklore', in P. Gilmore and A.A. Glatthorn (eds) *Children In and Out of School*, Washington, DC: Center for Applied Linguistics.

Beale, D. (1904) *History of the Cheltenham Ladies' College 1853–1904*, Cheltenham: 'Looker-on' Printing Works.

Becker, H.S. (1952a) 'The career of the Chicago public schoolteacher', *American Journal of Sociology* 57, 470–7.

——(1952b) 'Social-class variations in the teacher–pupil relationship', *Journal of Educational Sociology*, 25, 451–65.

——(1967) 'Whose side are we on?', *Social Problems*, 14, 3, 239–248.

——(1971) Footnote, added to the paper by M. Wax and R. Wax (1971) 'Great tradition, little tradition and formal education', in M. Wax, S. Diamond and F. Gearing (eds) *Anthropological Perspectives on Education*, pp. 3–27, New York: Basic Books.

——(1986) *Writing for Social Scientists: How to Start and Finish Your Thesis, Book or Article*, Chicago: University of Chicago Press.

——(1998) *Tricks of the Trade*, Chicago: University of Chicago Press.

Becker, H.S., Geer, B., Hughes E.C. and Strauss, A.L. (1961) *Boys in White*, Chicago: University of Chicago Press.

Becker, H.S., Geer, B. and Hughes, H.M. (1968) *Making the Grade*, Chicago: University of Chicago Press.

Behar, R. and Gordon, D. (eds) (1995) *Women Writing Culture*, Los Angeles: University of California Press.

Bell, C. and Encel, S. (eds) (1978) *Inside the Whale*, Rushcutters Bay: Pergamon.

Bell, C. and Newby, H. (eds) (1977) *Doing Sociological Research*, London: Allen and Unwin.

Bell, C. and Roberts, H. (eds) (1984) *Social Researching*, London: Routledge.

Bell, E.M. (1939) *Francis Holland School*, London: Waterlow.

Bennett, G. (1983) ' "Rocky the police dog: and other tales": traditional narrative in an occupational corpus', *Lore and Language*, 3, 8, 1–19.

Bernstein, B. (1971) 'On the classification and framing of educational knowledge', in M.F.D. Young (ed.) *Knowledge and Control*, London: Collier-Macmillan.

——(1974) 'Class and pedagogies: visible and invisible', in B. Bernstein, *Class Codes and Control*, vol. 3, London, Routledge and Kegan Paul.

Best, R. (1983) *We've All Got Scars: What Boys and Girls Learn in Elementary School*, Bloomington: Indiana University Press.

Bett, M. (1999) *Independent Review of Higher Education Pay and Conditions*, London: Stationery Office.

Beynon, J. (1983) 'Ways-in and staying-in: fieldwork as problem solving', in M. Hammersley (ed.) *The Ethnography of Schooling: Methodological Issues*, Driffield, N. Humberside: Nafferton Books.

——(1985) *Initial Encounters in the Secondary School*, London: Falmer Press.

——(1987) 'Zombies in dressing gowns', in N.P. McKeganey and S. Cunningham-Burley (eds) *Enter the Sociologist: Reflections on the Practice of Sociology*, Aldershot: Avebury.

Beynon, J. and Atkinson, P. (1984) 'Pupils as data-gatherers: mucking and sussing', in S. Delamont (ed.) *Readings on Interaction in the Classroom*, London and New York: Methuen.

Blatchford, P., Battle, S. and Mays, J. (1982) *The First Transition*, Windsor: NFER.

Bloom, S.W. (1973) *Power and Dissent in the Medical School*, New York: Free Press.

——(1979) 'Socialization for the physician's role', in E. Shapiro and L.M. Lowenstein (eds) *Becoming a Physician*, Cambridge, MA: Ballinger.

——(1988) 'Structure and ideology in medical education', *Journal of Health and Social Behaviour*, 29, 4, 294–306.

Bloor, M., Frankland, J., Thomas, M. and Robson, K. (2001) *Focus Groups in Social Research*, London: Sage.

Bluebond-Langer, M. (1978) *The Private Worlds of Dying Children*, Princeton, NJ: Princeton University Press.

Bogdan, R. and Taylor, S.J. (1975) *Introduction to Qualitative Research Methods*, New York: Wiley.

Boon, J.A. (1982) *Other Tribes, Other Scribes*, Cambridge: Cambridge University Press.

Booth, W.C., Colomb, G.G. and Williams, J.M. (1995) *The Craft of Research*, Chicago: University of Chicago Press.

Borman, K. (1981) 'Review of recent case studies on equity and schooling', in R.G. Corwin (ed.) *Research on Educational Organizations*, Greenwich, Conn.: JAI Press.

Bossert, S.T. (1979) *Tasks and Social Relationships in Classrooms: A Study of Institutional Organization and its Consequences*, Cambridge: Cambridge University Press.

Bowen, E. (1954) *Return to Laughter*, London: Gollancz.

Broadhead, R.S. (1983) *The Private Lives and Professional Identity of Medical Students*, New Brunswick: Transaction.

Brodribb, S. (1992) *Nothing Matters*, Melbourne: Spinifex.

Brooks, A. (1997) *Academic Women*, Buckingham: Open University Press.

Brown, P. (1987) *Schooling Ordinary Kids: Inequality, Unemployment and the New Vocationalism*, London: Tavistock.

Brunvand, J. (1983) *The Vanishing Hitchhiker*, London: Picador.

——(1984) *The Choking Doberman*, New York: W.W. Norton.

Bryan, K.A. (1980) 'Pupil perceptions of transfer', in A. Hargreaves and L. Tickle (eds) *Middle Schools*, London: Harper and Row.

Bryman, A. and Burgess, R.G. (eds) (1994) *Analysing Qualitative Data*, London: Routledge.

Bryman, A. and Hardy, M. (eds) (2002) *Handbook of Data Analysis*, London: Sage.

Buchan, J. (1916) *Greenmantle*, reprinted 1964, Harmondsworth: Peacock.

Bucher, R. (1970) 'Social process and power in a medical school', in M.N. Zald (ed.) *Power in Organizations*, Nashville: Vanderbilt University Press.

Bucher, R. and Stelling, J.G. (1977) *Becoming Professional*, Beverley Hills, CA: Sage.

Bullivant, D.M. (1978) *The Way of Tradition*, Victoria. Australian Council for Educational Research.

Burgess, R.G. (1983) *Experiencing Comprehensive Education*, London: Methuen.

——(1984a) *In the Field*, London: Allen and Unwin.

——(ed.) (1984b) *The Research Process in Educational Settings*, London: Falmer Press.

——(ed.) (1985a) *Field Methods in the Study of Education*, London: Falmer Press.

——(ed.) (1985b) *Strategies of Educational Research*, London: Falmer Press.

——(ed.) (1985c) *Issues in Educational Research*, London: Falmer Press.

——(1988a) 'Whatever happened to the Newsom course?', in A. Pollard, J. Purvis and G. Walford (eds) *Education, Training and the New Vocationalism: Experience and Policy*, Milton Keynes: Open University Press.

——(1988b) 'Examining classroom practice using diaries and diary interviews', in P. Woods and A. Pollard (eds) *Sociology and Teaching*, London: Croom Helm.

——(1989a) 'The politics of pastoral care', in S. Walker and l. Barton (eds) *Politics and the Processes of Schooling*, Milton Keynes: Open University Press.

——(ed.) (1989b) *The Ethics of Educational Research*, London, Falmer Press.

Burnet, J.F. (ed.) (1984) *Girls' School Yearbook*, London: Adam and Charles Black.

Burnett, J.H. (1973) 'Event description and analysis in the microethnography of urban classrooms', in F.A.J. Ianni and E. Storey (eds) *Cultural Relevance and Educational Issues*, Boston: Little, Brown.

Burrage, H. (1983) 'Women university teachers of natural science 1971–72', *Social Studies of Science*, 13, 147–60.

Cahill, S.E. (1985) 'Meanwhile backstage', *Urban Life*, 14, 1, 33–58.

Campbell-Jones, S. (1979) *In Habit: An Anthropological Study of Working Nuns*, London: Faber.

Carr, C. (1955) *The Spinning Wheel: City of Cardiff High School for Girls 1895–1955*, Cardiff: Western Mail and Echo.

Carter, I. (1990) *Ancient Cultures of Conceit*, London: Routledge.

Carter, K. and Delamont, S. (eds) (1996) *Qualitative Research: the Emotional Dimension*, Aldershot: Ashgate.

Casanova, U. (1991) *Elementary School Secretaries*, Newbury Park, CA.: Corwin Press.

Cesara, M. (1982) *Reflections of a Woman Anthropologist*, New York: Academic Press.

Chaff, S. (ed.) (1977) *Women in Medicine*, Lanham, MD: Scarecrow Press.

Charlton, J. and Hertz, R. (1989) 'Guarding against boredom – security specialists in the US Air Force', *Journal of Contemporary Ethnography*, 18, 3, 299–326.

Chase, S.E. (1995) *Ambiguous Empowerment*, Amherst: University of Massachusetts Press.

Chesnut, A. (1997) *Born Again in Brazil*, New Brunswick, NJ: Rutgers University Press.

Clarke, A.K. (1953) *A History of Cheltenham Ladies' College 1853–1953*, London: Faber and Faber.

——(1979) *A History of the Cheltenham Ladies' College 1853–1979*, Great Glemham, Saxmundham: John Catt.

Cleave, S., Jowett, S. and Bate, M. (1982) *And So to School*, Windsor: NFER-Nelson.

Clifford, J. and Marcus, G.E. (eds) (1986) *Writing Culture*, Berkeley: University of California Press.

Coffey, A. (1999) *The Ethnographic Self*, London: Sage.

Coffey, A. and Atkinson, P.A. (1996) *Making Sense of Qualitative Data*, Thousand Oaks, CA: Sage.

Coffey, A. and Delamont, S. (2000) *Feminism and the Classroom Teacher*, London: Falmer Press.

Coffield, F., Borrill, C. and Marshall, S. (1986) *Growing up at the Margins*, Milton Keynes: Open University Press.

Collier, J. (1997) *From Duty to Desire*, Princeton, NJ: Princeton University Press.

Collins, H. and Pinch, T. (1993) *The Golem*, Cambridge: Cambridge University Press.

——(1998) *The Golem at Large*, Cambridge: Cambridge University Press.

Colombotos, J. (1988) 'Continuities in the sociology of medical education', *Journal of Health and Social Behaviour*, 29, 4, 271–8.

Connolly, P. (1998) *Racism, Gender Identities and Young Children*, London: Routledge.

Connolly, P. and Troyna, B. (eds) (1998) *Researching Racism in Education*, Buckingham: Open University Press.

Conrad, P. (1988) 'Learning to doctor', *Journal of Health and Social Behaviour*, 29, 4, 323–32.

Coombs, R. H. (1978) *Mastering Medicine*, New York: Free Press.

Correll, S. (1995) 'The ethnography of an electronic bar: the lesbian café', *Journal of Contemporary Ethnography*, 24, 3, 270–98.

Corsaro, W. (1981) 'Entering the child's world – Research strategies for field entry and data collection in a preschool setting', in J.L. Green and C. Wallat (eds) *Ethnography and Language in Educational Settings*, Norwood, NJ: Ablex.

——(1997) *The Sociology of Childhood*, Thousand Oaks, CA: Pine Forge Press.

Cortazzi, M. (1991) *Primary Teaching: How It Is*, London: David Fulton.

——(1993) *Narrative Analysis*, London: Falmer Press.

——(2001) 'Narrative analysis in ethnography', in P.A. Atkinson, A. Coffey, S. Delamont, J. Lofland and L. Lofland (eds) *Handbook of Ethnography*, London: Sage.

Crapanzano, V. (1985) *Waiting*, London: Granada.

Croll, P. (1986) *Systematic Classroom Observation*, London: Falmer Press.

Cross, A. (1970) *Poetic Justice*, New York: Avon.

——(1971) *The Theban Mysteries*, New York: Avon.

——(1976) *The Question of Max*, London: Gollancz.

——(1981) *A Death in the Faculty*, London: Gollancz.

——(1984) *Sweet Death, Kind Death*, New York: Ballantine.

——(1988) *No word from Winifred*, London, Virago.

——(1990) *A Trap for Fools*, London: Virago.

——(1992) *The Players Come Again*, London: Virago,

——(1995) *An Imperfect Spy*, New York: Ballantine.

Cuba, L. and Cocking, J. (1994) *How to Write about the Social Sciences*, London: Harper and Row.

Cunningham, P. (1976) *Local History of Education in England and Wales: A Bibliography* (Educational Administration and History: Monograph no. 4), Leeds: Museum of the History of Education, University of Leeds.

Cusick, P. (1973) *Inside High School: the Students' World*, New York: Holt, Rinehart and Winston.

——(1983) *The Egalitarian Ideal and the American High School*, New York: Longmans.

Danforth, L.M. (1989) *Firewalking and Religious Healing*, Princeton: Princeton University Press.

Darmanin, M. (1990) 'Sociological perspectives on schooling in Malta', unpublished PhD thesis, University of Wales College of Cardiff.

Datnow, A. (1997) 'Using gender to preserve tracking's status hierarchy', *Anthropology and Education Quarterly* 28(2): 204–28.

  (1998) *The Gender Politics of Educational Change*, London: Falmer Press.

Davidson, J. (1997) *Courtesans and Fishcakes*, London: Fontana.

Davies, L. (1984) *Pupil Power: Deviance and Gender in School*, London and Philadelphia: Falmer Press.

Davis, J. (1987) *Libyan Politics*, London: Taurus.

Davis, N.Z. (1985) *The Return of Martin Guerre*, Harmondsworth: Penguin.

Davis, W. (1986) *The Serpent and the Rainbow*, London, Collins.

De Holmes, R.B. (1983) '*Shabono*: scandal or superb social science?', *American Anthropologist*, 85, 3, 65–9.

de Marrais, K.B. (ed.) (1998) *Inside Stories*, Mahwah, NJ: Erlbaum.

de Marrais, K.B., Nelson, P.A. and Baker, J.H. (1992) 'Meaning in mud', *Anthropology and Education Quarterly*, 23, 2, 89–107.

Deegan, M.J. (1987) 'Symbolic interaction and the study of women', in M.J. Deegan and M. Hill (eds) *Women and Symbolic Interaction*, London: Allen and Unwin.

——(1988) *Jane Addams and the Men of the Chicago School*, New Brunswick, NJ: Transaction Press.

——(1995) 'The second sex and the Chicago School', in G.A. Fine (ed.) *A Second Chicago School?*, Chicago: University of Chicago Press.

Del Vecchio Good, M.J. (1989) 'Disabling practitioners', *Orthopsychiatry*, 59, 303–9.

Delamont, S. (1973) 'Academic conformity observed', unpublished PhD thesis, University of Edinburgh.

——(1983) 'Salmon, chicken, cake and tears: deciphering the wedding breakfast', in A. Murcott (ed.) *Essays on the Sociology of Food*, Farnborough: Gower.

——(1984a) 'The old girl network: reflections on the fieldwork at St Luke's', in R. Burgess (ed.) *The Research Process in Educational Settings*, Brighton: Falmer Press.

——(1984b) 'Lessons from St Luke's: reflections on a study of Scottish classroom life', in B. Dockrell (ed.) *An Attitude of Mind*, Edinburgh: SCRE.

——(1987a) 'Three blind spots?', *Social Studies of Science*, 17, 1, 163–70.

——(1987b) 'Clean baths and dirty women', in N. McKeganey and S. Cunningham-Burley (eds) *Enter the Sociologist*, Aldershot: Avebury.

——(1989a) *Knowledgeable Women: Structuralism and the Reproduction of Elites*, London: Routledge.

——(1989b) 'The nun in the toilet: urban legends and educational research', *Qualitative Studies in Education*, 2, 3, 191–202.

——(1989c) 'The fingernail on the blackboard: a sociological perspective on science education', *Studies in Science Education*, 16, 25–46.

——(1991) 'The HIT LIST and other horror stories', *Sociological Review*, 39, 2, 238–59.

——(1992) 'Old fogies and intellectual women', *Women's History Review*, 1, 1, 38–61.

——(1993a) 'The beech-covered hillside', in G. Walford (ed.). *The Private Schooling of Girls*, London: Woburn Press.

——(1993b) 'Distant dangers and forgotten standards', *Women's History Review*, 2, 2, 233–52.

——(1997) 'Fuzzy borders and the fifth moment', *British Journal of Sociology of Education*, 18, 4, 601–6.

——(1999) 'Gender and the discourse of derision', *Research Papers in Education*, 14, 1, 3–21.

——(2000a) 'The anomalous beasts', *Sociology*, 34, 1, 95–112.

——(2000b) 'Confessions of a ragpicker', in H. Hodkinson (ed.) *Feminism and Educational Research Methodologies,* Manchester: Manchester Metropolitan University.

——(2001) 'Is the golem female?', unpublished paper.

Delamont, S. and Atkinson, P.A. (1995) *Fighting Familiarity*, Cresskill, NJ: Hampton.

Delamont, S. and Galton, M. (1986) *Inside the Secondary Classroom*, London: Routledge.

——(1987) 'Anxieties and anticipations', in A. Pollard (ed.) *Children and their Primary Schools*, London: Falmer Press.

Delamont, S., Atkinson, P.A. and Parry, O. (1997) *Supervising the PhD*, Buckingham: Open University Press.

——(2000) *The Doctoral Experience*, London: Falmer Press.

Delamont, S., Coffey, A. and Atkinson, P.A. (2000) 'The twilight years?', *Qualitative Studies in Education*, 13, 3, 223–38.

Dennis, N., Henriques, F. and Slaughter, C. (1959) *Coal is Our Life: an Analysis of a Yorkshire Mining Community*, London: Tavistock.

Denzin, N. and Lincoln, Y. (eds) (1994) *Handbook of Qualitative Research*, Thousand Oaks, CA: Sage.

——(eds) (2000) *Handbook of Qualitative Research* (2nd edition), Thousand Oaks, CA: Sage.

Dewalt, M.W. and Troxell, B.K. (1989) 'Old Order Mennonite one-room school: a case study', *Anthropology and Education Quarterly*, 20, 4, 308–19.

Dey, I. (1993) *Qualitative Data Analysis*, London: Routledge and Kegan Paul.

Dobbert, M.L. (1982) *Ethnographic Research*, New York: Praeger.

Donner, F. (1982) *Shabono*, London: Bodley Head.

Dumont, R.V. and Wax, M.L. (1971) 'Cherokee school society and the intercultural classroom', in *School and Society: A Sociological Reader*, London, Routledge and Kegan Paul.

Dunaway, D.K. and Baum, W.K. (eds) (1996) *Oral History: An Interdisciplinary Anthology*, Walnut Creek, CA: AltaMira.

Dunning, B. (ed.) (1931) *Graham Street Memories: Francis Holland Church of England School for Girls*, London: Hazell, Watson and Viney.

Duthie, G.I. and Duncan, H.M.E. (1967) *Albyn School Centenary*, Aberdeen: University of Aberdeen Press.

Dyhouse, C. (1995) *No Distinction of Sex?*, London: UCL Press.

Dyson, A. (1990) Paper presented at the AERA Meeting, Boston.

Eder, D. and Corsaro, W. (1999) 'Ethnographic studies of children and youth', *Journal of Contemporary Ethnography*, 28, 5, 520–31.

Edmondson, R. (1984) *Rhetoric in Sociology*, London: Macmillan.

Education Authorities Directory and Annual (1986) Merstham: School Government Publishing.

Edwards, A.D. and Westgate, D.P.G. (1994) *Investigating Classroom Talk* (2nd edition), London: Falmer Press.

Een, J.D. and Rosenberg-Dishman, M.B. (eds) (1978) *Women and Society – Citations 3001 to 6000, an Annotated Bibliography*, Beverley Hills: Sage.

Eggleston, J. and Delamont, S. (1983) *Supervision of Students for Research Degrees with a Special Reference to Educational Studies*, Kendall: Dixons Printers for British Educational Research Association.

Eichler, M. (1988) *Nonsexist Research Methods: a Practical Guide*, Boston: Allen and Unwin.

Eichna, L.W. (1980) 'Medical school education 1975–1979', *New England Journal of Medicine*, 303, 13, 727–34.

Eickelman, D. (1978) 'The art of memory', *Comparative Studies in Sociology and History*, 20, 4, 485–516.

——(1985) *Knowledge and Power in Morocco*, Princeton, NJ: Princeton University Press.

Eisner, E. (1997) 'The promise and perils of alternative forms of data representation', *Educational Researcher*, 26, 6, 4–10.

Eisner, E. and Peshkin, A. (eds) (1990) *Qualitative Inquiry in Education*, New York: Teachers College Press.

Ellis, C. and Bochner, A.P. (eds) (1996) *Composing Ethnography*, Walnut Creek, CA: AltaMira.

Ellis, R. and Delamont, S. (1979) *Statutory and Voluntary Response to Domestic Violence in Wales: a Pilot Study*, Sociological Research Unit, University College, Cardiff (Final Report to WO/DHSS).

Emerson, R.M., Fretz, R.I. and Shaw, L.L. (1995) *Writing Ethnographic Fieldnotes*, Chicago: University of Chicago Press.

——(2001) 'Participant observation and fieldnotes', in P. Atkinson, A. Coffey, S. Delamont, J. Lofland and L. Lofland (eds) *Handbook of Ethnography*, London: Sage.

Epstein, D. (1998) 'Are you a girl or are you a teacher?', in G. Walford (ed.) *Doing Research about Education*, London: Falmer Press.

Epstein, D. and Johnson, R. (1998) *Schooling Sexualities*, Buckingham: Open University Press.

Epstein, D., Elwood, J., Hey, V. and Maw, J. (eds) (1998) *Failing Boys?*, Buckingham: Open University Press.

Eskola, K. (1992) 'Women and the media-related intellectual public sphere', in N. Kauppi and P. Sulkunen (eds) *Vanguards of Modernity*, Jyvaskyla: University of Jyvaskyla Press.

Evans, D. and Wragg, E.C. (1969) 'The use of a verbal interaction analysis technique with severely subnormal children', *Journal of Mental Subnormality*, December.

Evetts, J. (1996) *Gender and Career in Science and Engineering*, London: Taylor & Francis.

Fabian, J. (1983) *Time and the Other*, New York: Columbia University Press.

Fermor, P.L. (1958) *Mani*, London: John Murray.

——(1966) *Roumeli*, London: John Murray.

——(1986) *Between the Woods and the Water*, London: John Murray.

Festinger, L., Riecken, W. and Schachter, S. (1964 [1956]) *When Prophecy Fails*, New York: Harper and Row.

Field, D. (1989) *Nursing the Dying*, London: Tavistock.

Fielding, N. (2001) 'Computer applications in qualitative research', in P. Atkinson, A. Coffey, S. Delamont, J. Lofland and L. Lofland (eds) *Handbook of Ethnography*, London: Sage.

Fielding, N.G. and Fielding, J.L. (1986) *Linking Data*, Beverley Hills, Sage.

Finders, M.J. (1997) *Just Girls*, New York: Teachers College Press.

Fine, G.A. (1981) 'Rude words', *Maledicta*, 5, 51–68.

——(1983) *Shared Fantasy*, Chicago: University of Chicago Press.

——(1985) 'Occupational aesthetics', *Urban Life*, 14, 1, 3–32.

——(1987) *With the Boys*, Chicago: University of Chicago Press.

——(1988) 'Good children and dirty play', *Play and Culture*, 1, 43–56.

——(1992) 'The culture of production: aesthetic choices and constraints in culinary work', *American Journal of Sociology*, 97, 1268–94.

——(ed.) (1995) *A Second Chicago School?*, Chicago: University of Chicago Press.

——(1996) *Kitchens*, Berkeley, CA: University of California Press.

——(1998) *Morel Tales*, Cambridge, MA: Harvard University Press.

Fine, G.A. and Sandstrom, K.L. (1988) *Knowing Children*, Beverley Hills, CA: Sage.

Fine, M. (1991) *Framing Dropouts*, Albany, NY: State University of New York Press.

——(1993) 'Sexuality, schooling and adolescent females', in L. Weis and M. Fine (eds) *Beyond Silenced Voices*, Albany, NY: State University of New York Press.

Fine, M. and Weis, L. (1998) *The Unknown City*, Boston: Beacon Press.

Fine, M., Weis, L., Powell, L.C. and Wong, L.M. (eds) (1997) *Off-White*, New York: Routledge.

Fitzgerald, F. (1987) *Cities on a Hill*, London: Picador.

Flanders, N.A. (1970) *Analysing Teaching Behavior*, New York: Addison Wesley.

Flecker, J.E. (1922) *Hassan. The Story of Hassan of Baghdad and How He Came to Make the Golden Journey to Samarkand*, London: Heinemann.

——(1947) *Collected Poems*, London: Secker and Warburg.

Fletcher, S. (1984) *Women First*, London: Athlone Press.

Fordham, S. (1993) 'Those loud Black girls: (Black) women, silence and gender "passing" in the Academy', *Anthropology and Education Quarterly* 24(1): 3–32.

——(1996) *Blacked Out*, Chicago: University of Chicago Press.

Foster, P., Gomm, R. and Hammersley, M. (1996) *Constructing Educational Research*, London: Falmer Press.

Fox, M.F. (ed.) (1985), *Scholarly Writing and Publishing: Issues, Problems and Solutions*, Boulder, CO: Westview.

Francis, B. (1998) *Power Plays*, Stoke-on-Trent: Trentham Books.

Fredericks, M.A. and Munday, P. (1976) *The Making of a Physician*, Chicago: Loyola University Press.

Freeman, S.T. (1970) *Neighbors: the Social Contract in a Castilian Hamlet*, Chicago: University of Chicago Press.

——(1979) *The Pasiegos: Spaniards in Noman's Land*, Chicago: University of Chicago Press.

French, J. and French, P. (1984) 'Sociolinguistics and gender divisions', in S. Acker, J. Megarry, S. Nisbett and E. Hayle (eds) *Women and Education*, London: Kogan Page.

Furlong, V. (1976) 'Interaction sets in the classroom: towards a study of pupil knowledge', in M. Hammersley and P. Woods (eds) *The Process of Schooling: a Sociological Reader*, London: Routledge and Kegan Paul.

Galton, M. and Delamont, S. (1976) *Final Report on PhD/PGCE Chemistry Courses*, Leicester: Leicester University School of Education.

——(1985) 'Speaking with forked tongue? Two styles of observation in the Oracle project', in R.G. Burgess (ed.) *Field Methods in the Study of Education*, London: Falmer Press.

Galton, M. and Willcocks, J. (1983) *Moving from the Primary Classroom*, London: Routledge and Kegan Paul.

Gamradt, J. (1998) 'Studying up in educational anthropology', in K.B. de Marrais (ed.) *Inside Stories*, Mahwah, NJ: Lawrence Erlbaum.

Geer, B. (1964) 'First days in the field', in P. Hammond (ed.) *Sociologists at Work*, New York: Basic Books.

——(1966) 'Occupational commitment and the teaching profession', *School Review* 77, 1, 31–47.

——(ed.) (1972) *Learning to Work*, Beverley Hills, CA: Sage.

General Medical Council (1993) *Tomorrow's Doctors*, London: GMC.

Gewirtz, S., Ball, S. and Bowe, R. (1995) *Markets, Choice and Equity in Education*, Buckingham: Open University Press.

Gibson, M. (1987a) 'The school performance of immigrant minorities', *Anthropology and Education Quarterly*, 18, 4, 262–75.

——(1987b) 'Punjabi immigrants in an American high school', in G. Spindler and L. Spindler (eds) *Interpretive Ethnography of Education: At Home and Abroad*, Hillsdale NJ: Erlbaum.

——(1988) *Accommodation without Assimilation*, Ithaca, NY: Cornell University Press.

Gilbert, J. and Watts, D.M. (1983) 'Concepts, misconceptions and alternative conceptions', *Studies in Science Education*, 10, 61–98.

Gilmore, P. and Glatthorn, A.A. (eds) (1982) *Children In and Out of School*, Washington, DC: Center for Applied Linguistics.

Glaser, B.G. and Strauss, A.L. (1967) *The Discovery of Grounded Theory*, Chicago: Aldine.

Gleeson D. and Mardle, G. (1980) *Further Education or Training? A Case Study in the Theory and Practice of Day-Release Education*, London: Routledge and Kegan Paul.

Gluck, S.B. and Patai, D. (eds) (1991) *Women's Words: the Feminist Practice of Oral History*, London: Routledge.

Godber, J. and Hutchins, I. (eds) (1982) *A Century of Challenge: Bedford High School 1882–1982*, Bedford: Bedford High School.

Goetz, J.P. and LeCompte, M.D. (1984) *Ethnography and Qualitative Design in Educational Research*, New York: Academic Press.

Goffman, E. (1959) *The Presentation of Self in Everyday Life*, Harmondsworth,: Penguin.

——(1961) *Asylums: Essays on the Social Situation of Mental Patients and Other Inmates*, Harmondsworth: Penguin.

——(1971) *Relations in Public: Microstudies of the Public Order*, Harmondsworth: Penguin.

——(1992) 'An interview with Erving Goffman, 1980', *Research on Language and Social Interaction*, 26, 3, 317–48.

Good, B. (1994) *Medicine, Rationality and Experience*, Cambridge: Cambridge University Press.

Good, B. and Del Vecchio Good, M.J. (1993) 'Learning medicine', in S. Lindenbaum and M. Lock (eds) *Knowledge, Power and Practice*, Berkeley, CA: University of California Press.

Goodson, I. (1995) 'The story so far: personal knowledge and the political', *Qualitative Studies in Education*, 8, 89–98.

Gordon, T., Holland, J. and Lahelma, E. (2000) *Making Spaces*, London: Macmillan.

Gornick, V. (1990) *Women in Science*, New York: Touchstone.

Goto, S.T. (1997) 'Nerds, normal people and homeboys', *Anthropology and Education Quarterly*, 28, 1, 7–84.

Grant, C and Sleeter, C. (1986) *After the School Bell Rings*, London: Falmer Press.

Graves, R. (1960) *The Greek Myths* (two volumes), Harmondsworth: Penguin.

Grugeon, E. (1988a) 'Children's oral culture – a transitional experience?', in M. MacClure, T. Philips and A. Wilkinson (eds) *Oracy International*, Milton Keynes: Open University Press.

——(1988b) 'Underground knowledge: what the spies missed', *English in Education*, 22, 2 (Summer), 9–17.

Gussow, Z. (1964) 'The observer–observed relationship as information about structures in small group research', *Psychiatry*, 27, 236–47.

Guthrie, G.P. (1985) *A School Divided*, Hillsdale, NJ: Erlbaum.

Haas, J. and Shaffir, W. (1987) *Becoming Doctors*, Greenwich, CT: JAI Press.

Hafferty, F.W. (1988) 'Cadaver stories', *Journal of Health and Social Behaviour*, 29, 4, 344–56.

——(1991) *Into the Valley*, New Haven, CT: Yale University Press.

Hale, E.M. (1959) *Landsdowne House School, Murrayfield, Edinburgh 1879–1950*, Edinburgh: Landsdowne House Old Girls Guild.

Hall, T. (2000) 'At home with the young homeless', *International Journal of Social Research Methodology*, 3, 2, 121–33.

Hamilton, D. (1977) *In Search of Structure: Essays from a New Scottish Open-Plan Primary School*, London: Hodder and Stoughton.

Hammersley, M. and Atkinson, P. (1983) *Ethnography: Principles in Practice*, London: Tavistock.

——(1995) *Ethnography: Principles in Practice* (2nd edition). London: Routledge.

Hammond, P.E. (ed.) (1964) *Sociologists at Work: Essays on the Craft of Social Research*, New York: Basic Books.

Harding, S. (1986) *The Science Question in Feminism*, Milton Keynes: Open University Press.

Hargreaves, A. (1980) 'Synthesis and the study of strategies', in P. Woods (ed.) *Pupil Strategies*, London: Croom Helm.

——(1984) 'Contrastive rhetoric and extremist talk', in A. Hargreaves and P. Woods (eds) *Classrooms and Staffrooms*, Milton Keynes: Open University Press.

Hargreaves, D.H. (1967) *Social Relations in a Secondary School*, London: Routledge and Kegan Paul.

——(1980) 'The occupational culture of teachers', in P. Woods (ed.) *Teacher Strategies*, London: Croom Helm.

Hargreaves, D.H., Hester, S.K. and Mellor, F.J. (1975) *Deviance in Classrooms*, London: Routledge and Kegan Paul.

Hart, C. (1998) *Doing a Literature Review*, London: Sage.

Hart, R.A. (1979) *Children's Experience of Place*, New York: Irvington.

Hatch, A. (1987) 'Impression management in kindergarten classrooms', *Anthropology and Education Quarterly*, 18, 2, 100–15.

Haw, K. (1998) *Educating Muslim Girls*, Buckingham: Open University Press.

Haywood, P. and Wragg, E.C. (1978) *Evaluating the Literature, Rediguide 2*, Nottingham: University of Nottingham School of Education.

Heath, S.B. (1983) *Ways with Words*, Cambridge: Cambridge University Press.

Heiberg, M. (1989) *The Making of the Basque Nation*, Cambridge: Cambridge University Press.

Hemmings, A. (1996) 'Conflicting images', *Anthropology and Education Quarterly* 27(1): 20–50.

Herbert, C. (1989) *Talking of Silence*, London: Falmer Press.

Herzfeld, M. (1983) 'Semantic slippage and moral fall', *Journal of Modern Greek Studies*, 1, 1, 161–72.

Hey, V. (1997) *The Company She Keeps*, Buckingham: Open University Press.

Heyl, B. (1979) *The Madam as Entrepreneur: Career Management in House Prostitution*, New Brunswick, NJ: Transaction Books.

Hicklin, S. (1978) *Polished Corners 1878–1978*, Hatfield: Stellar Press.

Hillerman, T. (1971) *The Fly on the Wall*, New York: Harper and Row.

Hilliard, D.C. (1987) 'The rugby tour', in G.A. Fine (ed.) *Meaningful Play, Playful Meaning*, Champaign, IL: Humanities Publishers.

Hirschon, R. (1989) *Heirs of the Greek Catastrophe*, Oxford: Clarendon Press.

Hitchcock, G. and Hughes, D. (1989) *Research and the Teacher*, London: Routledge.

Hobbs, D. (1988) *Doing the Business*, Oxford: Clarendon Press.

Hockey, J. (1990) *Experiences of Death*, Edinburgh: Edinburgh University Press.

Hodkinson, P. and Bloomer, M. (2000) 'Stokingham Sixth Form College', *British Journal of Sociology of Education*, 21, 2, 187–202.

Holland, D.C. and Eisenhart, M.A. (1990) *Educated in Romance*, Chicago: University of Chicago Press.

Hollingshead, A.B. (1947) *Elmtown's Youth*, New York: John Wiley and Sons.

Hornsby-Smith, M.P. (1987) *Roman Catholics in England: Studies in Social Structure since the Second World War*, Cambridge: Cambridge University Press.

Horobin, G. and Davis, A. (eds) (1977) *Medical Encounters*, London: Croom Helm.

Hostetler, J.A. and Huntington, G.E. (1971) *Children in Amish Society: Socialisation and Community Education*, New York: Holt, Rinehart and Winston.

Hughes, H.M. (1961) *The Fantastic Lodge*, London: Arthur Barker.

Humphries, L. (1970) *Tearoom Trade: A Study of Homosexual Encounters in Public Places*, London: Duckworth.

Hymes, D. (1996) *Ethnography, Linguistics, Narrative Inequality*, London: Taylor & Francis.

Jackson, A. (ed.) (1987) *Anthropology at Home*, London: Tavistock.

Jackson, B. (1964) *Streaming: an Education System in Miniature*, London: Routledge and Kegan Paul.

Jackson, C. and Warin, J. (2000) 'The importance of gender as an aspect of identity at key transition points in compulsory education', *British Educational Research Journal*, 26, 3, 375–92.

Jackson, J.E. (1990) 'Déjà entendu: the liminal qualities of anthropological fieldnotes', *Journal of Contemporary Ethnography*, 19, 1, 8–43.

Jacob, E. (1987) 'Qualitative research traditions: a review', *Review of Educational Research*, 57, 1, 1–50.

James, A., Hockey, J. and Dawson, A. (eds) (1997) *After Writing Culture*, London: Routledge.

Jessor, R., Colby, A. and Shweder, R.A. (eds) (1996) *Being Changed by Cross-Cultural Encounters*, Chicago: University of Chicago Press.

Johnson, D.C. (1983) *Physicians in the Making*, San Francisco: Jossey-Bass.

Jones, B. and Balsom, D. (eds) (2000) *The Road to the National Assembly for Wales*, Cardiff: University of Wales Press.

Jordan, S., Boston, P., Macnamara, F. and Kozolanka, K. (2000) 'Some signposts for medical and nursing educational policy formulation for aboriginal healthcare', *Qualitative Studies in Education*, 13, 3, 307–24.

Jordon, R.A. and Kalcik, S.J. (eds) (1985) *Women's Folklore, Women's Culture*, Philadelphia: University of Pennsylvania Press.

Kalman, J. (2000) 'Learning to write in the street', *Qualitative Studies in Education*, 13, 2, 187–204.

Karakasidou, A. (1997) *Hills of Blood, Fields of Wheat*, Chicago: University of Chicago Press.

Karp, D.A. (1980) 'Observing behaviour in public places', in W.B. Shaffir, R.A. Stebbins and A. Turowetz (eds) *Fieldwork Experience*, New York: St Martin's Press

Kaufman, A. (1985) *Implementing Problem-Based Medical Education*, New York: Springer.

Keiser, R.L. (1979) *The Vice Lords: Warriors of the Streets* (fieldwork edition), New York: Holt, Rinehart and Winston.

Kelle, U. (ed.) (1995) *Computer-Aided Qualitative Data Analysis*, London: Sage.

Keller, E.F. (1985) *Reflections on Gender and Science*, London: Yale University Press.

——(1995) 'The origin, history and politics of the subject called "Gender and Science"', in S. Jasanoff, G. Markle, J. Peterson and T. Pinch (eds) *Handbook of Science and Technology Studies*, Thousand Oaks, CA: Sage.

Kendall, L. (2000) 'Oh no! I'm a nerd!' *Gender and Society*, 14, 2, 256–74.

Kenna, M.E. (1992) 'Changing places and altered perspectives', in J. Okely and H. Callaway (eds) *Anthropology and Autobiography*, London: Routledge.

King, R.A. (1978) *All Things Bright and Beautiful*, Chichester: Wiley.

Klass, P. (1987) *A Not Entirely Benign Procedure*, New York: Putnams.

Kleinfeld, J.S. (1979) *Eskimo School on the Andreafsky*, New York: Praeger.

Konner, M. (1987) *Becoming a Doctor*, New York: Viking.

Koromila, M. (1994) *In the Trail of Odysseus*, Norwich: Michael Russell.

Krieger, S. (1979) 'Research and the construction of a text', in N.K. Denzin (ed.) *Studies in Symbolic Interaction*, vol. 2, pp. 167–87, New York: JAI Press.

Kronenfeld, J.J. (1985) 'Publishing in journals', in M.F. Fox. (ed.) *Scholarly Writing and Publishing*, Boulder, CO: Westview Press.

Labov, W. (1972) 'The logic of nonstandard English' in A. Cashdan and E. Grugeon (eds) *Language in Education: a Source Book*, London: Routledge and Kegan Paul.

Lacey, C. (1970) *Hightown Grammar*, Manchester: Manchester University Press.

——(1977) *The Socialisation of Teachers*, London: Methuen.

Ladson-Billings, G. (1994) *The Dreamkeepers*, San Francisco: Jossey-Bass.

Langley, E. (1997) *The Lusty Lady*, Zurich: Scalo.

Lareau, A. and Shultz, J. (eds) (1996) *Journeys Through Ethnography*, Boulder, CO: Westview.

Larkin, R.W. (1979) *Suburban Youth in Cultural Crisis*, New York: Oxford University Press.

Lash, S. and Urry, J. (1993) *Economies of Signs and Space*, London: Sage.

Lawton, D. (1968) *Social Class, Language and Education*, London: Routledge and Kegan Paul.

Le Compte, M. and Preissle, J. (1994) *Ethnography and Qualitative Design in Educational Research*, New York: Academic Press.

Le Compte, M., Millroy, L. and Preissle, J. (eds) (1992) *Qualitative Research in Education*, New York: Academic Press.

Leacock, S. and Leacock, R. (1972) *Spirits of the Deep*, New York: Doubleday.

Lee, C.F. (1962) *The Real St Trinnean's: with Tributes to the School by Former Pupils*, Edinburgh: W. Brown.

Leech, B. (1986) *Full Circle*, Risca, Gwent: Starling Press.

Lees, S. (1986) *Losing Out*, London: Heinemann.

Leserman, J. (1981) *Men and Women in Medical School*, New York: Praeger.

Lesko, N. (1988) *Symbolising Society*, London: Falmer Press.

Levi, P. (1980) *The Hill of Kronos*, London: Zenith.

Lichtenstein, R. and Sinclair, I. (1999) *Rodinsky's Room*, London: Granta.

Liebow, E. (1967) *Tally's Corner*, Washington, DC: Little, Brown.

Light, D. (1980) *Becoming Psychiatrists*, New York: W.W. Norton.

——(1988) 'Towards a new sociology of medical education', *Journal of Health and Social Behaviour*, 29, 4, 307–22.

Lightwood, J. (1980) *The Park School 1880–1980*, Glasgow: Robert MacLehose.

Lipka, J. and McCarty, T.L. (1994) 'Changing the culture of schooling: Navajo and Yup'ik cases', *Anthropology and Education Quarterly*, 25, 3, 266–84.

Llewellyn, M. (1980) 'Studying girls at school: the implications of confusion', in R. Deem (ed.) *Schooling for Women's Work*, London: Routledge and Kegan Paul.

Lloyd, B. and Duveen, G. (1992) *Gender Identities and Education*, New York: Harvester Press.

Lodge, D. (1978) *Changing Places*, Harmondsworth: Penguin.

——(1980) *How Far Can You Go?*, Harmondsworth: Penguin.

——(1984) *Ginger, You're Barmy* (revised edition), Harmondsworth: Penguin.

——(1985) *Small World*, Harmondsworth: Penguin.

——(1989) *Nice Work*, Harmondsworth: Penguin.

Lofland, J. (1971) *Analysing Social Settings*, Belmont, CA: Wadsworth.

——(1974) 'Analysing qualitative data', *Urban Life*, 3, 3, 307–62.

Lofland, J. and Lofland, L. (1984) *Analysing Social Settings* (2nd edition), Belmont, CA: Wadsworth.

——(1995) *Analysing Social Settings* (3rd edition), Belmont, CA: Wadsworth.

Loizos, P. (1981) *The Heart Grown Bitter*, Cambridge: Cambridge University Press.

Lopata, H. (1995) 'Postscript', in G.A. Fine (ed.) *A Second Chicago School?*, Chicago: University of Chicago Press.

Lubeck, S. (1985) *Sandbox Society*, London: Falmer Press.

Ludmerer, K.M. (1999) *Time to Heal*, New York: Open University Press.

Lurie, A. (1975) *Nowhere City*, London: Heinemann.

——(1978) *Imaginary Friends*, Harmondsworth: Penguin.

Lustig, D.F. (1998) 'Of Kwanzae, Cinco de Mayo and whispering', *Anthropology and Education Quarterly* 28(4): 574–92.

Mac an Ghaill, M. (1988) *Young, Gifted and Black*, Milton Keynes: Open University Press.

——(1989) 'Beyond the white norm', *Qualitative Studies in Education*, 2, 3, 175–89.

——(1994) *The Making of Men*, Buckingham: Open University Press.

McCrone, D. (1992) *Understanding Scotland*, London: Routledge.

McCrone, D., Morris, D. and Kiely, R. (1995) *Scotland – the Brand*, Edinburgh: Edinburgh University Press.

McCrone, D., Stewart, R., Kiely, R. and Bechhofer, F. (1998) 'Who are we?', *Sociological Review*, 46, 4, 629–52.

MacDonald, B. (1948) *The Plague and I*, Harmondsworth: Penguin.

McDonald, M. (1987) 'The politics of fieldwork in Brittany', in A. Jackson (ed.) *Anthropology at Home*, London: Tavistock.

——(1989) *We are not French!: Language, Culture and Identity in Brittany*, London: Routledge.

MacDonald, S. (ed.) (1993) *Inside European Identities*, Oxford: Berg.

McKechnie, R. (1993) 'Becoming celtic in Corsica', in S. MacDonald (ed.) *Inside European Identities*, Oxford: Berg.

McKeganey, N.P. and Cunningham-Burley, S. (1987) *Enter the Sociologist: Reflections on the Practice of Sociology*, Aldershot: Avebury.

McLaren, P. (1986) *Schooling as a Ritual Performance*, London: Routledge and Kegan Paul.

McNamara, D (1980) 'The outsider's arrogance', *British Educational Research Journal*, 6, 2, 113–26.

McNamara, R.P. (ed.) (1995) *Sex, Scams and Street Life*, Westport, Conn: Praeger.

Maines, D.R., Shaffir, W. and Turowetz, A. (1980) 'Leaving the field in ethnographic research: reflections on the entrance—exit hypothesis', in W.B. Shaffir, R.A. Stebbins and A. Turowetz (eds) *Fieldwork Experience: Qualitative Approaches to Social Research*, New York: St Martin's Press.

Mannix, D. (1951) *Memoirs of a Sword Swallower*, London: Hamish Hamilton.

Marqusee, M. (1994) *Anyone but England*, London: Verso.

Martin, W.B. (1976) *The Negotiated Order of the School*, New York: Maclean and Hunter.

Masingila, J. (1994) 'Mathematics practice in carpet laying', *Anthropology and Education Quarterly*, 25, 4, 430–62.

Maso, I. (1987) *Kwalitatief onderzoek (Qualitative Research)*, Amsterdam: Boom.

——(1990) 'Preliminary negotiations as an indicator of the context and the utilization of research', unpublished paper.

Mayerhoff, B. (1978) *Number Our Days*, New York: Simon and Schuster.

Measor, L. (1984) 'Gender and the sciences', in M. Hammersley and P. Woods (eds) *Life in School*, Milton Keynes: Open University Press.

——(1985) 'Interviewing: a strategy in qualitative research', in R.G. Burgess (ed.) *Strategies of Educational Research*, London: Falmer Press.

——(1989) 'Are you coming to see some dirty films today?', in L. Holly (ed.) *Girls and Sexuality*, Milton Keynes: Open University Press.

Measor, L. and Woods, P. (1983) 'The interpretation of pupil myths', in M. Hammersley (ed.) *The Ethnography of Schooling*, Driffield, Yorks: Nafferton Books.

——(1984) *Changing Schools*, Milton Keynes: Open University Press.

Mehan, H., Hubbard, L. and Villanueva, I. (1994) 'Forming academic identities', *Anthropology and Education Quarterly* 25(2): 66–85.

Merryfield, M.M. (2000) 'Why aren't teachers being prepared to teach for diversity, equity and global interconnections? A study of lived experiences in the making of multicultural and global educators', *Teaching and Teacher Education*, 16, 4, 429–44.

Merton, D.E. (1994) 'The cultural context of aggression: the transition to Junior High School', *Anthropology and Education Quarterly*, 25, 1, 29–43.

——(1996) 'Burnout as cheerleader', *Anthropology and Education Quarterly* 27(1): 51–70.

Merton, R., Reader, G. and Kendall, P.L. (1957) *The Student Physician*, Cambridge, MA: Harvard University Press.

Messerschmidt, D. (ed.) (1982) *Anthropologists at Home in North America*, Cambridge: Cambridge University Press.

Metz, M.H. (1978) *Classrooms and Corridors: the Crisis of Authority in Desegregated Secondary Schools*, Berkeley, CA: University of California Press.

——(1984) 'Editor's foreword', *Sociology of Education*, 57, 4, 199.

——(1986) *Different by Design*, New York: Routledge and Kegan Paul.

Middleton, S. (1993) *Educating Feminists*, New York: Teachers College Press.

——(1998) *Disciplining Sexuality: Foucault, Life Histories and Education*, New York: Teachers College Press.

Miles, M. and Huberman, M. (1983) *Qualitative Data Analysis*, Beverley Hills, CA: Sage.

Miller, S.J. (1970) *Prescription for Leadership*, Chicago: Aldine.

Mills, C.W. (1959) *The Sociological Imagination*, New York: Oxford University Press.

Mitchell, J. (1993) *Up in the Old Hotel*, New York: Vintage Books.

Mizrahi, T. (1980) *Getting Rid of Patients*, New Brunswick, NJ: Rutgers University Press.

Moffat, N. (1989) *Coming of Age in New Jersey*, New Brunswick, NJ: Rutgers University Press.

Moon, W.L.H. (1982) *Blue Highways*, New York: Fawcett Crest.

Morgan, D.H.J. (1981) 'Men, masculinity and the process of sociological enquiry', in H. Roberts (ed.) *Doing Feminist Research*, London: Routledge.

Morgan, D.L. (1991) *Focus Groups as Qualitative Research*, London: Sage.

——(1993) *Successful Focus Groups*, London: Sage.

Morgan, K. and Mungham, G. (2000) *Redesigning Democracy*, Bridgend: Seren.

Morin, E. (1971) *Rumour in Orleans*, London: Weidenfeld.

Morley, L. (1999) *Organising Feminisms: the Micropolitics of the Academy*, London: Macmillan.

Morley, L. and Walsh, V. (eds) (1995) *Feminist Academics*, London: Taylor & Francis.

——(eds) (1996) *Breaking Boundaries*, London: Taylor & Francis.

Mosley, W. (2000) 'Holiday is not an option', *Guardian*, 26 July, 12–13.

Mulkay, M. (1985) *The Word and the World*, London: Allen and Unwin.

Muller, J. (1992) 'Shades of blue', *Social Science and Medicine*, 34, 8, 885–98.

Mumford, E. (1970) *Interns*, Cambridge, MA: Harvard University Press.

Munro, P. (1998) *Subject to Fiction*, Buckingham: Open University Press.

Murcott, A. (1983a) (ed.) *A Sociology of Food and Eating*, Aldershot: Gower.

——(ed.) (1983b) *Essays on the Sociology of Food*, Farnborough: Gower.

——(ed.) (1998) *The Nation's Diet*, London: Longman.

Nash, R. (1973) *Classrooms Observed*, London: Routledge and Kegan Paul.

——(1977) *Schooling in Rural Societies*, London: Methuen.

Neel, J. (1993) *Death among the Dons*, London: Constable.

Nias, J.(1991) 'Primary teachers talking', in G. Walford (ed.) *Doing Educational Research*, London: Routledge.

Nisbet, J. (2000) 'When the "rot" set in', *British Educational Research Journal*, 26, 3, 409–22.

Noble, D. (1992) *A World without Women?*, New York: Oxford University Press.

Nordstrom, C. and Robben, A.C.G.M. (eds) (1995) *Fieldwork under Fire*, Berkeley, CA: University of California Press.

O'Brien, O. (1993) 'Good to be French?', in S. Macdonald (ed.) *Inside European Identities*, Oxford: Berg.

——(1994) 'Ethnic identity, gender and life cycle in North Catalonia', in V.A. Goddard, J.R. Llobera and C. Shore (eds) *The Anthropology of Europe*, Oxford: Berg.

Okely, J. and Callaway, H. (eds) (1992) *Anthropology and Autobiography*, London: Routledge.

Osmond, J. (1994) *A Parliament for Wales?*, Cardiff: Gomer.

Paley, V.G. (1981) *Wally's Stories*, Chicago: University of Chicago Press.

——(1984) *Boys and Girls*, Chicago: University of Chicago Press

——(1986) *Mollie is Three*, Chicago: University of Chicago Press.

Pardo, I. (1996) *Managing Existence in Naples*, Cambridge: Cambridge University Press.

Parker, H. (1974) *View from the Boys*, Newton Abbot: David and Charles.

Parry, O. (1987) 'Uncovering the ethnographer', in N.P. McKeganey and S. Cunningham-Burley (eds) *Enter the Sociologist*, Aldershot: Avebury.

Pearson, G. (1983) *Hooligan*, London: Macmillan.

Peshkin, A. (1986) *God's Choice*, Chicago: University of Chicago Press.

Phillips, E.M. and Pugh, D.S. (2000) *How to Get a Ph.D.: Managing the Peaks and Troughs of Research* (3rd edition), Buckingham: Open University Press.

Phillips, S.U. (1987) *The Invisible Culture*, New York: Longman.

Picchi, D. (1983) 'Review of *Shabono*', *American Anthropologist*, 85, 3, 674–5.

Pilcher, J. (1999) *Women of Their Time?*, Aldershot: Ashgate

Pilcher, J., Delamont, S., Powell, G., Rees, T. and Read, M. (1989) 'Evaluating a women's careers convention: methods, results and implications', *Research Papers in Education*, 4, 1, 57–76.

Pitkin, D. (1985) *The House that Giacomo Built*, Cambridge: Cambridge University Press.

Plummer, K. (1983) *Documents of Life*, London: Allen and Unwin.

——(2000) *Documents of Life 2*, London: Sage.

——(2001) 'The call of life stories in ethnographic research', in P. Atkinson, A. Coffey, S. Delamont, J. Lofland and L. Lofland (eds) *Handbook of Ethnography*, London: Sage.

Popkewitz, T.S. and Tabachnick, B.R. (1981) *The Study of Schooling: Field Based Methodologies in Educational Research and Evaluation*, New York: Praeger.

Potts, A. (1997) *College Academics*, Charleston, NSW: William Michael Press.

Prendergast, S. (1989) 'Girls' experience of menstruation', in L. Holly (ed.) *Girls and Sexuality*, Milton Keynes: Open University Press.

Prior, L. (1989) *The Social Organisation of Death*, London: Macmillan.

Prout, A. (1986) 'Wet children and little actresses', *Sociology of Health and Illness*, 8, 2, 111–36.

Prout, A. and James, A. (1997) 'A new paradigm for the sociology of childhood?', in A. James and A. Prout (eds) *Constructing and Reconstructing Childhood*, London: Falmer Press.

Pugsley, L. (1996) Unpublished MSc thesis, University of Wales, Cardiff.

——(1998) 'Throwing your brains at it', *International Studies in Sociology of Education*, 8, 1, 71–90.

Pugsley, L., Coffey, A. and Delamont, S. (1996a) 'Daps, dykes, five mile hikes', *Sport, Education and Society*, 1, 2, 133–46.

——(1996b) 'I don't eat peas anyway', in I. Shaw and I. Butler (eds) *A Case of Neglect?*, Aldershot: Ashgate.

Pyke, R. (1934) *Edgehill College 1884–1934*, London: Epworth Press.

——(1957) *Edgehill College 1884–1957: a Triumph of Faith*, London: Epworth Press.

Quicke, J. (1988) 'Using structured life histories', in P. Woods and A. Pollard (eds) *Sociology and Teaching*, London: Croom Helm.

——(1993) 'A yuppie generation?', in I. Bates and G. Riseborough (eds) *Youth and Inequality*, Buckingham: Open University Press.

Rabinow, P. (1979) *Reflections on Fieldwork in Morocco*, Berkeley: University of California Press.

Raikes, E. (1908) *Dorothea Beale of Cheltenham*, London: Archibald Constable.

Randall, G.F. (1969) *Rugby High School Golden Jubilee (1919–1969)*, Rugby: George Over.

Ranson, S., Bryman, A. and Hinings, B. (1977) *Clergy, Ministers and Priests*, London: Routledge and Kegan Paul.

Rapport, N. (1993) *Diverse World-Views in an English Village*, Edinburgh: Edinburgh University Press.

Reed-Danahay, D. (1987) 'Farm children at school: educational strategies in rural France', *Anthropological Quarterly*, 60, 2, 83–9.

——(1996) *Education and Identity in Rural France*, Cambridge: Cambridge University Press.

——(ed.) (1997) *Auto/Ethnography*, Oxford: Berg.

Regis, E. (1987) *Who Got Einstein's Office?*, London: Simon and Schuster.

Renold, E. (2000) 'Coming out', *Gender and Education*, 12, 3, 309–26.

Richardson, L. (1990) *Writing Strategies*, Newbury Park: Sage.

Riseborough, G. (1988) 'Pupils, recipe knowledge, curriculum and the cultural production of class, ethnicity and patriarchy: a critique of one teacher's practices', *British Journal of Sociology of Education*, 9, 1, 39–54.

——(1993a) 'Learning a living or living a learning?', in I. Bates and G. Riseborough (eds) *Youth and Inequality*, Buckingham: Open University Press.

——(1993b) 'GBH – the Gobbo Barmy Army', in I. Bates and G. Riseborough (eds) *Youth and Inequality*, Buckingham: Open University Press.

Robb, N.A. (1968) *A History of Richmond Lodge School*, Belfast: Richmond Lodge School.

Roker, D. (1994) 'Gaining the edge', in I. Bates and G. Riseborough (eds) *Youth and Inequality*, Buckingham: Open University Press.

Rose, S. (1988) *Keeping Them out of the Hands of Satan*, London: Routledge and Kegan Paul.

Rosenberg, H.G. (1988) *A Negotiated World*, Toronto: University of Toronto Press.

Rosenberg, M.B. and Bergstrom, L.V. (eds) (1975) *Women and Society: a Critical Review of the Literature with a Selected, Annotated Bibliography*, Beverley Hills, CA: Sage.

Rosenfeld, G. (1971) *Shut Those Thick Lips: a Study of Slum School Failure*, New York: Holt, Rinehart and Winston.

Rossiter, M. (1982) *Women Scientists in America: Struggles and Strategies to 1940*, Baltimore: Johns Hopkins University Press.

——(1995) *Women Scientists in America: Struggles and Strategies 1940–1972*, Baltimore: Johns Hopkins University Press.

Roth, J. (1963) *Timetables*, Indianapolis: Bobbs–Merrill.

——(1966) 'Hired hand research', *American Sociologist*, 1, 190–6.

Salamone, S.D. (1987) *In the Shadow of the Holy Mountain*, Boulder, CO: East European Monographs.

Sanjek, R. (ed.) (1990) *Fieldnotes: The Making of Anthropology*, Ithaca, NY: Cornell University Press.

Saran, R. (1981) 'Negotiating machinery as an expression of power relationships', in P. Robbins and H. Thomas (eds) *Research in Educational Management and Administration*, London: BEMAS.

——(1982) 'The politics of bargaining relationships during Burnham negotiations', *Educational Management and Administration*, 10, 2, 39–43.

——(1985) 'The use of archives and interviews in research on educational policy', in R.G. Burgess (ed.) *Strategies of Educational Research*, London: Falmer Press.

Saran, R. and Trafford, V. (1990) *Research in Educational Management and Policy*, London: Falmer Press.

Sayers, D.L. (1935) *Gaudy Night*, London: Gollancz.

Sayre, A. (1975) *Rosalind Franklin and DNA*, New York: W.W. Norton.

Schiebinger, Londa (1989) *The Mind has No Sex?*, Cambridge, MA: Harvard University Press.

——(1993) *Nature's Body*, Boston: Beacon.

——(1999) *Has Feminism Changed Science?*, Cambridge, MA: Harvard University Press.

Schneider, JoAnne (1997) 'Dialectics of race and nationality', *Anthropology and Education Quarterly*, 28, 4, 494–507.

Schoem, D. (1982) 'Explaining Jewish student failure', *Anthropology and Education Quarterly*, 13, 4, 308–22.

Schultz, K. (1996) 'Between school and work', *Anthropology and Education Quarterly* 27(4): 517–44.

Schutz, A. (1971) *Collected Papers II: Studies in Social Theory*, The Hague: Martinus Nijhoff.

Sconzert, K., Lazzetto, D. and Purkey, S. (2000) 'Small-town college to big-city school', *Teaching and Teacher Education*, 16, 4, 465–90.

Scaford, H.W. (1991) 'Addressing the creationist challenge', *Anthropology and Education Quarterly*, 21, 2, 160–6.

Sedgewick, F. (1990) 'Despairing of drab glossies', *Times Educational Supplement*, 16 March, 19.

Serbin, L.A. (1978) 'Teachers, peers and play preferences: an environmental approach to sex typing in the preschool', in B. Sprung (ed.) *Perspectives on Non-sexist Early Childhood Education*, New York: Teachers College Press.

——(1984) 'Teachers, peers and play preferences: an environmental approach to sex typing in the preschool', in S. Delamont (ed.) *Readings on Interaction in the Classroom*, London: Methuen.

Sewell, T. (1997) *Black Masculinities and Schooling*, Stoke on Trent: Trentham.

——(1999) 'Loose canons?', in D. Epstein, J. Elwood, V. Hey and J. Maw (eds) *Failing Boys?*, Buckingham: Open University Press.

Shaffir, W.B., Stebbins, R.A. and Turowetz, A. (eds) (1980) *Fieldwork Experience: Qualitative Approaches to Serial Research*, New York: St Martin's Press.

Shapiro, M. (1978) *Getting Doctored*, Ontario: Between the Lines.

Sharp, R. and Green, A.G. (1975) *Education and Social Control*, London, Routledge and Kegan Paul..

Sharpe, T. (1978) *Wilt*, London: Pan Books.

Shaw, A.M. (1984) *When You Were There*, South Molton, Devon: G.P. Printers.

Shaw, C.R. (1966) *The Jack-roller: A Delinquent Boy's Own Story*, Chicago: University of Chicago Press.

Shepley, N. (1988) *Women of Independent Mind*, Edinburgh: St George's School.

Shields, C. (1993a) *The Republic of Love*, London: Flamingo.

——(1993b) *Mary Swann*, London: Fourth Estate.

Shipman, M. (1976) (ed.) *The Organisation and Impact of Social Research*, London: Routledge and Kegan Paul.

Shultz, J. and Florio, S. (1979) 'Stop and freeze', *Anthropology and Education Quarterly*, 10, 3, 166–91.

Shuval, J.T. (1980) *Entering Medicine*, Oxford: Pergamon.

Sikes, P., Measor, L. and Woods, P. (1985) *Teacher Careers*, London: Falmer Press.

Silverman, D. (1985) *Qualitative Methodology and Sociology: Describing the Social World*, Aldershot: Gower.

——(1995) *Qualitative Methodology and Sociology* (2nd edition), London: Sage.

Simonite, V. (2000) 'The effects of aggregation method and variations in the performance of individual students on degree classifications in modular degree courses', *Studies in Higher Education*, 25, 2, 197–210.

Sinclair, S. (1997) *Making Doctors*, Oxford: Berg.

Singleton, J.C. (1967) *Nichu: a Japanese School*, New York: Holt, Rinehart and Winston.

Slater, C. (1986) *Trail of Miracles*, Berkeley, CA: University of California Press.

——(1990) *City Steeple, City Streets*, Berkeley, CA: University of California Press.

——(1994) *Dance of the Dolphin*, Chicago: University of Chicago Press.

Smith, L.M. (1982) 'Ethnography', in H. Mitzel (ed.) *The Encyclopaedia of Educational Research* (5th edition), New York: Macmillan (4 vols).

Smith, L.M. and Geoffrey, W. (1968) *The Complexities of an Urban Classroom: an Analysis toward a General Theory of Teaching*, New York: Holt, Rinehart and Winston.

Smith, L.M. and Keith, P. (1971) *Anatomy of Educational Innovation*, London: Wiley.

Smith, L.M., Kleine, P.F., Prunty, J.P. and Dwyer, D.C. (1986) *Educational Innovators*, London: Falmer Press.

Smith, L.M., Prunty, J.P., Dwyer, D.C. and Kleine, P.F. (1987) *The Fate of an Innovative School*, London: Falmer Press.

Smith, L.M., Dwyer, D.C., Prunty, J.P. and Kleine, P.F. (1988) *Innovation and Change in Schooling*, London: Falmer Press.

Snodgrass, J., with Geis, G., Short, J.F. Jr, Koburi, S. and the Jackroller himself (1982) *The Jack-roller at Seventy – A Fifty Year Follow Up*, Lexington, MA: Lexington Books.

Solorzano, D.G. (1998) 'Critical race theory, race and gender microaggressions, and the experience of Chicana and Chicano scholars', *Qualitative Studies in Education*, 11, 1, 121–36.

Sonnert, G. and Holton, G. (1995) *Gender Differences in Science Careers*, New Brunswick, NJ: Rutgers University Press.

Sontag, S. (1966) 'The anthropologist as hero', in E.N. Hayes, and T. Hayes (eds) *Claude Levi-Strauss: the Anthropologist as Hero*, Cambridge, MA: MIT Press.

Spindler, G. (ed.) (1982) *Doing the Ethnography of Schooling*, New York: Holt, Rinehart and Winston.

Spindler, G. and Spindler, L. (eds) (1987) *Interpretive Ethnography of Education: At Home and Abroad*, Hillsdale, NJ: Erlbaum.

Spradley, J.P. (1969) *Guests Never Leave Hungry*, London: Yale University Press.

——(1979) *The Ethnographic Interview*, New York: Holt, Rinehart and Winston.

——(1980) *Participant Observation*, New York: Holt, Rinehart and Winston.

Spring, M. (1994) *Every Breath You Take*, London: Orion.

Stake, R. and Easley, W. (eds) (1978) *Case Studies in Science Education*, Urbana, IL: CIRCE, University of Illinois.

Stanley, J. (1989) *Marks on the Memory*, Milton Keynes: Open University Press.

Stanley, L. and Wise, S. (1983) *Breaking Out*, London: Routledge and Kegan Paul.

——(1993) *Breaking Out Again*, London: Routledge.

Steinberg, D.L., Epstein, D. and Johnson, R. (eds) (1997) *Border Patrols*, London: Cassell.

Stewart, C. (1991) *Demons and the Devil*, Princeton, NJ: Princeton University Press.

Stillman, A. and Maychell, K. (1984) *School to School: LEA and Teacher Involvement in Educational Continuity*, Windsor: NFER Nelson.

Stoeckle, J. (1987) 'Physicians train and tell', *Harvard Medical School Alumni Bulletin*, 61, 9 11.

Strahan, J.E. (1998) *Managing Ignatius: the Lunacy of Lucky Dogs and Life in the Quarter*, Baton Rouge, LA: Louisiana State University Press.

Strauss, A., Schatzman, L., Bucher, R., Erlich, D. and Sabsheri, M. (1964) *Psychiatric Ideologies and Institutions*, New York: Free Press.

Strauss, A.L. (1987) *Qualitative Analysis for Social Scientists*, Cambridge: Cambridge University Press.

Sussmann, L. (1977) *Tales out of School: Implementing Organizational Change in the Elementary Grades*, Philadelphia, PA: Temple University Press.

Sutherland, M. (1985) *Women Who Teach in Universities*, Stoke-on-Trent: Trentham Books.

Sutton, D.E. (1998) *Memories Cast in Stone: the Relevance of the Past in Everyday Life*, Oxford: Berg.

Swidler, A. (1979) *Organization without Authority: Dilemmas of Social Control in Free Schools*, Cambridge, MA: Harvard University Press.

Taylor, B. and Thomson, K. (eds) (1999) *Scotland and Wales: Nations Again*, Cardiff: University of Wales Press.

Tesch, R. (1990) *Qualitative Research: Analysis Types and Software Tools*, London: Falmer Press.

Tescione, S.M. (1998) 'A woman's name: implications for publication, citation and tenure', *Educational Researcher*, 27, 8, 38–42.

Tey, J. (1947) *Miss Pym Disposes*, London, Peter Davies.

——(1954) *The Daughter of Time*, Harmondsworth: Penguin.

Thomas, M. (1999) 'Foreign affairs', unpublished PhD thesis, University of Wales, Cardiff.

Thomas, W.I. (1923) *The Unadjusted Girl*, Boston, MA: Little, Brown.

Thorne, B. (1993) *Gender Play*, Buckingham: Open University Press.

Thrasher, F.M. (1927) *The Gang*, Chicago: University of Chicago Press.

Thubron, C. (1968) *The Hills of Adonis*, Harmondsworth: Penguin.

——(1986) *Journey into Cyprus*, Harmondsworth: Penguin.

Tobias, S. (1990) *They're Not Dumb, They're Different*, Tucson, AZ: Research Corporation.

Tuchman, B.W. (1979) *A Distant Mirror*, Harmondsworth: Penguin.

——(1981) *Practising History*, New York: Knopf.

Ulin, R.C. (1996) *Vintages and Traditions*, Washington, DC: Smithsonian Institution Press.

Upton, G., Beasley, F., Atkinson, P. and Delamont, S. (1988) *The Effectiveness of Locational Integration for Children with Moderate Learning Difficulties*, Cardiff: HMSO/Welsh Office.

Urban Life (1974) (October) 3, 3, 307–62.

Valli, L. (1986) *Becoming Clerical Workers*, London: Routledge.

Varenne, H. (1982) 'Jocks and freaks', in G. Spindler (ed.) *Doing the Ethnography of Schooling*, New York: Holt, Rinehart and Winston.

Vaughan, J. (1982) 'Searching the literature: additional sources of information and how to keep up to date', in A. Hartnett (ed.) *The Social Sciences in Educational Studies: a Selective Guide to the Literature*, London: Heinemann Educational Books.

Vaz, K.M. (ed.) (1997) *Oral Narrative Research with Black Women*, Thousand Oaks, CA: Sage.

Verhoeven, J. (1992) 'Backstage with Erving Goffman', *Research on Language and Social Interaction*, 26, 3, 307–16.

Vidich, A.J. (1955) 'Participation and the collection and interpretation of data', *Amerian Journal of Sociology*, 60, 354–60.

Walford, G. (1983) 'Research state and research style', *CORE*, 7, 1.

——(ed.) (1987) *Doing Sociology of Education*, London: Falmer Press.

——(ed.) (1991) *Doing Sociology of Education*, London: Falmer Press.

——(ed.) (1994) *Researching the Powerful in Education*, London: UCL Press.

——(1995) 'Classification and framing in English public boarding schools', in P. Atkinson, W.B. Davies and S. Delamont (eds) *Discourse and Reproduction*, Cresskill, NJ: Hampton Press.

——(ed.) (1998) *Doing Research about Education*, London: Falmer Press.

Walker, J.C. (1988) *Louts and Legends: Male Youth Culture in an Inner City School*, Sydney: Allen and Unwin.

Walker, R. (1985) *Doing Research: a Handbook for Teachers*, London: Methuen.

Walker, R. and Adelman, C. (1976) 'Strawberries', in M. Stubbs and S. Delamont (eds) *Explorations in Classroom Observation*, Chichester: Wiley.

Warde, A., Martens, L. and Olsen, V. (1999) 'Consumption and the problem of variety', *Sociology*, 33, 1, 105–28.

Waterhouse, S. (1991) *First Episodes*, London: Falmer Press.

Watson, J. (1968) *The Double Helix*, London: Weidenfeld and Nicholson.

Weis, L. (1985) *Between Two Worlds*, London, Routledge.

——(1990) *Working Class without Work*, New York: Routledge.

Welland, T. and Pugsley, L. (eds) (2001) *The Ethics of Qualitative Research*, Aldershot: Ashgate.

Welsh, B.W. (1939) *After the Dawn: a Record of the Pioneer Work in Edinburgh of the Higher Education of Women*, Edinburgh and London: Oliver and Boyd.

Wertheim, M. (1997) *Pythagoras' Trousers*, London: Fourth Estate.

Westaway, K.M. (ed.) (1932) *A History of Bedford High School*, Bedford: Hockliffe.

——(1945) *Old Girls in New Times (1939–1945)*, Bedford: Hockliffe.

——(ed.) (1957) *Seventy-Five Years: the Story of Bedford High School, 1882–1957*, Bedford: Diemer and Reynolds.

Wexler, P. (1992) *Becoming Somebody*, London: Falmer.

Whitty, G., Rowe, G. and Aggleton, P. (1993) 'Subjects and themes in the secondary-school curriculum', *Research Papers in Education*, 9, 2, 159–81.

Willes, M. (1983) *Children into Pupils*, London: Routledge and Kegan Paul.

Williams, M. (2000) Unpublished material supplied to the author.

Williams, R. (1975) *The Country and the City*, St Albans: Paladin.

Willis, P. (1977) *Learning to Labour*, Farnborough: Saxon House.

——(1978) *Profane Culture*, London: Routledge and Kegan Paul.

Wilson, A. (1980) 'Group session', *British Journal of Guidance and Counselling*, 8, 2, 231–41.

Wilson, E. (1980) *Only Halfway to Paradise*, London: Tavistock.

Witherall, K. and Noddings, N. (eds) (1991) *Narrative and Dialogue in Education*, New York: Teachers College Press.

Wolcott, H.F. (1977) *Teachers versus Technocrats*, Eugene, OR: Centre for Educational Policy and Management, University of Oregon.

——(1981) 'Confessions of a "trained" observer', in T.S. Popkewitz and B.R. Tabachnick (eds) *The Study of Schooling*, New York: Praeger.

——(1990) *Writing Up Qualitative Research*, Newbury Park, CA: Sage.

——(1994) *Transforming Qualitative Data*, Thousand Oaks, CA: Sage.

Wolf, M. (1992) *The Thrice Told Tale*, Berkeley, CA: University of California Press.

Woods, P. (1975) ' "Showing them up" in secondary school', in G. Chanan and S. Delamont (eds) *Frontiers of Classroom Research*, Windsor: NFER.

——(1979) *The Divided School*, London: Routledge and Kegan Paul.

——(1985a) 'Conversations with teachers', *British Education Research Journal*, 11, 1, 13–26.

——(1985b) 'Sociology, ethnography and teacher practice', *Teaching and Teacher Education*, 1, 1, 51–62.

——(1986) *Inside Schools*, London, Routledge.

——(1994) 'Teachers under siege', *Anthropology and Education Quarterly*, 25, 3, 250–65.

——(1996) *Researching the Art of Teaching*, London: Routledge.

Woods, P. and Hammersley, M. (eds) (1993) *Gender and Ethnicity in Schools*, London: Routledge.

Wright, T. and Cochrane, R. (2000) 'Factors influencing successful submission of PhD theses', *Studies in Higher Education*, 25, 2, 181–96.

Yates, P.D. (1987a) 'Figure and section: ethnography and education in the multicultural state', in G. Spindler and L. Spindler (eds) *Interpretive Ethnography of Education: At Home and Abroad*, Hillsdale, NJ: Erlbaum.

——(1987b) 'A case of mistaken identity: interethnic images in multicultural England', in G. Spindler and L. Spindler (eds) *Interpretive Ethnography of Education: At Home and Abroad*, Hillsdale, NJ: Erlbaum.

Young, M.F.D. (ed.) (1971) *Knowledge and Control*, London and New York: Collier-Macmillan.

Zuckerman, H., Cole, J.R. and Bruer, J.T. (eds) (1991) *The Outer Circle*, New York: W.W. Norton.

Index